NIETZSCHE'S PHILOSOPHY OF RELIGION

In his first book, *The Birth of Tragedy*, Nietzsche observes that Greek tragedy gathered people together as a community in the sight of their gods, and argues that modernity can be rescued from 'nihilism' only through the revival of such a festival. This is commonly thought to be a view which did not survive the termination of Nietzsche's early Wagnerianism, but Julian Young argues, on the basis of an examination of all of Nietzsche's published works, that his religious communitarianism in fact persists through all his writings. What follows, it is argued, is that the mature Nietzsche is neither an 'atheist', an 'individualist' nor an 'immoralist': he is a German philosopher belonging to a German tradition of conservative communitarianism – though to claim him as a proto-Nazi is radically mistaken. This important reassessment will be of interest to all Nietzsche scholars and to a wide range of readers in German philosophy.

JULIAN YOUNG is Professor of Philosophy at the University of Auckland and honorary Research Professor at the University of Tasmania. His many publications include *Heidegger: Off the Beaten Track* (2002) edited and translated with Kenneth Haynes, *Heidegger's Later Philosophy* (2002) and *Heidegger's Philosophy of Art* (2001, 2004).

D0933380

NIETZSCHE'S PHILOSOPHY OF RELIGION

JULIAN YOUNG

CAMBRIDGE
UNIVERSITY PRESS

CAMBRIDGE UNIVERSITY PRESS
Cambridge, New York, Melbourne, Madrid, Cape Town, Singapore, São Paulo

Cambridge University Press
The Edinburgh Building, Cambridge CB2 2RU, UK

Published in the United States of America by Cambridge University Press, New York

www.cambridge.org
Information on this title: www.cambridge.org/9780521681049

© Julian Young 2006

First published 2006

Printed in the United Kingdom at the University Press, Cambridge

A catalogue record for this publication is available from the British Library

ISBN-13   978-0-521-85422-1 hardback
ISBN-10   0-521-85422-9 hardback
ISBN-13   978-0-521-68104-9 paperback
ISBN-10   0-521-68104-9 paperback

For
David Montgomery

Contents

Acknowledgements

I am grateful to the German Academic Exchange Service, the University of Auckland Research Committee and the University of Auckland Arts Faculty for grants which supported the writing of this book. And to Christoph Jamme of the University of Lüneburg and Günter Seubold of the University of Bonn (where Nietzsche was briefly a student) for useful discussions of the substance of the work. I am grateful to Kathleen Higgins for helpful references to secondary literature concerning *Zarathustra's* 'Ass Festival', and to Friedrich Voit for enlightening background information that only a Germanist would know. I am particularly grateful to my colleagues in the Auckland Philosophy Department, Robert Wicks, Markus Weidler, Rosalind Hursthouse and especially Christine Swanton who helped make my thoughts a lot clearer than they would otherwise have been. My greatest debt, however, is to the German historian Thomas Rohkrämer of the University of Lancaster who generously allowed me to read portions of the unpublished manuscript of his forthcoming study of the roots of National Socialism within the tradition of right-wing German thought, a study that is certain to become essential reading on the topic.

Abbreviations

Nietzsche's works are cited using the following abbreviations: roman numerals refer to major parts of the works; arabic numerals refer to sections, not pages. The exceptions to this are (i) references to extraneous material included in translations of Nietzsche's published works (generally editorial comments and excerpts from the *Nachlass*) in which case I cite page numbers, and (ii) references to KSA which I cite by volume number followed by the notebook number and, in brackets, the note number (e.g. 13 14 [204]). For bibliographical details of the works cited see pp. 216–17 below. Sometimes I have preferred my own translation to that provided in the translation cited.

A	*The Antichrist*
BGE	*Beyond Good and Evil*
BT	*The Birth of Tragedy*
D	*Daybreak*
EH	*Ecce Homo*
GM	*On the Genealogy of Morals*
GS	*The Gay Science*
HH	*Human, All-too-Human*
KSA	*Sämtliche Werke: Kritische Studienausgabe in 15 Bänden*
NCW	*Nietzsche contra Wagner*
TI	*Twilight of the Idols*
UM	*Untimely Meditations*
WC	*The Case of Wagner*
WP	*The Will to Power*
Z	*Thus Spoke Zarathustra*

Schopenhauer's works are cited as follows:

FR	*The Fourfold Root of the Principle of Sufficient Reason*
PP	*Parerga and Paralipomena*
WR	*The World as Will and Representation*

Introduction

In his first book, *The Birth of Tragedy* (1872), Nietzsche presents the tragic art of fourth-century Greece as a religious festival which gathered the community together as community in the presence of its divinities. And he further argues that without a religion which both unites a culture and provides answers to the fundamental existential questions faced by all individuals, society decays. So, he concludes, the hope for a redemption of modernity from the decadence – the dis-integration – into which it has fallen, lies in the rebirth of Greek tragedy promised by Richard Wagner's projected Bayreuth Festival.

Two features distinguish this early thinking. First, it is *communitarian* thinking in the sense that the highest object of its concern is the flourishing of the community as a whole. And second, it is *religious* thinking in that it holds that without a festive, communal religion, a community – or, as Nietzsche frequently calls it, a 'people' – cannot flourish, indeed cannot properly be said to *be* a community.

This book originated in the question: what happened to this early religious communitarianism in Nietzsche's later works? What happened to Nietzsche's 'Wagnerianism'?

In 1876 two people departed, as if in panic, midway through the first Bayreuth Festival. One was poor, 'mad' King Ludwig, Wagner's patron, and the other was Friedrich Nietzsche. After his flight, Nietzsche turned from being Wagner's ardent disciple to being his most virulent critic. But what was it that he rejected? Was it just the *music,* or did he also reject the *ideal* he had once taken the music to fulfil? Did he abandon his view of the relation between community and religion, or did he perhaps abandon his concern for community?

Realising I had no answer to these questions I undertook a systematic rereading of the texts for a graduate seminar at Auckland in the first semester of 2004. The – to me, at least – initially startling answer that emerged is that Nietzsche in fact *never* abandoned his religious communitarianism. To the end – such is the argument of this book – Nietzsche's fundamental concern, his highest value, lies with the flourishing of community,[1] and to the end he believes that this can happen only through the flourishing of communal religion.

In two ways, this reading runs counter to nearly all Anglophone interpretations of Nietzsche. First, while most conclude from his scathing assaults on established religions in general and on Christianity in particular, as well as from the naturalistic tenor of his later thought, that Nietzsche was, *quite obviously*, an 'atheist',[2] I hold that he *never* was. Though atheistic with respect to the *Christian* God, Nietzsche, I hold, ought to be regarded as a religious *reformer* rather than an enemy of religion. Second, while most readings take Nietzsche to be an 'individualistic' philosopher I take his concern to lie, first and foremost, with community.

Let me be more specific on this point. There are, it seems to me, at least two ways in which Nietzsche might be regarded as an 'individualist'. The first sees him as focused exclusively on individual psychic 'health'. On this view, like, in their various ways, Freud, Pilates (of Pilates callisthenics) or Atkins (of the Atkins diet), Nietzsche has nothing to say about communal life (save, perhaps, that psychic health requires a few, challenging friends), has nothing to say about it for the reason that it is just 'not his department'. This is the view set forth in Walter Kaufmann's enormously influential *Nietzsche: Philosopher, Psychologist, Antichrist* (1950) according to which 'the leitmotiv of Nietzsche's life and thought [was] the theme of the antipolitical individual who seeks self-perfection far from the modern

---

1 It needs to be made clear that there is no *incompatibility* between this highest value and the flourishing of individuals, the reason being that, according to the kind of communitarianism I shall attribute to Nietzsche, the flourishing of individuals *presupposes* the flourishing of community. In greater detail, what Nietzsche holds, I shall suggest, is that individuals only truly flourish, *when their own highest commitment is to the flourishing of the community as a whole*, when, that is, their highest personal goal is the communal good. (This kind of communitarianism is, I suspect, what Lee Kuan Yew intended to affirm when he claimed that Asians have 'little doubt that a society with communitarian values where the interests of society take precedence over that of the individual suits them better than the individualism of America'.) It might be suggested that what follows from this is that Nietzsche's highest value actually turns out to be the flourishing of *individuals*, his point being merely that they can do this only by standing in a certain relation to community. But that would have the peculiar consequence of excluding *Nietzsche himself* from flourishing. The fact of the matter is, as we shall see, that Nietzsche is not a disengaged observer commenting on how individuals best flourish, but a thoroughly engaged individual who himself has community (in fact world-community) as his highest goal.

2 See for example, Leiter (2002) p. 266, Wicks (2002) p. 75.

world' (p. 418). More recently it has found a celebrated embodiment in Alexander Nehamas' *Nietzsche: Life as Literature* (1985). Concerned, as Nehamas is, to present Nietzsche's literary construction of himself as an exemplary model of self-creation (and hence of 'health'), it is revealing to note that such collectivist notions as 'politics', 'culture' and even 'society' achieve not a single entry in his index.

A second way in which Nietzsche is interpreted as an 'individualist' – an 'elitist' or 'aristocratic' individualist – admits, unlike the first, that Nietzsche is crucially concerned with culture, with 'cultural greatness'. But it reduces this to individualism by reading him as holding that cultural greatness consists, not in some characteristic of society as a whole, but simply in the existence of a few 'excellent persons' or 'higher types' such as Beethoven or Goethe.[3] The proper role for the rest of society (which, if left to its own devices, is likely to prove a serious impediment to the appearance of such individuals) is simply to configure itself as a support-system for the production of these *übermenschlich* types.

This second version of the individualist reading is certainly more plausible than the first since it at least avoids suppressing Nietzsche's concern for 'culture', an unmistakable feature of the texts. But it is the aim of this book to argue that it is none the less mistaken. Though the 'higher types' are of unmistakably central importance to Nietzsche, the 'aristocratic individualist' reading, in my view, gets things precisely round the wrong way. On my reading, it is not the case that the social totality is valued for the sake of the higher types. Rather, the higher types are valued for the sake of the social totality.

Much of the recent attention paid to Nietzsche within the Anglophone world has treated him as a stimulating new contributor to discussions

---

3 Leiter (2002) pp. 206, 233, 299, 302. (Beethoven is actually a somewhat problematic example here, since Nietzsche often criticises him for being a 'romantic' (WP 106, 838, 842).) Another proponent of this reading is Keith Ansell-Pearson. Nietzsche, he asserts in his introduction to the Cambridge translation of *On the Genealogy of Morals*, is not a 'liberal' but an 'aristocratic individualist'. Nietzsche is committed to 'the "enhancement" of man' but this has nothing to do with the condition of the majority but only 'with the production of a few, striking, superlatively vital "highest exemplars" of the human species' (GM pp. ix–x). A further subscriber to the aristocratic individualist interpretation is Bruce Detweiler, who writes (sourly and, as we shall see, quite implausibly) that Nietzsche has 'an uncommon inability to affirm the life of this world except in those rare instances where its embodiments approach perfection' (Detweiler (1990) p. 194). The final subscriber to this interpretation I shall mention – one who gives it a political twist – is Frederick Appel, who holds that Nietzsche's concern is exclusively 'for the flourishing of those few whom he considers exemplary of the human species' and has as his highest aim 'a new, aristocratic political order in Europe in which the herdlike majority . . . are . . . under the control of a self-absorbed master caste whose only concern is for the cultivation of its own excellence' (Appel (1999) pp. 1–2).

within analytic moral philosophy. Hence his alleged 'elitism' has been taken to be a fundamental, and perhaps 'immoral', challenge to foundational assumptions concerning the equality of all persons before the moral law. Though this approach is legitimate up to a point, it tends, through decontextualisation, to disguise Nietzsche's central concerns.

For the fact is, of course, that Nietzsche is not a recent arrival on the Anglophone moral-philosophy scene. (*Zur Genealogie der Moral* is *not* an anonymous text, written in English, that washed up one day on a North American beach.) Rather, Nietzsche is a late nineteenth-century *German* thinker whose preoccupations were those of late nineteenth-century German thinkers. Specifically, the root of Nietzsche's thinking lies in the dismay that afflicted him, along with a great many other German thinkers, at the effects of modernisation, in particular of industrialisation, that took place in Germany during the nineteenth century. The starting-point of Nietzsche's thinking, that is to say, is 'cultural criticism', a sustained and still-relevant critique of the cultural world of industrial modernity.

The crucial fact about Nietzsche's critique of modernity is that it issues from the standpoint of the conservative, past-oriented right rather than from that of the socialist, future-oriented left. This places Nietzsche in proximity to the so-called 'Volkish'[4] tradition in German thinking.

As I shall discuss in some detail in the Epilogue, Volkish thinking grew out of the response of romanticism to the Enlightenment in general and to the birth of its offspring, industrialised modernity, in particular. Receiving an initial impetus from romantic thinkers such as Herder, Hölderlin, Novalis, Schelling and Fichte, early figures of importance in the Volkish movement proper were Nietzsche's near contemporaries Heinrich Riehl, Paul de Lagarde and, crucially, Richard Wagner. Nietzsche's friends Franz Overbeck and Heinrich von Stein also thought along Volkish lines.

Volkish thinkers were appalled by the alienated, materialistic, mechanistic, secular, urban, creepingly democratic, mass culture of modernity which they saw as the product of Enlightenment rationalism. In the quest for a more spiritual, less alienated society they looked to an idealised

---

4 From '*Volk*', meaning 'people' or 'folk'. The term is coined in George Mosse's classic study of the tradition (Mosse (1964)). Its nearest German equivalent is '*völkisch*'. In today's German, however, this term has come to be a near synonym for 'Nazi'. Since Mosse's interest as an historian is in showing how Nazism *grew out of* the Volkish tradition he evidently does not want it to be true by definition that Volkish thinkers are Nazis. The term is therefore, in some degree, a term of art.

image of the pre-Enlightenment past. What they found in that past was the spiritual unity of a Volk.

A Volk was conceived as a quasi-personal entity with a particular 'will', 'mission' or 'destiny'. It was thought of as prior to the state: as the vehicle of the Volk, the state's laws are justified to, but only to, the extent they reflect the ethos of the Volk. And it was thought of as prior to the individual: as an organic totality, its well-being takes precedence over – or, better put, constitutes – the well-being of individuals, so that the meaning and highest value of individual lives lie in their contribution to the well-being of the whole. As the First World War approached, Volkish thinkers were thus disposed to contrast Germany as a nation of '*Helden* (heroes)' with England – which they saw as epitomising the degeneracy of atomised, materialistic modernity – as a nation of '*Händler* (traders)'. As an organism such as the human body is made up of different organs, some subservient to others, so Volkish thinkers wished to preserve social differences, more specifically social hierarchy. Many saw the medieval estates as a social ideal.

Nietzsche's proximity to the Volkish tradition, in his later as much as his early work, is something I shall be concerned to argue at length in the later chapters of this book. An initial clue as to this proximity, however, I shall mention now: the interesting linguistic fact that though Nietzsche has, for reasons I shall investigate in some detail, a number of highly abusive terms for social collectivities – '*Pöbel* (mob or rabble)', '*Gesindel* (mob or rabble)' and to a lesser degree '*Herde* (herd)' – there is *nowhere* in the published works where he uses '*Volk*' (in the sense of ethnic unity) except as a term of utmost respect.

As the Volkish movement progressed many of its adherents became viciously nationalistic, militaristic and anti-Semitic. A great many (conspicuously Martin Heidegger) became Nazis. And a great deal of the vocabulary of Nazism – '*Volksgemeinschaft*', '*Volksgenossenschaft*', '*Volkskörper*', '*Volk-in-seinem-Staat*' and so on – was drawn from the Volkish tradition.

An unavoidable consequence of my reading is, therefore, to reraise the hoary suspicion that Nietzsche stands in too close a relation to Nazism, that those Nazi Nietzsche-scholars like Ernst Bertram and Alfred Bäumler who appropriated Nietzsche to the Nazi cause understood him, in fact, all too correctly. Fortunately, however, as I shall argue in the Epilogue, though there is a genuine and significant overlap between Nietzsche and the Volkish tradition, at the same time deeply embedded aspects of his thinking make it, in reality, a radical opponent of Nazism.

By no means all who, in the 1920s and 1930s, thought in Volkish ways became Nazis. Oswald Spengler, Ernst Jünger and Stefan George did not. And, moreover, many Volkish thinkers who had initially supported Hitler became appalled when it became clear just *what* they had supported. I have argued elsewhere that Martin Heidegger falls, in the end, into this category.[5] A clearer and less controversial case is Claus von Stauffenberg, a member of Stefan George's 'Circle' of disciples, who was hanged for trying to assassinate Hitler in July 1944. There is, I think, a moral to be drawn in the case both of Nietzsche's philosophy and of von Stauffenberg's heroism, a moral I shall be concerned to substantiate by the end of this book: there is no *essential* connexion between Volkish thinking as such and Nazism, no essential connexion, that is to say, between German communitarianism on the one hand and nationalism or fascism or totalitarianism or anti-Semitism on the other.

A word about the focus of this work. The most salient aspect of Nietzsche's thinking about religion is, of course, his critique of Christianity: of its metaphysics, but more particularly of its morality. Yet Nietzsche also holds that 'only as creators can we destroy' (GS 58), that, for the genuine philosopher, critique must always be a prelude to construction. Since Nietzsche's critique of Christian morality has been discussed in countless works, I shall attend to it only peripherally, only in so far as it is necessary to understanding his *constructive* thinking about religion. My focus is on the positive rather than the destructive aspect of Nietzsche's philosophy of religion.

Finally, some words about methodology. In my *Nietzsche's Philosophy of Art* (1992) I read through all the Nietzsche texts in chronological order, attending specifically to what each had to say about art. I propose to do the same here, attending, this time, to what they have to say about community and religion. For several reasons, I take this chronological approach to be good 'philological' practice. First, because it is how Nietzsche reads himself (in *Ecce Homo* in particular). Second, because the discovery of what are, as we shall see, surprisingly strong continuities in his thinking enables one to interpret with confidence passages that are unclear or whose meaning is in dispute. Induction, that is to say, is a

---

5 Young (1997).

useful philological tool: if on many occasions Nietzsche clearly affirms X then on the unclear occasion one can infer with some confidence that he probably means X. A third and connected reason for favouring the chronological approach is that it strongly discourages the 'ink-blot' technique of interpretation – picking a single text, or part of a text, or a fragment of an unpublished note, and projecting onto it one's most (or least) favourite philosophy.[6] A final reason in favour of the comprehensively chronological approach is that it is fascinating: to watch the birth, growth and refinement of a great thinker's thought is, to my mind, much more exciting than receiving the finished product in one neatly packaged lump. And, as Hegel points out, living with the development of a philosophy enables one to understand it better.

As in *Nietzsche's Philosophy of Art*, my focus is strongly on the works Nietzsche himself chose to publish; I dip only very discretely into the *Nachlass* (which includes that portion collected by his sister and published as *The Will to Power*). Nietzsche wanted the *Nachlass* destroyed at his death – understandably since it contains a great deal of weak material. As he says of Beethoven, a glance into his notebooks reveals that real artistry consists not in sudden and perfect inspiration but in the production of a great deal of material, most of it of indifferent quality, so that what is really important is a high work rate together with good critical taste (HH I 155). Nietzsche exercised his critical taste in deciding what, and what not, to publish.

Finally, again as in *Nietzsche's Philosophy of Art*, I devote my first chapter to Arthur Schopenhauer, and centrally to a work called 'On Man's Need for Metaphysics'. Since Nietzsche calls Schopenhauer his 'first and only educator' (HH II Preface I) and refers continually to 'the metaphysical need', Schopenhauer's views on religion can be guaranteed to provide an important background to the development of his own views.

---

6 Steven Aschheim's fascinating account of Nietzsche's German legacy after 1890 (Aschheim (1992)) shows how, using the ink-blot technique, just about *everyone* – Nazis, Zionists, Volkists, socialists, communists, feminists, eroticists, vegetarians, dancers, Protestants, Catholics, deconstructionists, and so on – discovered Nietzsche to have pronounced precisely *their* message.

CHAPTER I

Schopenhauer and 'Man's Need for Metaphysics'

Nietzsche describes Schopenhauer's *The World as Will and Representation* (1818), which he discovered in a second-hand book shop in Leipzig in 1869, as a book written especially for him (UM III 2). *The Birth of Tragedy* he describes as written 'in his [Schopenhauer's] spirit and to his honour' (BT 5). Even after his break with decadent 'romanticism' represented, as he saw it, by both Schopenhauer and Wagner, he continued to regard the former, his 'first and only educator', as both a 'great thinker' and a great human being (HH II Preface 1). Even in the middle of attacking everything Schopenhauer stands for, in *On the Genealogy of Morals*, Nietzsche still pauses to call him 'a genuine *philosopher* . . . a man and a knight with a brazen countenance who has the courage to be himself, knows how to stand alone and does not wait for the men in front and a nod from on high' (GM III 5).

In this chapter I shall very briefly sketch Schopenhauer's general philosophy, acquaintance with which is necessary, *inter alia*, to understanding the development of Nietzsche's metaphysics, before turning to what Schopenhauer has to say specifically about religion.

IDEALISM AND PESSIMISM

The basis of all Schopenhauer's thinking is, as he understands it, Kantian idealism. The everyday world of space and time, a product of the way in which the human mind processes the raw material it has received from external reality, is, he holds, mere 'appearance' or 'representation', in the final analysis a 'dream'. Beyond it lies 'noumenal' or 'intelligible' reality, the 'thing in itself'. Kant held that the thing in itself was unknowable by us and, some of the time, Schopenhauer agrees with this. One thing, however, he is quite certain we do know about it: that it is 'beyond plurality', in some sense 'One'. This is because individuality, and hence plurality, is dependent on space and time which together constitute the *'principium individuationis'*. But these, as Kant proved, are nothing but 'forms' which the mind imposes on experience – as it were, irremovable, tinted glasses through which it perceives the world – and are not features of reality in itself. So plurality is merely 'ideal' and reality in some sense 'One'.

The other important idea in Schopenhauer's general philosophy is 'the will to life'. Sometimes, particularly in the first edition of *The World as Will and Representation*, he seems, while claiming to be a good Kantian, also to want to deny that the thing in itself is unknowable. On the contrary, he seems to want to say, the thing in itself is the will to life. In later editions, however, recognising the contradictory nature of his earlier position, he withdraws the will to the appearance side of the appearance/reality dichotomy. 'Will' provides a deeper account of the world than is provided either by everyday experience or by science, but it still does not get to the absolute heart of things.[1]

Whatever its exact metaphysical status, will is the human essence. Unless something very extraordinary happens – so extraordinary that it can be described as a transcendence of human nature – we are incapable (save when asleep, and sometimes not even then) of not willing, incapable of inaction. And this means that life is, on balance, a miserable affair. For if the will is unsatisfied then we suffer. Hunger for example is the unsatisfied will to eat. But if the will is satisfied we suffer something even worse: boredom, a state in which the essential vanity and futility of life become inescapably present to us.[2] Schopenhauer's solution to the problem – somewhat reminiscent of Stoicism – is asceticism, 'denial of the will', the cessation of willing, which implies, in the end, of course, death.

RELIGION

It is against this background of pessimism that Schopenhauer expounds his mainly sympathetic account of religion. This occurs principally in chapter 17 of the second volume of his great work, a chapter entitled 'On Man's Need for Metaphysics'. That Nietzsche refers constantly to 'the metaphysical need' (in HH 1 26 he actually places the phrase in quotation marks) shows the importance of this chapter as a background to understanding his own philosophy of religion.

---

1 For a detailed discussion of these matters see Young (2005) chapter 4.
2 This is almost a parody of an argument which in fact contains, as Iris Murdoch puts it, a 'depth of humane wisdom'. For a detailed discussion see Young (2005) chapter 8.

Another reason, however, for prefacing my discussion of Nietzsche's philosophy of religion with a discussion of 'On Man's Need' is that Schopenhauer's account of what it is that constitutes the essence of religion is, in my view, in broad outline, *correct*. The chapter is, in fact, one of the great classics of philosophy, not only in style and wit but in insight into its subject matter. If I am right about its essential correctness it follows that the chapter provides us with a standard for assessing whether there is anything in Nietzsche's positive thinking that counts as genuinely *religious* thinking.

Schopenhauer asks us to be amazed – as if we were alien historians, surveying earth from a distant galaxy – at all 'the temples and churches, pagodas and mosques, in all countries and ages, in their splendour and spaciousness' (WR II p. 162). Why should such buildings be so universal and so dominant? What on earth could be their function?

His answer is that religion is 'popular metaphysics', that it is an expression *in sensu allegorico* of what philosophy or metaphysics proper expresses in *sensu stricto et proprio* for the benefit of that 'great majority of people who are not capable of thinking but only of believing, and are susceptible not to arguments, but only to authority'. It is, in other words, metaphysics for 'children' rather than for 'adults'. By 'metaphysics', Schopenhauer explains, he means the attempt at knowledge of that which is 'beyond nature or the given phenomenal appearance of things, in order to give information about that by which, in some sense or other, this nature is conditioned, or in popular language, about that which is hidden behind nature and renders nature possible'; about, in other words, the thing in itself (WR II pp. 162–6). 'Metaphysics', then, whether popular or strict, whether for intellectual 'children' or for 'adults', is the study of the supra-natural. But why should this be of such universal interest?

Because, Schopenhauer answers (sounding like Heidegger), unlike the non-human animals, the human being, at a certain point in its growth to adulthood, ceases to take itself 'as a matter of course' and instead 'asks itself what it is. And its wonder is the more serious, as here, for the first time, it stands consciously face to face with *death*' (WR II p. 160). Only human beings, that is, are condemned to live in the light of mortality, in the light of that 'dark . . . nothingness' which we must one day become and which (here Schopenhauer plagiarises Francis Bacon's famous simile) 'we fear as children fear darkness' (WR I p. 411).

Schopenhauer takes it, then, that the need for a 'solution' to the 'riddle' of death, some kind of denial of its finality, is an inescapable part of the human condition.[3] From which it follows that it is the promise of immortality rather than the existence of gods that constitutes the true heart of any fully fledged religion. Usually, of course, gods and immortality go together. But were they to be shown to be somehow incompatible, men 'would soon sacrifice the gods to their own immortality and be eager for atheism'. (In a witty parody of scholastic metaphysics, Schopenhauer even suggests an argument for their incompatibility: immortality, the argument might run, presupposes 'originality'. But this would be incompatible with God's status as the first cause (WR II p. 161).)

So dealing with death is the first, and most essential, function of any authentic religion. Historically speaking, he suggests, it is usually only the most primitive societies that lack a religion in this sense. Judaism and (Graeco-Roman) 'paganism' he regards as failed religions since they lack a properly developed doctrine of immortality. This is the reason they were supplanted by or absorbed into Christianity (WR II p. 170). Schopenhauer adds that finding a 'consolation' for, an 'antidote' to, the certainty of death is also the principal task of philosophy. As Socrates remarks in the *Phaedo*, at bottom, authentic philosophy is a 'preparation for death' (WR II p. 463).

As observed, Schopenhauer is a pessimist. Happiness – that brief pause between the two forms of suffering – is the exception, suffering the rule of life. It follows that the second aspect of 'the unfathomable and ever-disquieting riddle of life' (WR II p. 171) is pain. Its dominating presence threatens us with 'nausea' and 'despair', something from which we desperately need 'redemption' (WR II p. 170). This constitutes the second major function of any properly developed religion. Over and above the 'physical', that is to say, we need to believe in a 'metaphysical' domain, the character of which will reconcile us to at least the *grand* narrative

---

3 He would therefore have been entirely unsurprised at Jacques Derrida's confession to *Le Monde* during the final days of his last illness that 'I have not yet learnt to accept death', given Derrida's earlier remark that 'learning to live should also mean learning to die, taking into account and accepting the absolute nature of mortality with neither resurrection nor redemption' (quoted in an obituary for Derrida in the *Jerusalem Post* of 10 October 2004). *Of course*, Schopenhauer would say, Derrida could not accept death since the conditions he sets up for doing so – accepting the 'absolute' nature of mortality yet facing death without fear – are impossible for human beings to fulfil.

of our existence by reducing the painful part to but a brief chapter. Again, Schopenhauer thinks of Judaism and 'paganism' as, in this respect, inadequate religions.

The third essential function a religion is required to fulfil concerns society as a whole rather than the existential predicament of the individual. A religion provides social cohesion, creates community, by supporting morality.[4] There are two aspects to this.

First, it provides 'sanctions' for moral injunctions. Without sanctions, morality has neither sense nor force. The idea of a 'categorical' imperative is, Schopenhauer believes, a conceptual absurdity. Instilling moral rules and embedding them in a framework of sanctions is, he observes, a major part of childhood training.

The second aspect is that of showing what morality is. Religions have the essential function of providing 'a guiding star for . . . [people's] actions, as the public standard of integrity and virtue' (WR II p. 167). Obviously, the exemplary status of the life of, for instance, Jesus and the saints is an important part of what Schopenhauer has in mind here.

The final feature Schopenhauer sees as essential to any religion is *mystery*. Part of the reason for the allegorical nature of religious language – as opposed to the literalness aimed at by philosophy – is, as we have seen, that the latter would be beyond the comprehension of the uneducated masses. But part of the reason that religion needs mysteries, even contradictions, is to show that it is dealing with an order of things so profound as inevitably to distort the language that tries to talk about it. So, for example, Augustine's and Luther's mysteries are greatly to be preferred to the 'trite and dull comprehensibility' of Pelagianism. This, Schopenhauer observes, is what Tertullian was getting at when he wrote 'It is thoroughly credible because it is absurd . . . it is certain because it is impossible' (WR II pp. 166–7). In a word, Schopenhauer is against the 'demythologising' of religion – a theme which, as we will see, reappears in Nietzsche's critique of David Strauss in the first of the *Untimely Meditations*.

What Schopenhauer is really getting at, here, is – as Dostoevsky's Grand Inquisitor observes – that, unlike temporal power, religion needs mystery to provide it with authority. Mystery creates authority by utilising our awe before the unknown.

---

4 Emile Durkheim defines religion *solely* in terms of the use of the sacred to create 'one single moral community' (Durkheim (1995) p. 47). This failure to recognise the essential role played by the task of overcoming death in all world-religions makes his account inferior, I think, to Schopenhauer's.

In sum then, according to Schopenhauer's paradigm, a religion is something with four central and interconnected features: it provides a 'solution' to the problem of death, a solution to the problem of pain, an exposition and sanctioning of the morality of the community of believers, and, finally, it is pervaded by a sense of mystery. I want to turn now to Nietzsche, and to the question of the degree to which we can discover this same paradigm in his thinking about religion.

CHAPTER 2

The Birth of Tragedy

THE PROBLEM

In two ways, *The Birth of Tragedy* stands in Schopenhauer's shadow. First, the metaphysical framework on which it is constructed is Schopenhauer's version of Kantian idealism: Schopenhauer's view that the manifest world is mere 'appearance', ultimately a 'dream', behind which stands the metaphysically real, the 'thing in itself'. Second, it assumes the truth of Schopenhauer's pessimism. In our heart of hearts, Nietzsche believes, we all really know that pain is the rule and joy the occasional exception, so that we are permanently liable to experience a paralysing 'nausea' (BT 7) in the face of life. In our heart of hearts we are all acquainted, too, with life's 'absurdity' (*ibid.*). We all know that however fine a life we build up, however pretentious a bubble we blow, it will inevitably suffer the fatal prick of death; and so we succumb to the what's-the-point-of-it-all feeling. The contrast between the earnestness with which we pursue our projects and the inexorability of death reveals that, like the serious-faced clown slipping on a banana-skin, there is a tragic yet 'comic' (*ibid.*) aspect to human existence.

The Greeks, says Nietzsche, were especially aware of this, 'exquisitely' sensitive to the 'terrors and horrors' and absurdity of life. This is the evidence of their myths: the fate of Oedipus, the wisest of men who had solved the riddle of the Sphinx yet was destined to kill his father and sleep with his mother, the fate of Prometheus condemned on account of his love of man to have an eagle feed on his liver, and most directly the 'wisdom of Silenus'. Captured by King Midas and finally forced to speak, the forest daemon declares 'with a cackle' that for humans, 'The very best thing is . . . not to have been born, not to *be*, to be *nothing*. However, the second best thing for you is: to die soon' (BT 3). Yet the Greeks survived and, from the Homeric age to the fourth century, thrived. Nietzsche's question is: how did they do it?

Nietzsche identifies four possible responses to 'nausea' and 'absurdity', to pain and death. Ostensibly he is commenting, *qua* historian, on the ancient world. But since ancient history is only interesting in so far as it provides a 'polished mirror' in which to view ourselves (HH II a 218), in so far as it is 'relevant', he is, at the same time, speaking about *us* and *our* possible responses to these universal phenomena.

First, a culture may have no solution at all to the problems of pain and death. Such is true of certain 'dark' ages; of, for example, the age of the Titans that preceded that of Homer and the Olympians, an age in which the wisdom of Silenus was 'popular philosophy'. And it is true of the Fijian Islands where 'compassionate genocide' was widespread (BT 4, 15).[1]

Second, there is the 'Apollonian' art of, above all, Homer. Shortly, I shall look at just what Apollonian art is and at how it constitutes a 'solution' to pain and death, but for the moment let me just note that the key idea is that of 'discovering joy *in* appearances' (BT 17) through a 'veiling' of life's horrors and terrors.

Third, there is the 'Dionysian' art of Sophocles and Aeschylus which is distinguished from the Apollonian by the fact that it provides a '*metaphysical* comfort', teaches us 'to seek joy not in the appearances but behind them' (BT 17).

A final attempted solution to the nauseous and absurd is 'Socratism'. This is the conviction, which Nietzsche attributes to Socrates, that human reason, especially science and its offspring, technology, has in principle the capacity to solve every human problem.

THE QUESTION OF NIETZSCHE'S OWN ATTITUDE

Camus famously claimed that *the* problem of philosophy is suicide – whether life is worth living or not. Nietzsche *seems* to be dealing with this issue since he talks a great deal about the problem of 'justifying' life. He claims, for example, that 'only as *aesthetic phenomenon* is existence . . . *justified*' (BT 5). (What this means will be examined shortly.) When, however, he repeats this key sentence towards the end of the book it undergoes a significant change; 'only', it now reads, 'as aesthetic phenomenon does existence *appear* justified' (BT 24; my emphasis). Another startling passage occurs at the beginning of section 18, where Nietzsche says that Socratism, Apollonianism and Dionysianism are *all* 'illusions

---

1 How Nietzsche could possibly believe this of a South Sea island paradise is a mystery. Perhaps he did not know where Fiji was.

(*Illusionen*)' through which the unconscious 'will' that underlies all of life 'tricks' us into continued existence.

What all this adds up to is the fact that the youthful Nietzsche, following his mentor, Schopenhauer, actually believes that human life is *not* worth living. As Raymond Geuss says in his introduction to Ronald Speirs' excellent new translation of *The Birth*, Nietzsche's answer to the question 'Is life worth living?' is 'No' (BT p. xi). That is his answer to *Camus'* question. Another question, however, remains: given that the 'will to live' (Nietzsche agrees with Schopenhauer that this is the human essence) is a non-rational impulse which we cannot, save in very exceptional circumstances, escape, what did the Greeks – what can we – do about the pain and absurdity of life, what can we do to make its worthlessness at least *tolerable*? And in answer to this question, Nietzsche holds, three types of 'illusion' – Socratic, Apollonian and Dionysian – can be classified as more or less effective responses to the problem. Let us now look at these three responses in detail.

APOLLONIANISM

In *The Birth* Nietzsche speaks of Apollonian *art*. But since it is about the gods it is, like of course virtually all pre-modern art, *religious* art. In the unpublished 'The Dionysian World View' (1870) he explicitly calls the world view that appears in Homer a 'religion'; a 'religion of life, not one of duty or asceticism or spirituality' (BT p. 124). (As a paradigm of the art of 'asceticism and spirituality' one might call to mind the weightless, bloodless, boneless, sexless, eyes-turned-heavenward figures set against a background of lightning flashes and thunderclouds in El Greco's Counter-Reformation imaginings of saints and martyrs.)

The key word for the Apollonian is 'dream' (as the key word for the Dionysian is 'intoxication (*Rausch*)'). Nietzsche uses this word because, at least initially, the key contrast the Apollonian/Dionysian distinction is intended to capture, a contrast taken over from Schopenhauer, is the contrast between the representational arts on the one hand and music – 'absolute', purely instrumental, music – on the other. What the non-musical arts do is to produce *images* – which is what we do in dreams. (Presumably this same connexion is made by the Australian Aborigines, who call the time of the origin of the visible world 'the dreaming'.)

One thing that particularly attracts Nietzsche to the 'dream' metaphor is the fact that in dreams, as in good art, 'all forms speak to us: nothing is superfluous or unnecessary' (BT 1). 'Dream', that is to say, is a better word than 'image' because it provides him with a criterion of *good* art. After he has recovered from his infatuation with the formless rhapsody of Wagnerian music, Nietzsche always maintains that good art must be clear, simple, economical and logical – 'classical' as he calls it, in recognition of Greek Apollonianism as its supreme exemplification.

A severe disadvantage of the 'dream' metaphor, however, is that in encountering art we know we are confronting a fictive image – even when the 'willing suspension of disbelief' sets in – whereas in dreams we do not. This forces Nietzsche to claim, implausibly, that all dreams are 'lucid' – are such that the dreamer knows he is dreaming (BT 1). This appears to reflect a peculiarity of Nietzsche's own dream-life. In later works he abandons the representation–dream connexion, perhaps through coming to realise the atypical character of his dreaming.

On balance, I think, one should forget the 'dream' metaphor and say, simply, that Apollonian art is 'imaging' – or 'imag-ining' – art.

One confusing feature of *The Birth* is that it uses 'Apollonian' in two senses. In the first it just means the everyday world, the world which, following Schopenhauer, Nietzsche calls the world of the '*principium individuationis*'. Apollo, that is to say, he regards as the god of boundary drawing, justice, individuality and plurality (BT 1, 2, 9). So the everyday world is 'Apollonian' because it is a world of individual *things*: a boundary, as Heidegger observed, is more perspicuously understood as where a thing *starts* than as where it finishes.

In the second sense, 'Apollonian' refers to this same world raised to a state of glory in Homeric art. It is its 'perfection', 'apotheosis', 'transfiguration' (BT 1, 4, 16). Christian art (for example, the art of El Greco mentioned above) erects a non- and so anti-human ideal. Since none of *us* can have a virgin birth or escape sexual desire we are tainted by original sin from the start. But Apollonian art does the opposite. It 'deifies [incorporates into its portraits of the gods] everything [human] whether good or evil' (BT 3; compare BT p. 124). It was a radiant portrait of *themselves* the Greeks constructed in Apollonian art, the 'ideal image of their own existence'.[2] Thus do the gods 'justify the life of man by

---

2 Nietzsche's emphasis on the strong continuity between men and gods experienced by the Greeks (see, further, p. 71 below) has received recent support from Jasper Griffin, who points out that in the original Olympic games there were no prizes for coming second or third, that, unlike its nineteenth-century re-creation, what was important was winning, not taking part. 'The victor was', he continues, 'in his moment of victory, supreme. So supreme was he, in fact, that the line distinguishing mortal men from the gods was drawn, at times, into question. Pindar compares his

living it themselves – the only satisfying theodicy!' (BT 3). In this way, Nietzsche observes, the Greeks 'overcame . . . or at any rate veiled' (BT 3) the terrors and horrors of existence. In this way they 'seduced' themselves into continued existence. 'Existence under the bright sunshine of such gods is regarded as desirable in itself' (*ibid*).

What exactly is the character of this 'transfiguration' of human life? Frequently Nietzsche says it is a matter of 'illusion' and 'lies' (BT 3, 7, 16, 18). The world view of Apollonian art stands to reality, he says, as does 'the ecstatic vision of the tortured martyr to his torments' (BT 3). In 'The Dionysian World View' he speaks of the cross behind the roses (BT 124). Drawn as they are from Christian iconography these images are aesthetically inappropriate in a work that is already, as *Ecce Homo* observes, quietly yet profoundly 'hostile' to Christianity (EH IV 1). But what makes them positively misleading is that they conjure up the idea of falsification, a view of life with all the unpleasant bits covered over, cast into oblivion. In fact, however, this cannot be Nietzsche's view, first, because Homer's stories are *war* stories packed full of death and destruction, and, second, because Nietzsche explicitly acknowledges this, saying that in Homer, 'all things whether good *or evil* are deified' (BT 3; my emphasis). So *concealing* the 'terrors and horrors' of life cannot be the intended account of transfiguration.

Nietzsche speaks of Apollonian art as 'transform[ing] the most terrible things by joy in mere appearance and redemption through mere appearance' (BT 12). And he speaks of the Apollonian artist as one who – unlike the scientist, who always wants to 'uncover', get to the bottom of, things – 'cling[s] with rapt gaze on what remains even after such uncovering' (BT 15). Even after the uncovering of unpleasant truth, the Apollonian artist takes delight in the beautiful, delight in 'beautiful forms' (BT 16).

This suggests that the art of the Homeric epic – and the corresponding attitude to life – is a matter not of elimination, but rather of focus. It suggests an attitude in which one is inclined to describe life as 'terrible but magnificent'. In Uccello's *Battle of San Romano*, for example, the ground is littered with bodies and body parts. But what captures one's attention is the magnificence of the horses, the athleticism of the combatants, the sheen on the armour and the vibrant colour of the pennants fluttering proudly in the breeze. (This is an apposite comparison since at one point Nietzsche compares human existence to that of soldiers in an oil-painting

victorious athletes to the heroes of myth, sons of gods and goddesses, to Achilles and Ajax and Heracles' (*New York Review of Books* 51 no. 16, 21 October 2004, p. 20).

of a battle scene (BT 5).) Were one to look for a modern instance of Apollonian art, what might come to mind is the Western: death and destruction are all about, but what one focuses on is the cool courage and the sheer 'style' of its heroes. On a more debased level, the same phenomenon is exhibited by the space-invaders game and the 'woman's' magazine. In the latter, terrible things – drunkenness, disease, divorce and death – happen to its gods and goddesses (minor royals, rock musicians and football stars), but through it all the glamour remains, their stardom shines on.

The Apollonian outlook on life – in the Preface to *The Gay Science* Nietzsche calls it 'being superficial – *out of profundity*' – requires a strongly external approach both to others and to oneself. (Schopenhauer makes the same observation about the Homeric world: objects and events are portrayed, he says, with a unique 'objectivity', are untouched, that is to say, by human moods and feelings (PP II p. 444).) The outlook requires that death be, as in the space-invaders game, bloodless and painless. It requires a kind of inner anaesthesia. This, I think, is why Nietzsche associates it with 'illusion' and (in an 'extra-moral', non-judgmental way) 'lie': it is, as it were, a three-dimensional object represented two-dimensionally. Though there is no censorship of *facts*, there is, none the less, censorship: of *perspectives*. The inner perspective, how it feels to be on the *inside* of loss, injury and mortality, is not allowed to be seen.

The heart of the 'lie' concerns death. What Apollonianism represents is, in Heideggerian language, an 'inauthentic' attitude to death. By treating all death in an equally 'objective' way, it evades what *Being and Time* calls the 'mineness (*Jemeinigkeit*)' of death, pretends that death is always someone *else's* problem. This means that what Schopenhauer plausibly identifies as the most important function of religion is not satisfied by the Apollonian outlook. Since it pretends that *my* death never happens it can never provide me with a 'consolation' for it. And so, as Nietzsche records in 'The Dionysian World View', when his own death inevitably approaches, Apollonian man is without recourse: 'the pain of Homeric man related to departure from this existence, above all to imminent departure' (BT p. 125). The good death, in the sense of dying *my* death well, is impossible for Apollonian man.

This is, I think, the major reason Nietzsche ultimately prefers the Dionysian 'solution' to the terrors and horrors of existence. For, as we shall see, it does have something important to say by way of consoling us in the face of death.

DIONYSIANISM

The religious/artistic outlook of Apollonianism is, therefore, inadequate: inadequate in terms of Schopenhauer's account of a fully functioning religion and inadequate from *our* point of view – remember that what we are really thinking about, in the 'polished mirror' of the Greeks, is ourselves. I turn now to the Dionysian outlook which Nietzsche takes to be embodied in Greek tragedy.

What, first of all, does Dionysus stand for? Exactly how is Dionysianism distinguished from Apollonianism?

At its first introduction, as we saw, whereas Apollonian art is image-making, the Dionysian is image-less music. This way of painting the contrast is, however, inadequate if, as Nietzsche does, one wishes to speak of Apollonian *epochs* as well as outlooks. For obviously, music was as present in Homeric Greece as it was in later times. This leads Nietzsche to draw a distinction between Apollonian and Dionysian *music*, the latter being, he claims, unknown to the Homeric Greeks (BT 2).

What is the difference between the two? Apollonian music is, says Nietzsche, the 'wave-like rhythm' of the cithara. It is the self-restraint of Doric architecture translated into sound. It engages only the voice – apart, presumably, from the mechanics of playing the cithara. Dionysian music, on the other hand, is 'dithyrambic', performed out of a state of rapture. It engages not just the mouth but the whole body, moves its devotees to *dance* (a key Nietzschean word) (BT 2).[3]

So, remembering that *Rausch* is the one-word summation of the Dionysian, the contrast seems to be between restrained and intoxicated music. Examples of the latter supplied by Nietzsche include not only the chorus of Greek tragedy but also the 'Dionysian enthusiasts' of the Middle Ages – the roaming throngs, singing and dancing in celebration of St John or St Vitus (BT 1).

To these examples, one might perhaps add the rock festival and charismatic Christian worship. (The latter offers, perhaps, a hint of a 'post-death-of-God' Christianity, a Christianity that might to a large degree *agree* with Nietzsche's critique of its traditional form.)

---

3 Since all music has a rhythm it might well be argued that all music is 'dance' music, is at least repressed dance. This suggests that Nietzsche's distinction between the two kinds of music ought to be regarded as a distinction of degree rather than kind.

Another characterisation of the Apollonian/Dionysian dichotomy is made in terms of Schopenhauer's metaphysics. Since Apollo is the god of boundary-drawing – both ethical and conceptual – he is the god of the *principium individuationis*. But the world of the *principium individuationis* is an ideal world. Beyond the 'dream' of plurality, reality itself is 'One'. So Dionysian 'intoxication' is a transcendence of everyday consciousness in which we overcome individuality and so, of course, the mortality that attaches to it.

Nietzsche distinguishes what we may call the *pure* Dionysian state – that which was experienced by the 'barbarians' of the ancient world – from the *modified* Dionysian state – that which was experienced in Greek tragedy.

The pure state is Janus-faced. On the one hand there is the feeling of universal 'brotherhood' as expressed in Beethoven's (or Schiller's) 'Hymn to Joy'. When all the 'rigid, hostile barriers' which 'necessity, caprice, or "impudent fashion"' have established between one human being and another have dematerialised, one has the sense of belonging to a 'higher community', feels 'on the brink of flying and dancing up and away into the air above' (BT 1). But on the other hand the pure state can as easily express itself as a release of the beast in man, as the 'witches brew' of 'sensuality and cruelty' which periodically swept over the 'barbarian' world, destroying the 'statutes' of family life (BT 2). Why cruelty? Because if identity is universal then the sacrifice of an individual is as trivial as the cutting of one's toenails. The individual may, indeed, be sacrificed precisely as an affirmation of the supra-individual identity possessed by all things.

Not just the life of the family, but also that of the state is rendered impossible by pure Dionysianism. 'Dionysian outbursts' are accompanied by a 'dwindling of the political instinct', by indifference, even hostility, to everyday, collective life in the world: 'the state and the sense of home-land (*Heimatsinn*)', 'the original male lust for struggle', cannot survive without the 'assertion of individual personality' (BT 21).

That pure Dionysianism is incompatible with the state is relatively obvious. If one ascends to a 'higher community', if one's kingdom is not of this world, then the kingdoms that are of this world cannot interest one. This is why Nietzsche says that the 'ecstatic brooding' of pure Dionysianism 'leads a people . . . along the road towards Indian Buddhism', engenders 'apathy' towards 'worldly' things (BT

21).[4] One has no motive to engage in the Apollonian business of law-making and law-following.

That 'homeland' also involves Apollonian division and individuation, however, is perhaps not so obvious. But what Nietzsche is talking about here is, I think, 'identity politics'. I cannot have a sense of a cultural place, and so cannot have a sense of *my* place, without a boundary, a division, an opposition between it and the foreign. I cannot be a Greek without a concept of 'the barbarian' (or at least the non-Greek). Homeland, no less than the state, is dependent on division and individuation, a point to which I shall return at the very end of this book.

Given that pure Dionysianism is incompatible with communal life, the Greeks had – one has – an obvious motive for seeking to modify it. The modified state is embodied, Nietzsche holds, in Greek tragedy, the focal point of Greek culture at its highest point.

Greek tragedy grew, Nietzsche observes, out of the Dionysian festival. Originally the festival consisted in the communal singing of hymns to Dionysus. Later, action and actors were 'born' out of the music in somewhat the way in which the idea of 'moonlight' might be born out of the music of Beethoven's piano sonata.[5] Finally, a distinction grew up between chorus and audience. The chorus became, as it were, professionalised.

In two ways, says Nietzsche, Greek tragedy is quite unlike modern theatre. First, there are no 'spectators' in the modern sense. Though physically separate, 'the audience of Attic tragedy identified itself with the chorus on the *orchestra*, so that there was fundamentally no opposition between public and chorus'. True to its origins in communal singing, 'the whole is just one sublime chorus' (BT 8). Second, the audience was no tiara-and-ball-gowned elite parading its wealth and cultivation. Rather, as one looked down, the 'whole . . . world' was assembled on the terraces

---

4 There seems to be a certain tension, here, between orgy and apathy, between the idea of Dionysianism as the *smashing* of statutes and the idea of it as *indifference* to them. The thought must be that these are two *different* manifestations of pure Dionysianism, or possibly two *phases*, so that a complete process might start with orgy and end in apathy.

5 The original, full title of Nietzsche's book is *The Birth of Tragedy out of the Spirit of Music*. Nietzsche's basic idea of the way in which music gives birth to text and action is, he acknowledges, taken over from Schopenhauer (BT 5). Schopenhauer's idea, in a nutshell, is that purely instrumental music describes the inner, object-less phenomenology of an emotion which, because it lacks an intentional object, is universal. Words and actions, if they authentically grow out of the music, fit a specific outer 'example' to that universal inner feeling. (See WR 1 section 52 and, for a detailed discussion, see Young (2005) chapter 6.)

(*ibid.*). *Everyone* (except possibly women and slaves) was there. The modern rock concert or football match (which are increasingly merging into one other) provides, in fact, more of an approximation to Greek tragedy than modern theatre or cinema. Yet even they provide only a distant approximation. One was, as Raymond Geuss points out in his introduction (BT p. xi), paid to attend the tragic festival as one is paid for modern jury service, a fact which indicates how different Greek tragedy was from anything that might be produced by the modern 'entertainment industry'.

Nietzsche is quite clear that tragedy was a 'religious' occasion. 'Purely religious' in origin (BT 7), its coming into being was, he says, 'the most important moment in the history of Greek religion' (BT 2). Sophocles, in particular, is a profoundly 'religious writer' (BT 9). So bearing in mind Schopenhauer's account of the essential characteristics of a religion, let us ask what tragedy has to offer as a consolation for nausea and absurdity, for pain and death.

Nietzsche's answer comes by way of an account of the 'tragic effect' (essentially a repetition of Schopenhauer's account[6]), an account of the seeming paradox of our deriving satisfaction from witnessing the destruction of figures who, in most ways, represent what is finest and wisest among us.

Because, as Greeks, we identify with the chorus rather than with the figures engaged in the action, tragedy produces in us, says Nietzsche, the 'metaphysical solace' that 'in the ground of things and despite all changing appearances, life is indestructibly mighty and pleasurable' (BT 7).[7] This is because we transcend the everyday: the world of individuals becomes 'unreal' (BT 8), individuals become like soldiers in a painting (BT 5). Instead of identifying with anything *in* the world of the *principium individuationis*, 'for a brief moment' we become

the primordial being itself and we feel its unbounded greed and lust for being: the struggle, the agony, the destruction of appearances, all this now seems to us to be necessary given the uncountable excess of forms of existence thrusting and pushing themselves into life, given the exuberant fertility of the world-will. (BT 17)

From this it follows that

---

6 See WR II chapter 37. For a detailed discussion, see Young (2005) chapter 6.
7 In other words, it satisfies the Schopenhauerian 'metaphysical need'. Though we shall soon see Nietzsche arguing that the 'need' is something to be *exterminated*, here, clearly, he thinks of it as something to be *satisfied*.

Only as aesthetic phenomenon do existence and the world appear justified; which means that tragic myth in particular must convince us that even the ugly and disharmonious is an artistic game which the [Schopenhauerian] Will in the fullness of its delight plays with itself. (BT 24)

This, then, is the 'solace', the 'consolation' for pain and death brought to us by tragedy. For a brief moment one has intuitive insight into the truth of Schopenhauerian idealism. Pain and death, I realise, are not *my* problem since, while they belong to the realm of mere appearance, what I, in truth, am is the thing in itself, the 'primordial unity', the 'world-will'. Pain and death are not my problem since they are just parts of the epic movie with respect to which I am, not a participant, but rather – given my identification with the 'world-building force' that 'the dark Heraclitus' compared to a child building sandcastles and then knocking them over again (BT 24) – 'the sole author and spectator' (BT 6). Not just parts but *necessary* parts since, as Margaret Atwood ruefully observes, there is no narrative without conflict, a plot can never encompass the new without destroying the old.[8]

So that is the Dionysian solace: the solace we find not, as in Apollonian solace, *in* a glorified world of appearance but rather 'behind' it (BT 17). Tragedy 'relieves us of the greedy thirst for this existence' by reminding us of a 'higher delight' for which the tragic hero 'prepares himself not by his victories but by his destruction' (BT 21).

But if this is the nature of the tragic effect, does not the supposedly 'modified' Dionysian state turn out to be exactly the same as the 'pure'

---

8 This theodicy-like idea – crudely, the proverb that you can't make an omelette without breaking eggs – might seem to turn Schopenhauer's pessimism on its head. Whereas for Schopenhauer pain and death are supreme *objections* to life, *The Birth*, one might be tempted to conclude, turns them into *necessities*. This is what Nietzsche suggests in the 1886 'Attempt at a Self-Criticism' (sections 1 and 6) with which he prefaced the reissue of *The Birth*. Already in 1872, he claims, he had discovered his later 'pessimism of strength', though spoiling his 'Dionysian intuitions' with 'Schopenhauerian formulations'. In place of Schopenhauer's interpretation of the tragic outlook as leading to 'resignation', *The Birth* already interprets it, he suggests, in terms of a pessimism which '*demands* the terrifying as foe' – a pessimism which, as he later puts it, affirms life even in the face of, indeed precisely on account of, that which is 'most terrible and questionable . . . evil, absurd and ugly' (GS 370) in it. This, however, is a confusion. Schopenhauer's pessimism teaches resignation from *human* life. And that is precisely what *The Birth* teaches as, in Silenus' words, 'the best thing'. That pain and death are indispensable to *life as an entertainment for the primal unity* sitting back comfortably in its padded seat in the cosmic movie theatre does nothing at all to justify life to those who – like Christians in the Roman arena – have the misfortune to have to be *parts of* the entertainment. As I have already suggested, to the question of whether *life as a human individual* is worth living, *The Birth* replies with the same 'No' as does Schopenhauer. The 'romantic' Nietzsche is, in short, every bit as much a 'resignationist' as are Schopenhauer, Tristan, and Isolde.

Dionysian state? Not so. There are two ways in which the latter undergoes modification.

The first consists in the fact that, as Nietzsche puts it in 'The Dionysian World View', the Greeks 'spiritualised' the Dionysian festival (BT p. 123). ('Spiritualisation', which becomes a central notion in later Nietzsche and is very probably the origin of Freud's notion of 'sublimation', is a matter of finding a surrogate object to replace the natural object of a given impulse.) Whereas the barbarians made actual human sacrifices in ec-static affirmation of their supra-individual identity, the Greeks did it in art, 'in effigy', as *Daybreak* puts the idea (D 94). By removing it from the arena where it could destroy the 'statutes' of social life they *civilised* the Dionysian, made it, for the first time, *safe*.

The second modification concerns the fact that pure Dionysianism leads, as we saw, towards worldly 'apathy', towards a Buddhistic 'longing for nothingness' (BT 21). 'Individuality' is, says Nietzsche, 'the primal cause of all suffering' (BT 10). It is only as individuals that we face mortality and only as individuals that we experience the disjunction between will and world that constitutes suffering. So once we escape the world of individuals we want to *stay* out of it. Sounding rather like a rebirthing therapist, Nietzsche speaks of there being a Dionysian 'joy' in a return to the 'womb of the Primordial Unity' (BT 22) – the joy, as it were, of coming home from an alien place. And he also says that no one could listen to the final act of Wagner's dithyrambic *Tristan* as a piece of absolute music (easy to do if one happens not to understand German) without 'suffocating as their soul attempted convulsively to spread its wings' (BT 21). The reference, of course, is to the account, in Plato's *Phaedrus*, of the soul's preparation for a return to the heavens as its regrowing its wings. Though the writing is overblown, what Nietzsche is getting at seems to me a genuine phenomenon: the feeling, in the words of Schubert's '*An die Musik*', of being 'transported to a better world' that one experiences when one *really* listens to, immerses oneself in, certain kinds of music.

But, importantly, the tragic effect is *not* a pure Dionysian feeling. There is also the Apollonian aspect of the tragic drama. This shields us from the full force of the Dionysian effect, 'restores the almost shattered individual with the healing balm of illusion'. We are subject to the 'noble deception' that the tragedy concerns only the fate of an individual in a world of individuals. In this way, we return to everyday life strangely comforted yet 'relieved of the burden' of understanding why we are comforted, relieved of the burden of Dionysian insight, and so able, once more, to act (BT 21). This is the true meaning of Hamlet's paralysis; it is grounded in the knowledge that action requires the 'veil of [Apollonian] illusion' (BT 7).

So, Nietzsche concludes, the total effect of tragedy, the fact that Greeks created a 'tragic culture', enabled them, placed geographically between India and Rome, to discover a spiritual *via media* between the two. On the one hand they avoided the 'ecstatic brooding', the pure Dionysianism, of India – Nietzsche always regards Dionysus as an immigrant from the East – while on the other, they avoided the 'debilitating chase after power and honour' of the pure Apollonianism of the Roman Imperium (BT 21). The fourth-century Greeks achieved, that is, a perfect balance between the active and the contemplative.

THE ROLE OF MYTH

Nietzsche says that the mythic figures of Greek tragedy are 'contracted' images which 'abbreviate appearances'. And that they are human *types* rather than individuals (the actors of course all wore masks), which endows them with universal significance (BT 23).

Mainly towards the end of *The Birth* he makes some further remarks about myth which seem to have to do with the importance of myth in general rather than being confined to the tragic myths that formed the subject-matter of tragic drama.

Religions die, he observes, when 'orthodox dogmatism' corrals myth into the 'narrow confines' of historical fact. They die because this destroys the natural tendency within myths 'to go on living and to throw out new shoots' (BT 10). I take this to be a point against religious fundamentalism and in favour of modernisation. To be a *living* myth its figures require constant reinterpretation in order to make sense in the current historical context. (This theme will reappear and will be discussed in greater detail in chapter 4 below.)

Nietzsche says that 'only a [living] mythic horizon unifies a culture', in other words *makes* it a genuine culture. Only myth provides it with a 'secure and sacred place of origin'. The 'images of myth', he continues,

must be the unnoticed but ever-present daemonic guardians under whose tutelage young souls grow up and by whose signs the grown man interprets his life and his struggles; even the state knows of no more powerful unwritten laws than the mythical fundament which guarantees its connection with religion and its emergence from out of mythic representations.

(In Sophocles' *Antigone*, Antigone appeals to 'the unwritten laws divine' to justify her resistance to the unjust laws of Creon's state.)

Notice the appearance, in this quotation, of the Volkish doctrine of the priority of Volk to state (see p. 5 above.) 'Art and nation (*Volk*), myth and morality', Nietzsche concludes, are 'necessarily . . . entwined'. A 'people' is only properly a people if it can impose a mythic, 'eternal' view on its experience. Neither a people nor an individual human being can thrive without there being 'gods of the hearth' to constitute its 'mythical home' (BT 23).

What does all this mean? What Nietzsche is talking about is the importance of what his fellow radical German conservative, Martin Heidegger, calls (in section 76 of *Being and Time*) 'heritage'. As Heidegger conceives it, heritage is the ethical tradition of a community. It is embodied not in a book of rules but rather in narratives of the lives of exemplary 'heroes' or, as I shall call them, 'role models'.[9] (Hence for him, too, the 'laws' of heritage are 'unwritten'.) Heritage is the ultimate unifier, the creator of a culture, people or nation, and the ultimate court of appeal in which the laws of the state must find their legitimation.

Actually, it is no surprise that Heidegger's ideas concerning heritage and heroes can be used to explicate Nietzsche since, as he explicitly acknowledges, he derives those ideas from Nietzsche's 'penetrating' discussion in the second of his *Untimely Meditations*.[10] As we shall shortly see, what Nietzsche is talking about at the end of *The Birth* is what in the second *Meditation* he calls the 'monumental' use of history.

In sum, then, having addressed the problem of pain and death in discussing the Dionysian aspect of Greek culture, he is addressing here what Schopenhauer identifies as the second main function of religion: that of providing an exposition of a fundamental ethos which unifies a culture and gives its members a sense of community, rootedness, identity and meaning. Shortly, I shall show how the accomplishing of this task represents, for Nietzsche, the true significance of Apollonian art.

THE DEATH OF TRAGEDY

Eccentrically, Nietzsche thinks that Greek tragedy died at the hand of Euripides. It was killed by his 'putting the spectator on the stage' (BT 11).

---

9 Since 'role model' suggests the modelling of some specific role whereas ethical heroes are models for one's life as a whole, 'life model' would be a more appropriate term. I shall, however, stick with 'role model' for the sake of its catchy familiarity.
10 See Heidegger (1962) p. 448.

The hidden hand behind this murderous act, Nietzsche alleges, was Socrates.

What he means by 'putting the spectator on the stage' is that Euripides made drama into nothing but a representation of everyday life, thereby expelling the Dionysian element. He did this because, influenced by Socrates, he held 'reason to be the root of all enjoyment and creation'. He distrusted the 'puzzling depth', the 'comet's tale' of 'significance' trailed after them by the characters of his predecessors, Aeschylus and Sophocles. He particularly distrusted, and so eliminated, the mysterious, dithyrambic chanting of the chorus. Above all, therefore, Euripides represents the death of the chorus. All this is in the spirit of Socrates, is 'aesthetic Socratism', the conviction that to be beautiful is to be 'reasonable' (BT 11).

'Socratism' as such – Heidegger talks about 'Enlightenment' in a similar way – Nietzsche identifies with the rational, the logical, with the joy in 'unveiling', in getting beneath the surface of things to find out what makes them tick. 'Socratic man' (also 'Alexandrian man' and 'theoretical man') is one who, like, according to Nietzsche, the historical Socrates, has the 'imperturbable belief [i.e. *faith*] that thought, as it follows the thread of causality [i.e. of scientific reason], reaches down into the deepest abysses of being, and that it is capable, not simply of understanding existence, but even of *correcting* it' (BT 15). It is in other words the faith that science and its offspring, technology, has, in principle, the capacity to solve every human problem. As a consequence, it makes existence seem 'justified' and is therefore 'optimistic', believing (like *Zarathustra*'s 'last man') in the possibility of 'earthly happiness for all' (BT 18).

It is, therefore, not difficult to see why, from the 'Socratic' point of view, tragedy, the Dionysian, had to go. It undermines faith in reason, the key to human happiness.

Nietzsche makes two important claims about Socratism. First, that it is not merely ungrounded *faith*, but that it is actually *false*. This is revealed by science (in the broad, German sense) itself. Thanks to 'the extraordinary courage and wisdom of Kant and Schopenhauer', thanks, in other words, to idealism, which confines causality to the realm of mere appearance, we know that ultimate reality is *not* accessible to, and hence not 'correctible' by, natural science (BT 18). What this means is that a Socratic culture is liable to catastrophic traumas as *moira*, fate (BT 3), the 'child-god', smashes one of his sandcastles (see p. 24 above), traumas for which it is entirely unprepared. Nietzsche's second claim is that Socratism is the way that we of the post-Enlightenment West are now. (9/11 might be thought of as just such a trauma.) *Modern* man is 'Socratic man', 'theoretical man'.

To these claims Nietzsche adds a third: Socratic culture is *degenerate* culture. Why should this be so?

WHAT IS WRONG WITH THE WAY WE ARE NOW?

Nietzsche claims that two things are wrong with Western modernity. First, through the loss of the Dionysian 'maternal womb' we are deprived of the 'metaphysical solace' for the fact of death that is possessed by a tragic culture (BT 23). The implication is that anxiety about death has to be a constant undertone to modern culture, a life-degrading undertone since, as Derrida remarks, learning to live means learning to die.[11] Through living in a secular, scientistic culture, we find ourselves without anything to replace the first of the two main functions of religion, that of providing a solution to the 'riddle' of death. Though Socratism might purport to offer in the long term a solution to the problem of pain, it offers nothing at all when it comes to death.[12]

The second thing wrong with our Socratic culture, according to Nietzsche, is that it kills myth (BT 23), destroys the foundation on which authentic community depends. His grounds for holding this are, however, somewhat difficult to decipher, the reason being, I think, that without properly distinguishing them, he has in fact two lines of explanation. Both of these have to do with art. The first concerns the *existence* of art in the modern age, the second concerns its *use*.

Nietzsche says that the 'foundations of art and Volk, myth and morality' are 'necessarily and closely intertwined' (BT 23). What he has particularly in mind at this point, I think, is *Apollonian* art – or the Apollonian side of art which combines the Apollonian with the Dionysian.

Apollonian art, as we know, 'transfigures', 'glorifies'. Through the techniques of the trade – pushing the not-so-attractive out of focus, pushing the attractive into focus, through dramatic and partial lighting

---

11 See footnote 3 of chapter 1.

12 Sensing that if it is ever going to replace the need for religion it *has* to promise immortality, certain of the more speculative of contemporary scientists talk of our age as the first in which the achievement of eternal life – eternal, embodied, individual existence – represents a realistic project. It is doubtful, however, that the idea is ultimately intelligible, and even more doubtful that eternal life would be desirable either for individuals or for humanity as a whole.

and so forth – it raises the mundane to a state of glory, makes it 'shine'.[13] By doing so it allows us, as Nietzsche's later meditation on Apollonian art puts it, to 'esteem the hero that is concealed in . . . everyday characters' (GS 78). But of course, to allow a figure to shine the artist is at the same time *discovering* that figure. So really, Apollonian art does two things: it *selects* certain figures as, in my abbreviating phrase, 'role models' and it endows them with the charismatic *authority* they require in order to inspire our lives. This is what Greek, or for that matter medieval, art does: it selects those figures which embody communal ethos and endows them with motivational power.

Nietzsche's first explanation of why the modern human being is 'myth-less man' is that, in our Socratic culture, nothing 'shines' any more. When, for example, we go to the theatre, we can no longer experience the '*miracle*' which, for children, happens as a matter of course (BT 23). Modernity, as Max Weber was later to put it, suffers from *Entzauberung* – *Ent-zauberung*, dis-enchantment. We have lost the magic, the magic, in particular, of art. The cause, according to Nietzsche, is that we have been overcome by the 'critical-historical spirit', have become 'Socratic, critical human beings' (*ibid.*). I shall have a great deal more to say about the 'critical-historical spirit' in the next chapter, but the idea, roughly, is that we have become oversophisticated. Overwhelmed by information about other cultural practices and about past practices of our own culture we have lost the naivety necessary to respond to the charisma of art. Childlike responsiveness has been replaced by 'scholarly', knowing detachment (*ibid.*).

Whether or not this analysis had some plausibility with respect to the 'modernity' of the nineteenth century, it seems, at least at first glance, to have little application to *our* modernity. For the fact is that many, in fact many *too* many, things 'shine' in modernity, and they shine precisely on account of art – otherwise known as 'the media': David Beckham, Princess Di (as immortal as any of the Olympians), Tom Cruise, this and that 'teenage idol', this week's winner of the 'reality' TV show, and so on.

This is that point anticipated with great prescience by Nietzsche's second explanation of the myth-lessness of modernity. 'Only by myth

---

13 In *The Gay Science* Nietzsche says that 'artists constantly glorify – they do nothing else' (GS 85). In his middle period the Apollonian–Dionysian dichotomy disappears from his writings, the reason being, I would argue, that he treats *all* (worthwhile) art as Apollonian. As we shall see, it is only in the final year of his productive life that Dionysian art is allowed to reappear (in TI IX 9–10).

can all the energies of fantasy and Apollonian dream be saved from aimless meandering' (BT 23) 'Aimless meandering' seems to me precisely to capture the fickle flickering of celebrity – 'Apollonian dream' – in the present age. And what this means, for Nietzsche, is that the Apollonian art of the present is devoid of 'mythic' content.

The important thing to notice here is that, for Nietzsche, 'myth' means something like 'unified, comprehensive and consistent myth'. For him a myth is something that can constitute 'the unity (*Einsein*) of Volk and culture', something that can constitute 'the noble core of [a] . . . people's character (*Volkscharakter*)' so that there could be such a thing as, for example, '*the* German myth' (BT 23; my emphasis).[14] So, for example, the entire panoply of Greek gods and heroes constitutes a *single* myth, the entire range of Christian divinities and saints another. From this point of view the problem with modernity is that we have, not a community-creating myth, but rather – as Nietzsche puts it in a related context – 'fragment and riddle and terrible accident': all we have is an incoherent and constantly changing chaos of myth-*fragments*, a 'pandemonium of myths . . . thrown into a disorderly heap' (*ibid.*), as Nietzsche puts it.

On the face of things, Nietzsche's two explanations of the myth-lessness of modernity are inconsistent with each other. The first, claiming that nothing 'shines' in modernity, seems to *deny the existence* of (Apollonian) art in modernity. The second, on the other hand, seems to say that art is there but lacks coherent *focus*. I do not know how Nietzsche would wish to remove this appearance of inconsistency, but one possibility is the following.

The death of awe before the magical that afflicts the (in contemporary terminology) 'deconstructive' spirit, Nietzsche may want to say, characterises the (supposedly) educated intelligentsia: those adherents of 'modern ideas' whom he constantly disparages. The 'aimless meandering' of Apollonian fantasy, on the other hand, characterises the uneducated masses, the wandering 'herd', in his later terminology. If this is right then Nietzsche's description of modernity is, in a word, cynicism of the few combined with the manipulable gullibility of the many.

---

14 Sounding very much like Hans Sachs at the end of Wagner's *Mastersingers*, Nietzsche calls, at the end of *The Birth*, for a '*rebirth of German myth*' (BT 23; Nietzsche's emphasis.) As soon as he has recovered from his infatuation with Wagner such nationalist sentiments disappear from Nietzsche's thought, become, indeed, anathema to it. (See, further, pp. 213–14 below.) What never disappears, however, as we shall see, is his commitment to the vital importance of communal myth.

In Nietzsche's view, modern culture is, then, 'myth-less'. In pointing to the specific consequences or symptoms of this, he develops the beginning of a 'cultural criticism' that proves to be remarkably consistent throughout his career.

The first such symptom is loss of unity. Since 'only a horizon surrounded by myths encloses and unifies a cultural movement', without it 'all cultures lose their healthy, creative, natural energy'. Community, that is, a common enterprise shaped by a shared conception of the good life, is replaced by a 'wilderness of thought, morals, and action', a 'home-less roaming about' (BT 23). Both communally and individually, life becomes meaningless.[15]

The second symptom is a 'greedy scramble to grab a place at the table of others', the quest for meaning in the supermarket of foreign religions and cultures (BT 23). One might think, here, of 'post-modernist' architecture. What Nietzsche is effectively pointing out (in 1872!) is that this kind of 'post-modernism', the raiding of past and alien cultures as a symptom of the hollowed-out emptiness of one's own, actually belongs to modernity.

The final symptom *The Birth* draws attention to is modernity's 'feverish agitation'. The loss of the eternal, mythical perspective on things, the loss of a 'meaning of life', leads to an 'enormous growth in worldliness', a 'frivolous deification of the present . . . of the "here and now"' or else 'a dull turning away from it' (BT 23). This is what modern German sociologists call the *Erlebnisgesellschaft* – the society of the frenzied quest for 'experiences', for cheap thrills. Without a communal ethos to give aspiration and meaning to one's life, the only way of keeping boredom at bay is in the frenzied search for cheap thrills. At the back of Nietzsche's mind, here, I suspect, is Schopenhauer's stress-or-boredom observation (see p. 9 above.) Without the (healthy) stress provided by an identity-defining ideal, life can only be preserved from boredom by the quest for ever more exotic thrills.

Nietzsche calls, in *The Birth*, for a living of Greek history in reverse (BT 19). So although he already accepts, and indeed already quietly celebrates, the 'death' of the Christian God, far from celebrating the disappearance of religion from our culture, far from celebrating secularism, he calls for

---

15 One might call to mind, here, the later Nietzsche's remark that 'If we possess our *why* of life we can put up with almost any *how*; man does not strive after happiness (*Glück*); only the [utilitarian] Englishman does that' (TI 1 12).

a religious *revival*. Specifically, he calls for something that will play the role in modern life that was played by religious myth, and in particular by the tragic myth and the tragic festival, in the lives of our 'radiant leaders', the Greeks (BT 23). He calls, in an oversimplifying nutshell, for a revival of 'Greek' religion. Religion is thus early Nietzsche's solution to the ills of modernity. The question for the remainder of this book is: what happens to this solution, this religious communitarianism, in the earthquakes and sea-changes that occur in the later works? Does it disappear without trace, survive with modifications, or survive virtually unmodified?

CHAPTER 3

Untimely Meditations

Discussions of Nietzsche typically move directly from the 'romanticism' of *The Birth* to the 'positivism' of *Human, All-too-Human*. The *Untimely Meditations*, poised, it is felt, in an uncomfortable no man's land, generally get short shrift. For two reasons, however, this is unfortunate. First, because they contain a great deal of very good philosophy. And second, because many later ideas have their origins in the *Meditations* and become much more intelligible when read in the light of those origins. I shall discuss the four *Meditations* in the obvious order. The question that guides each discussion is that of whether the conclusion of *The Birth*, that religion is essential to life, is preserved in the *Meditations*.

FIRST MEDITATION: 'DAVID STRAUSS: THE CONFESSOR AND THE WRITER'

David Strauss was a Hegelian who wrote a 'deconstructive'[1] *Life of Jesus* in 1835–6. By discovering inconsistencies between the gospels and establishing that a recognisably Christian faith only came into being after Jesus' death, this book probably made a significant contribution to Nietzsche's own abandonment of Christianity in 1865.[2] Though generally extremely rude about him, Nietzsche admits that Strauss had *once* been a fine scholar. In this, the first of the *Untimely Meditations* (1873), Nietzsche attacks the aged Strauss who offers Hegelian optimism – a kind of

---

1 In the second *Meditation* Nietzsche identifies 'Voltairean *écrasez* (Voltairean destruction)' as the essence of the 'critical-historical' examination of texts undertaken by scholars such as Strauss (UM II 7). Since, later on, he himself, in his 'genealogical' investigations, comes to deploy the critical-historical method, and since Derrida is on record as saying that his deconstruction is just Nietzschean genealogy, it seems appropriate here to speak of deconstruction.

2 And to George Eliot's abandonment of Christian metaphysics. She translated the book into English in 1846.

evolutionary pantheism – as an alternative religion. It affirms the 'rationality of the real' (UM 1 2) as leading to a 'heaven on earth' (UM 1 4). In *Ecce Homo*, Nietzsche says that the first of the *Meditations* is an 'attack on German culture' (EH v 1). So the 'assassination (*Attentat*)' (EH v 2) of Strauss is in a sense impersonal: Strauss is attacked as a representative of current German culture. Nietzsche has three main criticisms of his doctrine.

First, it is a 'stupid ease and contentment doctrine' written for the benefit of Strauss' 'we' (UM 1 6). Like Hegelianism in general, it is merely a 'deification of success', an 'apotheosis of the commonplace' (UM 1 7). As Nietzsche reads the Hegelianism of the 1870s, that is, Bismarck's Germany, bourgeois Prussia, replete with the triumph over France in the war of 1870–1, is taken to represent the final coincidence of the rational and the real, the 'end of history'. Nietzsche objects that this is an inauthentic pandering to Strauss' self-satisfied, bourgeois readership. Such pandering might perhaps have *something* to be said for it were there to be anything to admire about the culture of imperial Germany, but in fact there is nothing at all to admire about a bourgeois 'philistinism' which, like a worm, conceived of heaven as nothing higher than a 'fat carcass' (UM 1 6). Indeed, as we will see when we turn to the second of the *Meditations*, it does not actually count as an authentic culture at all.

Second, even if there is a primordial source of everything, how, Nietzsche asks, can it possibly be called 'God' and made an object of religious veneration since, as the source of everything, it is also the source of all *evil* (UM 1 7)? (This powerful objection to pantheism, as old as medieval theology, is repeated in *The Gay Science*. In the end, however, so I shall argue, Nietzsche himself comes to affirm a form of pantheism. An important task, therefore, will be to see how he seeks to overcome this fundamental objection.)

The third criticism of Strauss amounts to the claim that, in the language of *The Birth*, he is a 'Socratist', believing science to be capable of solving every human problem. There are two things Nietzsche objects to about this. First, he repeats the claim of *The Birth* that Socratism is shown to be false by Kantian philosophy. Strauss, he says, is one of those people who find it impossible to understand Kant. That he subscribes to 'the crudest kind of realism' shows he has no understanding of

Kant's critique of reason . . . no notion of the fundamental antinomies of idealism [Nietzsche means 'antinomies that are *resolved by* idealism'] or of the extreme relativity of all science and reason. Or: it is precisely reason that ought to tell him how little of the in-itself of things can be determined by reason.

(UM 1 6)[3]

From this reaffirmation of idealism it is reasonable to infer that Nietzsche has found no reason to abandon *The Birth*'s account of the tragic effect, no reason to abandon his 'Dionysian' solution to the 'riddle' of death.

Nietzsche's second objection to Strauss' scientism is that it is 'consciously dishonest'. An honest Socratist would tell his public: 'I have liberated you from a helpful and merciful God, the universe is only a rigid machine, take care you are not mangled in its wheels.' Instead of this, however, Strauss reacts 'religiously' and tries to build God into the machine. The result is bad science and bad religion (UM 1 7).

This is an important pointer to Nietzsche's later position on the science-versus-religion question. Even in the positivist period, as we will see, Nietzsche holds that one can perhaps have science *and* religion. But what one can never have – as Kant, too, insisted – is religion as *a part of* science, a 'scientific religion'. If science and religion are to co-exist, they must occupy different domains of life and thought.

SECOND MEDITATION: 'OF THE USES AND DISADVANTAGE OF HISTORY FOR LIFE'

As the title indicates, this 1874 book is about the uses and misuse of history – where 'history' is understood to mean not 'events in the past' but 'representations of the past'. His general argument is that while history of the right sort is essential 'for life', history of the wrong sort kills it. 'Life', here, seems to mean something like 'growth': good history is essential to the growth of a living thing 'whether this living thing be a

---

3 In view of this considered affirmation of idealism in 1873, I think Daniel Breazeale must be wrong to assert, in his introduction to the Cambridge edition of the *Meditations*, that private letters and papers show that 'by 1871 at the latest' Nietzsche 'had privately rejected not only Schopenhauer's world-negating pessimism, but also his fundamental . . . dualism of "appearance" . . . and "reality"', so that 'by the time he wrote the third *Meditation* he had long since jettisoned any allegiance he may once have had to the two most distinctive features of Schopenhauer's philosophical system' (UM p. xvii). Like all genuine thinkers, Nietzsche, throughout his career, reflected privately on objections and alternatives to his published views. But to slide, as Breazeale does, from Nietzsche's 'private' reservations to simply *Nietzsche's position* 'long' before he wrote *Schopenhauer as Educator* (1874) is surely perverse. Breazeale's story entails the – again surely perverse – view that (rather like a Democrat employed as a speech writer for George W. Bush) Nietzsche wrote *The Birth* as *pure* Wagnerian propaganda and, at bottom, didn't believe a word he said.

man or a people or a culture' (UM II 1): bad history stunts it. Nietzsche distinguishes three types of history that can be of value.

Monumental history

Representations of the past function 'monumentally' when they are used to provide (in my language) role models: figures that are 'exemplary and worthy of imitation' (UM II 2), models of self-'transfiguration', as the third of the *Meditations* puts it (UM III 4). Inspiring us to 'greatness' through imitation, they form the objects of celebration at 'popular festivals (*Volksfesten*) and at religious or military commemorations (*Gedenktagen*)'. They provide cultural 'solidity and continuity' in that they are a 'protest against the passing away of generations and the transitoriness of things' (UM II 2). In other words, they 'lead the eye away from becoming and towards that which bestows upon existence the character of the eternal and stable', and they do this through 'the eternal-izing powers of art and religion' (UM II 10). (Compare the well-known remark from the 1880s: 'To impose upon becoming the character of being – that is the supreme will to power' (WP 617).)

Monumental figures are always mythologised, that is, deindividualised. For two reasons. First, they need to be fairly sketchy and undetailed so as to create a space for that 'poetic invention' which allows figures from the past to make sense in the current context. Nietzsche speaks, here, of a healthy 'culture' or 'people' as one which possesses the 'plastic power' to 'incorporate . . . what is past and foreign', to 'recreate' the 'moulds' of the past in the language of the present (UM II 1). Figures from Greece inspired, for example, the Italian Renaissance but that did not entail wandering around in sandals and togas. Rather, Greek 'moulds' were 'recreated' in terms, as it were, of modern dress. The second reason monumental figures need to be deindividualised, need to be 'forced into a universal mould [with] . . . all its sharp corners and hard outlines broken up', is 'in the interest of agreement (*Übereinstimmung*)' (UM II 2).

As we saw in the previous chapter, it is the mythologised, exemplary figures, gods and heroes, who embody the 'unwritten laws' that constitute the ethos of a community. The reason their outlines must be fuzzy enough to apply to everyone and thereby create 'agreement', is, of course, that without commitment to a shared ethos there is no community, merely the 'aimless . . . roaming-about' of atomic individuals. In a word, then, the discussion of monumentalised history is a repetition – with added detail – of *The Birth*'s religious communitarianism: of its insistence that a healthy society needs a religion which provides it with a communal ethos.

Antiquarian history

A person with an 'antiquarian' stance to the past is 'the preserving and revering soul' (almost exactly the language used to describe the 'camel' in *Zarathustra*'s 'Three metamorphoses'), one who 'wants to preserve for those who . . . come after him the conditions under which he himself came into existence. An antiquarian person reveres the past *in toto*; his soul is indeed constituted by the totality of the past' (UM II 3).[4]

The antiquarian spirit, says Nietzsche, can be of great value as a restraining influence on monumental history. Since the latter hovers between producing an idealised representation of a past figure and a 'free poetic invention' with no genuine connexion to the past, it can cause enormous harm to the continuity of a culture, indeed destroy it. Revolutions typically happen, that is, through the *invention* of a monumental figure (usually the revolutionary leader himself: Hitler, Mao, Kim Jong-Il, and other creators of personality cults). The antiquarian spirit is a vital safeguard against this erection and worship of false 'idols' (UM II 2).

Another advantage of the antiquarian spirit is that it leads to contentment. It preserves its possessor from a 'restless cosmopolitanism', endows him with the contentment of 'the tree in its roots' (UM III 3).

On the other hand, since the antiquarian soul reveres *everything* that is past – even 'the trivial, circumscribed, decaying and obsolete acquire their own dignity and inviolability through the fact that . . . the soul of the antiquarian man has emigrated into them and there made its home' – it is blind to the need for *any* kind of change. And this refusal to recognise the need to do away with the 'decaying and obsolete' can lead to a 'mummification' which can cause great harm to both an individual and a community.[5]

Critical history

Only monumental history can be creative. It alone can embody a vision of the future, inspire 'architects of the future' (UM II 3, 6). Pure antiquarianism

---

4 Sartre's portrait of the person of 'bad faith' as someone captured by their 'facticity', someone for whom their '*Wesen*' (essence) is '*was gewesen ist*' (what has been), may well take its inspiration from Nietzsche's portrait of the 'antiquarian spirit'.

5 Effectively, the charge of 'pure antiquarianism' is the content of Donald Rumsfeld's neoconservative sneer concerning 'Old Europe's' refusal to see the necessity of the Second Gulf War.

on the other hand paralyses creation. Here it becomes clear, says Nietzsche, that 'critical' history is also necessary 'in the service of life'. To flourish, that is to say, 'man must possess and from time to time employ the strength to break up and dissolve a part of the past'. (If the antiquarian spirit is the ancestor of *Zarathustra*'s 'camel', the critical spirit is, surely, the ancestor of the 'lion'.) How, however, does the critical spirit judge which aspects of the past need to be abandoned? Not on the basis of 'justice' – justice in a society is, after all, always defined by past practice so that innovation is always 'unjust' – but on the basis of 'life' alone. Life, 'that dark driving power that insatiably thirsts for itself', decides the matter (UM II, 3). (As we shall see, Nietzsche's own fundamental criticism of Christianity is that it 'poisons' life.)

Nietzsche says that all three types of history, provided they interact in the right way, 'serve life'. Monumental history inspires cultural change, change which, ideally, through continuity with the past, preserves the identity of a culture. The antiquarian spirit, on the other hand, by placing a brake on the wilder uses of the 'monument', helps to ensure that cultural change *is* identity-preserving, that it takes the shape of reform rather than 'revolution' (UM II, 2). The critical spirit, by contrast, counteracts the ossifying effects of pure antiquarianism, creates the ground on which alone effective monuments can be constructed.

This sophisticated theory of cultural (as we may call it) 'health' is very important to the argument of this book. I want to make two claims about it which the rest of the book will attempt to substantiate. First, that in essence, it, and above all the crucial significance it attaches to the 'monumental' role model, stayed with Nietzsche all his life, later developments – for example the definition of 'life' as the 'will to power' and the mutation of the 'critical' into the 'free' spirit – representing refinements rather than rejections. Second, that the discussion reveals the communitarian heart of Nietzsche's thinking, that his overriding concern is for 'people' or 'culture' – which has the consequence that his later concern for the production of exceptional individuals must derive from a conception of them as, in some way, promoters of communal 'health'.

History not in the service of life

The second *Meditation* continues the cultural criticism initiated by *The Birth*, and in particular *The Birth*'s critique of the 'critical-historical' spirit of our times (see p. 30 above). Modernity, Nietzsche says, is oversaturated with knowledge of the past. Historiography has become 'objective science'. While the interplay of the three previously discussed forms of history he regards as value-affirming 'art', modern historiography prides itself on being value-free 'science'. The result is that modern culture has ceased to be a genuine culture at all but is merely an 'encyclopaedia' of scraps of past and foreign cultures (UM II 4).

This is an important passage because, though Nietzsche talks a great deal about 'culture' throughout his career, he rarely explains what he means by the term. But in the *Meditations* he does.

In the first *Meditation* he defines 'culture', which he says requires neither 'knowledge' nor 'learning',[6] as 'above all, unity of artistic[7] style in all the expressions of the life of a people' (UM I 1). And he complains that by this standard, modernity is literally culture-less, that it amounts to 'the opposite of culture, barbarism' since all we have is a 'fairground motley', a 'chaotic jumble' of confused and different styles (UM I 1). This characteristic of modernity is, of course, the reason that the town that is the object of Zarathustra's love and scorn is called 'Motley Cow'. Its inhabitants, while 'cow'- or 'herd'-like, also live a chaotic jumble of different lifestyles.[8] The 'motley' criticism is a repetition of the observation made in *The Birth*, that (in my own language) there is nothing 'post' about so-called 'post-modernism', the phenomenon belonging, rather, to the essence of modernism itself. *En passant* it may be noticed that the 'motley' criticism strongly echoes Plato's critique of 'democracy' as, while superficially attractive on account of its bright variety of different colours, actually the worst possible form of government – barring the tyranny to which it naturally tends – on account of its inability to pursue concerted communal action.

In the second *Meditation* Nietzsche defines 'culture' in a way similar to the first's definition of it as unity of 'artistic style'. He calls it a 'unity of

---

6 This should give pause to those who identify Nietzsche's concern for 'culture' with the production of a few individual artists and scientists of genius.

7 Nietzsche always connects 'art' very closely to 'beautiful'. Indeed the German language does: 'fine art', in German, is 'the beautiful arts'. So what he is talking about here, I think, is a shared 'style' of *beauty*, a shared conception of the outlines of a 'beautiful life', of, in other words, a virtuous life.

8 How can a 'herd' be 'motley'? As we shall see, Nietzsche identifies anti-Semitism, jingoistic nationalism and idolisation of the state as herd-like features of Bismarck's Germany. So what he may be pointing to is the *manipulability* – by politicians, for example – of the Germans of his time. His point would then be that modern culture is a combination of 'motley' individualism with a disposition to mass hysteria – the latter, of course, being in no way the same as the capacity for 'long-willed', concerted action created by authentic communal ethos.

feeling among a people' (UM II 4). And he complains about a double lack of culture, a double 'barbarism', in contemporary German society. First, those who pride themselves on the famous German 'inwardness (*Inner-lichkeit*)', because there is no unity to it, are never able to express it in coherent outwardness, in action. And secondly, contemporary society is marked by a strong division between the so-called cultivated and the uncouth. But for there to be a genuine culture, unity of feeling (i.e. commitment to communal ethos) must permeate and unify an *entire* society (*ibid.*).[9]

How is such all-pervading 'unity of feeling' to be created and preserved? Evidently through, in the language of *The Birth*, the possession of homeland gods, 'gods of the hearth', who provide a 'mythical home' for the Volk as a whole (BT 23; see p. 27 above). Only, that is, through the embodiment of communal ethos in monumental figures – figures who are of course updated, where necessary, so that they continue to *live* in the current context – can communal 'feeling' be preserved.

What, however, is actually wrong with 'post-modernism', with being dominated by the 'critical-historical' spirit? Why should such a spirit be culture-destroying? What is wrong, Nietzsche says, is that by presenting us with a smorgasbord of lifestyle options but with no evaluative ranking of them, it produces a mood of irony, cynicism and bewilderment which turns us into spectators rather than actors. Our culture becomes 'senile' since the critical-historical spirit destroys life's 'plastic powers' – its ability to employ its past so as to nourish its future (UM II 10).

Consider, for example, religion. Under the guise of historical objectivity, scientific history (i.e. deconstructive history *à la* David Strauss) actually kills religion, by revealing how much there is that is false, crude, inhuman and absurd in it. Some truths, says Nietzsche – sounding a major theme – are deadly. Religion can only be a *living* religion within a mood of 'pious illusion (*Illusions-Stimmung*)'. Indeed *we* can only flourish within such a mood. All living things require an atmosphere around them, a mysterious misty vapour. Life itself is only possible within pious illusions – within religion – but an excess of history kills them (UM II, 7).[10]

---

9 Again, then, at least at this stage in his career, the idea that a culture or the human species could be redeemed merely through the production of a couple of Goethes is far removed from Nietzsche's thinking.

10 As already mentioned (footnote 1 above), Nietzsche calls the critical-historical method 'Voltairean *écrascez* (destruction)'. But in the immediate successor to the *Meditations*, *Human, All-too-Human*,

What does Nietzsche mean, here, by 'illusion'? Religion needs the pious illusion, he says, because

It is only in love, only when shaded by the illusion produced by love, that is to say in the unconditional faith in right and perfection, that man is creative. Anything that constrains a man to love less than unconditionally has severed the roots of his strength: he will wither away.

Nietzsche continues by saying that

In producing this [withering] effect, history is the antithesis of art: and only if history can endure to be transformed into a work of art will it perhaps be able to preserve instincts or even evoke them. (UM II 7)

The key to this passage is a much later remark about love and art. Art, the later Nietzsche argues, is sublimated sexuality since 'as [in love] a man sees a woman and, as it were, makes her a present of everything excellent, so the sensuality of the artist puts into one object everything else that he honours and esteems – in this way he *perfects* an object ("idealises" it)' (WP 806). What this shows, I think, is that in talking of religious 'illusion' Nietzsche is not thinking of falsification, as when the straight stick half submerged in water is taken to be bent. Rather, he is speaking, in very much the vein of *The Birth*, of the glamourising power of art – specifically of what, in *The Birth*, is categorised as 'Apollonian' art.

So the memorialised figures which embody the ethos which creates and preserves a community are given charismatic authority, become objects of veneration and imitation (acquire 'soft power', as one might say), through the 'transfigurative', 'glorifying' powers of art. As in *The Birth*, art is an essential adjunct to religion.

In sum, then, Nietzsche's stance on religion in the second of the *Meditations* remains essentially that of *The Birth*. A thriving community, and hence the possibility of thriving individuals living meaningful lives, needs a living religion which creates and preserves it as a community, a Volk, by expounding and empowering its foundational ethos. What is new is the development of the conception of the objects of festive worship and celebration by means of the ideas of 'antiquarian' and 'critical' and, above all, 'monumental' history.

---

he employs the method of 'historical philosophy' – later to be called 'genealogy' – precisely to destroy Christianity. A way of describing the great 'turn' in Nietzsche's thinking that took place after his break with Wagner and Schopenhauer in 1876 would be to say that after 1876 he came to see a way in which, deployed against the right targets in the right way, the 'critical-historical' approach could be used to promote rather than destroy 'life'.

THIRD MEDITATION: 'SCHOPENHAUER AS EDUCATOR'

Structurally, *Schopenhauer as Educator* (1874) is probably the weakest of all Nietzsche's published works. It lacks a clear focus. The reason for this, I think, is that it tries to do too many things at the same time: to perform an act of homage to his 'first and only educator' (HH II, Preface 1), to remodel Schopenhauer's philosophy into something more congenial to himself (which involves pretending that the last quarter of *The World as Will and Representation*, which contains Schopenhauer's doctrine of 'salvation' through asceticism and life-'denial', was never written), to continue the discussion of 'role models' from the second *Meditation*, to construct an idealised portrait of himself, to criticise the sorry state of contemporary society, and finally to construct the dim outlines of a healthier future society and an equally dim account of how we might get there. In what follows I try to present parts of the discussion in a reasonably organised manner. This, however, it should be said, somewhat flatters the work by failing to reproduce its rambling quality.

Schopenhauer as Educator has comparatively little to say about religion as such. It is however important to this study since it contains some of the most extreme statements of what *appears* to be Nietzsche's 'aristocratic individualism'. Since the thesis of this book is that Nietzsche is not an individualist of any kind (in his own, explicit words, 'my philosophy does not aim . . . at an individualistic morality' (WP 287)), it is important for me to put these remarks in their proper context.

The way we are now Educator

Education, Nietzsche asserts, is in crisis. Obsessed, as it is, by inhuman, value-free, 'science', it no longer provides any training in morality. The result is that we are simply squandering the 'moral capital' accumulated by our grandfathers without in any way adding to it. The major contributor to modernity's moral crisis is Christianity. Through the exaltedness of its claims and the extravagance of its promises, it destroyed the 'naturalism' (*human* attainability) of the morality of the ancient world. But when Christianity declined, a wholehearted return to the naturalism of antiquity proved to be no longer possible. The result is that we are in an age of moral confusion and hence of 'low moral energy'. It is in 'an oscillation between Christianity and antiquity, between an imitated or hypocritical Christianity of morals and an equally despondent and timid revival of antiquity that modern man lives, and does not live very happily'

(UM III 2). (One might think here of nineteenth-century architecture's 'oscillation' between classical antiquity and medieval Christianity, between the classical and gothic revivals, as the most visible sign of the phenomenon Nietzsche is pointing to.)

So, of course, with no coherent ethos to unify it, modernity has degenerated into 'an age of atoms, of atomistic chaos'. Modern individuals, 'think[ing] with a precipitancy and with an exclusive preoccupation with themselves never before encountered in man . . . build and plant for their own day alone'. The modern age is one in which 'all men feel in themselves only the self-seeking worm', so that they have declined to the level of animals and even worse (here Nietzsche touches what will become a major theme in his critique of modernity, the mechanisation of man) to the level of 'automata' (UM III 4).

Surprisingly, Nietzsche opposes to the egoistic atomism of modernity the role of the Catholic Church in the Middle Ages. In the Middle Ages the competing egoisms of money makers, military despots and petty nationalisms

were held together by the Church and, through the strong pressure it exerted, to some extent assimilated with one another. The Reformation declared many things to be *adiaphora* [matters of indifference], domains where religion was not to hold sway; this was the price at which it purchased its existence. (UM III 4)

Already in *The Birth*, as we have observed, Nietzsche has a hostile attitude to the *content* of Christian morality. But for the medieval Church as a unifying *institution* he expresses here (and always retains) intense admiration. Correspondingly (though he has some difficulty making up his mind as to whether Luther himself was a good or a bad thing) he always retains a deep hostility towards the Reformation; first, because it created a partially secular society, and second, because it made religion an instrument of state power, hence reversing the proper relation between religion – that is to say the culture or ethos of a Volk – and the state (UM III 6).

What can be inferred from these remarks is that *The Birth*'s ideal of a festival-centred society, a society with a religious ethos that permeates and unifies the total life of the 'people', remains Nietzsche's conception of a healthy society. The disintegration of this ideal, the collapse of the West into a society of petty, atomistic egoisms (the degeneration of *Kultur* into mere *Civilization* as Volkish thinkers often put it), is the central *problem* confronted in the third *Meditation*. Notice that since the problem concerns *society as a whole* it would be very odd indeed were Nietzsche's *sole* concern to be the production of great individuals.[11] Though he certainly is thus concerned, what we should expect, to repeat, is that there will be some connexion between the production of exceptional individuals and the 'redemption' (UM III 5) of society as a whole.

Educators

Given the character of his problem, Nietzsche's central question is: what kind of a life should we lead that might have some relevance to the redemption of contemporary society?

Obviously, given the decadent nature of the times, such a life will be, an '*un*timely' one – out of step with the public opinion of the age.[12] But untimeliness is merely a negative characteristic. What might be said by way of offering a positive account of such a life?

One is, says Nietzsche – sounding a celebrated theme – to become one's 'self'. The self, however, is something not deep within but rather high above one – a task to become committed to rather than a pressure to be released. And to discover one's task one needs to ask what one has 'truly loved up to now', what it is, in other words, 'which has drawn [one's]. . . soul aloft' (UM III 1). But how is one to discover that?

At this point, the considerations of the third *Meditation* begin to coalesce with those of the second. To discover one's true love and task, one is to seek out a 'revered object' (role model) which will perhaps supply the 'fundamental law of [one's] . . . own true self'. In the second *Meditation* such heroes were described as 'monumental' figures. Here they are described as 'educators' (UM III 1).

Where, however, in these destitute times of dark 'bewilderment' (UM III 1) are we to find such educators? Where are we to find an '*image of man*' (UM III 4) that might have something to offer by way of redeeming the situation?

---

11 Were, indeed, Nietzsche's sole concern the production of 'great' individuals, it would be hard to see why he bothers with most of his 'cultural criticism' at all. Why, supposing that to be his sole concern, should he care one way or another that the great majority of the 'herd' live mechanised, harried, exhausted, meaningless lives? It is noteworthy that most of the 'individualist' interpreters of Nietzsche, apart from noting that he favoured hierarchy over democracy, pay little or no attention to his cultural criticism.

12 Notice that the value of 'untimeliness' is relative to the health of the times. In healthy times one would expect untimeliness to be a vice rather than a virtue. And indeed, as we shall see in chapter 11, Nietzsche acknowledges the possibility of an exceptional but 'timely' person; of indeed a 'timely' philosopher. Philosophical 'meditations' are not, in Nietzsche's view, *necessarily* 'untimely'.

Nietzsche says – somewhat wildly – that the modern age has thrown up just three 'images of man which will no doubt long inspire mortals to a transfiguration of their own lives': Rousseau, Goethe and Schopenhauer. But since Rousseau, the arouser of 'dangerous excitations', is too revolutionary and Goethe too passive, this leaves Schopenhauer as the only role model available to inspire the thoughtfully 'youthful soul' (UM III 4).

Before discussing just what inspiration Nietzsche takes from Schopenhauer it is important to take note of a difference between the monumental figures of the second and the 'educators' of the third *Meditation*. In the second, as in *The Birth*, Nietzsche's focal topic is the *healthy* society – antiquity, above all Greece, or its rebirth in the Italian Renaissance. 'Monumental' role models constitute the festive heart of such a healthy culture: they embody the ethos that unifies the community and are the object of *universal* reverence. In the third *Meditation*, however, the topic has changed to the destitute society, a society which is destitute precisely because there are no longer any society-binding 'monumental' figures, at best only 'educators'. Who, then, are the 'educators' to educate? For whom is the third *Meditation* written?

In later works, as we will see, Nietzsche is quite explicit that his books are not intended for just anyone, and not, in particular, for the hoi polloi. *Human, All-too-Human* is subtitled 'a book for free spirits [alone]', *The Gay Science* is written for Nietzsche's 'friends' (GS 381) and *The Antichrist*'s foreword says that the book 'belongs to the very few'. But the third *Meditation* is written, too, for a quite circumscribed audience. It is addressed to the 'youthful soul' (UM III 4), to a 'small . . . band' who, 'through continual purification and mutual support . . . help prepare within themselves and around them' for the redemption of culture (UM III 6). Various associations might come to mind here. The small band of Nietzsche's friends from boarding school at Pforta, Zarathustra's band of followers, Jesus' disciples, or, of course, Wagner's 'Bayreuth Circle'. Looking forward to Nietzsche's admirer Stefan George, one might think of the 'George Circle', a group of the poet's (mainly gay) disciples dismayed by the decay of modern language and culture, who thought of themselves as the avant-garde of a movement of regeneration the task of which was to create a new language and a new mythology inspired by the models of Dante, Goethe, and Nietzsche himself (see further pp. 210–11 below). The main point, however, is that educators are to educate only a small group of young and talented people who are to prepare the way for the birth of a new cultural health. Educators differ then in two ways from monumental figures: they are to be objects of reverence and inspiration not for everyone but only for a select band, and their function is to occupy a transitional stage between decadence and health.

Back, then, to Schopenhauer – Schopenhauer the 'living man' rather than the body of works, for only a living and rounded human being can be a model for *life* (UM III 2). What are his virtues? Nietzsche admits that the account he is about to provide is somewhat idealised (UM III 5), that it portrays as much the virtues he would like Schopenhauer to have had as the ones he actually had. (But mythologising, as we know, is essential to the creation of role models.) Nietzsche portrays Schopenhauer's virtues as a series of triumphs, 'self-overcomings' in his later language, the overcoming of deleterious tendencies latent in all of us.

First, Schopenhauer showed a marked independence from state and society. (In reality, of course, he had substantial private means.) He had the courage to enter into an adversarial relation to public opinion, but also, unlike Hölderlin or Kleist, the iron constitution that enabled him to accept the solitariness, the social ostracisation, which that entails (UM III 3).

Second, though tempted by 'sainthood' ('world-denial', 'Buddhist negation of the will', in the language of *The Birth*), Schopenhauer overcame this and lived a full and productive life.

Third, though like all philosophers working under the shadow of Kant's demonstration of the limits of human reason, Schopenhauer was tempted by 'scepticism and relativism', he overcame this and produced a rounded and positive account of the world, the message of which is sacrifice of the ego and compassion (UM III 3).

And finally, Schopenhauer had the 'heroism of truthfulness' to acknowledge the fact that a happy life is impossible, that the highest form of humanity is the 'heroic life', a life that accepts the '*suffering involved in being truthful*' (UM III 4).

Nietzsche now asks what 'circle of duties' can be drawn from this ideal. How can we show that it points towards 'practical activity', that is to say, really *educates* (UM III 5)? Nietzsche acknowledges that it is a 'hard . . . task' to show that *anything* practical follows from the 'loftiness' of 'Schopenhauerian man', that one might well take from him the rejection of 'any participation in the world of action'. None the less he does manage to find practical consequences of the Schopenhauerian ideal – though the fact that he gets there via a highly distorted summary of Schopenhauer's philosophy suggests that what was important to Nietzsche was the *answer* to the question of practical consequences rather than how he got there. The answer is that since 'nature' finds redemption only when it understands the metaphysical significance of life, redemption consists in those aspects of man that distinguish him from the animals. Its sole 'concern', that is, is with the production of 'true *men, those who are no longer animal, the philosophers, artists and saints*'. This then is the task: '*to promote the production of the philosopher, the artist and the saint within and without us and thereby to work at the perfecting of nature*' (UM III 5).

At the beginning of the next section of the work Nietzsche provides a summary of the above conclusion that is often quoted as one of the clearest expressions of his supposed elitist individualism: 'Mankind must work continually at the production of individual great men – that and nothing else is its task' (UM III 6). This certainly looks like elitism of the most radical sort: a couple of Goethes and 'nature's purpose' is completed. In fact, however, one only has to read the sentences that immediately follow it to get a quite different impression:

How much one would like to apply to society and its goals something that can be learnt from observation of any species of the animal or plant world: that its only concern is the individual higher exemplar, the more uncommon, more powerful, more complex, more fruitful – how much one would like to do this if inculcated fancies as to the goal of society did not offer such tough resistance! We ought really to have no difficulty in seeing that, when a species has arrived at its limits and is about to go over into a higher species, the goal of its evolution lies, not in the mass of its exemplars and their wellbeing . . . but rather in those apparently scattered and chance existences which favourable conditions have here and there produced. (UM III 6)

So, concludes Nietzsche, mankind ought to seek out and create the 'favourable conditions' under which those great redemptive men can come into existence. And for the rest of us, our lives acquire their 'highest value' when we live 'for the good of the rarest and most valuable exemplars' (*ibid.*).

Let us reflect upon this Darwinian[13] analogy. The first thing to note is that evolution of a species is evolution of *a total species* – not the consequence-less evolution of a couple of finer-than-usual exemplars. What

---

13 John Richardson's excellent book *Nietzsche's New Darwinism* (2004) appeared too late for me to make serious use of it in this study. Let me say, however, that Richardson's main theme – that Nietzsche's frequent abuse of Darwin disguises (and was probably intended to disguise) how much he had borrowed from him – seems to me absolutely correct and much in need of saying.

happens of course is that the 'random mutations' – a term I shall take over to apply to Nietzsche's exceptional individuals – adapt better and breed whereas those that do not tend to die out before reproducing. So gradually the characteristics of the 'higher' (more adaptive) type become the rule of the species rather than the exception. Later on, as we shall see, Nietzsche expresses considerable interest in eugenics. So it is possible that it is already in his mind as part of 'preparing within and around' oneself for the redemption of culture – though there is no explicit mention of 'breeding' in the third *Meditation* itself.

What the biological analogy strongly suggests, however, is that the appearance of the great individual is *not an end in itself but rather a means to the redemptive 'evolution' of the social totality.* (Later on we shall see Nietzsche developing a quite elaborate theory of cultural development in terms of the interaction between the 'norm' and the 'random mutation'.) And in fact, the *Meditation* makes it quite explicit that this is the case. How, he asks, can the great philosopher[14] be of 'universal utility' (UM III, 7)?

Nietzsche's answer is reminiscent of Plato's: 'the proper task of all great thinkers is to be lawgivers as to the measure, stamp and weight of things' (UM III 3). In *some* sense we need a philosophical *leadership*. Whether Nietzsche yearns for Plato's *Republic* with its philosopher-king or whether it is some different kind of philosophical leadership that he seeks is something we will need to investigate in later chapters. Here, his position is unclear. He mentions Plato's ideal state favourably, but without explicit endorsement (UM III 8). What is clear, however, is that the true philosopher, and by implication other forms of 'genius', must be of service to the social totality. Repeating Schopenhauer's criticism that 'university philosophers' are not true philosophers since, paid by the state, they play its tune,[15] he calls for 'freedom and again freedom' as the condition of philosophy's performing its proper task. But he adds that such 'freedom is in fact a heavy debt which can be discharged only with great deeds' (UM III 8). So far as the third *Meditation* is concerned, the freedom to enjoy the conditions under which genius flourishes entails heavy responsibility to the society which grants that freedom. Properly read, it contains no hint at all of the idea that the great individual is an end in itself.

---

14 For no visible reason those other great individuals, the artist and the saint, have suddenly disappeared from the discussion.

15 There are those, says Schopenhauer, who live *from* philosophy and those who live *for* it (FR p. 73).

FOURTH MEDITATION: 'RICHARD WAGNER AT BAYREUTH'

Published in July 1876 to coincide with the first Bayreuth Festival, the fourth *Meditation* was written with some difficulty. The reason is that, by the time of writing, his attitude to Wagner had changed from adulation to ambivalence. His private notebooks of the period ponder and reflect the suspicion that was later to become the foundation of his case against Wagner – that the composer is, in reality, nothing but a producer of cheap thrills for a work-weary audience and so not an *antidote to* but rather a *manifestation of* the ills of modernity.

The device Nietzsche adopts in order to be able to write out of such a divided state of mind is to compose an idealised biography of Wagner in which the composer's 'higher' self eventually triumphs over his 'lower' self. This enabled him to combine the hagiography Wagner demanded with a warning to him to remain true to his highest ideal. Thus Wagner is pictured, at the first stage in his career, as the producer of the empty 'effects' and 'revolting' 'artifices' of grand opera, but as graduating, with maturity, to the profound and significant art of the music drama (UM IV 8). The result is that the portrait of the mature Wagner presents what, in 1876, Nietzsche regards as the, as it were, 'inner truth and greatness'[16] of the Wagner phenomenon.

As in *The Birth*, Nietzsche thinks of that inner truth and greatness of Bayreuth as the rebirth of Greek tragedy.[17] 'The earth', he says, after its long domination by the 'orientalism', the alien spirit, of Christianity, 'longs again for the Hellenic' (UM IV 4). And it is the Hellenic that is (or ought to be) reborn in the Wagnerian music drama.

What then is a music drama and why is its revival of the Hellenic an important phenomenon? What does Nietzsche's 'Wagnerianism' of 1876 amount to? As with all the *Meditations*, the Wagner-discussion takes place against the background conviction that modern culture is seriously sick. So the underlying structure of the work is simple: it offers a diagnosis of the disease followed by an account of the Wagnerian cure.

---

16 This, of course, is the notorious phrase used by Heidegger in the *Introduction to Metaphysics*, to describe what he subscribed to in 1933 and what, as it turned out, he suggests, Hitler betrayed.

17 Of course, Wagner himself thought of his music dramas in this way and is quite explicit about it in his theoretical writings. The *Ring* cycle he presents not as mere theatre, but as 'a stage festival drama for three days and a fore-evening', self-consciously recalling the tragic festival of the Greeks.

The destitution of modernity

What, according to the fourth *Meditation*, is wrong with modernity? It is, Nietzsche observes, vulgar (*gemein*) and money-grubbing,[18] its denizens exhausted by overwork so that the typical demeanour of the passer-by in the city street is one of being 'harried' (UM IV 5). This is partly because, whereas formerly we looked at life from the eternal point of view,[19] we now live in a newspaper (media) culture which barrages us with the events and agitations of the moment (UM IV 6). Modern culture is permeated by boredom, 'industrious boredom' (UM IV 5) – because presumably (a) work is what we do nearly all of the time, and (b) modern work practices are intrinsically unsatisfying (see p. 61 below). That we are bored work-slaves generates a specific kind of art, in particular theatre. It is forced to become a 'lascivious antidote' to the worker's exhaustion and boredom (UM IV 8). What the audience wants – and gets – is 'bedazzlement, not art' (UM IV 6). (Referring to the same phenomenon, Berlioz says that the Italians take their opera as they take their pasta and Heidegger calls modern art the art of 'pastry cooks'.) This is a continuation of *The Birth*'s critique of modernity as an *Erlebnisgesellschaft*: a society given over to 'worldliness', as he again calls it (UM IV 4), a society in desperate search of cheap thrills.

So the first major critique is that we are a society of harried, exhausted, bored, industrialised, mechanised 'automata' (UM III 4) capable at best only of cheap *Erlebnisse*.

Nietzsche's second major criticism is that we have lost community. Though Nietzsche does not clearly distinguish them, it seems to me that there are actually two strands to this criticism. The first concerns community in the sense of shared commitment – what Nietzsche calls

---

18 For the classically educated, money and the 'trade' which produces it is vulgar because in Plato's *Republic* it corresponds to the basest element in the soul, sensual appetite.

19 Nietzsche speaks, remember, of 'the eternalizing power of art and religion' (UM II 10). And in *The Gay Science* he says that, for all its failings, we must at least 'concede' that Christianity had the 'merit' of 'surrounding man with the eternal perspective' (GS 78). What he means is that by disclosing everyday existence as a brief moment in the grand panorama of the life of one's immortal soul it endows one with a detachment from, and so equanimity in the face of, daily occurrences which is lacking in secular, and so 'harried', modernity. It is possible, however, that Nietzsche has a further contrast in mind. Like other Volkish thinkers he has an intense dislike of the big city. So it is possible that he also has in mind a contrast between the 'eternal recurrence' of the cycles of the rural life of the past and the 'harried' existence of the modern city-dweller which is exacerbated by the information overload brought by 'newspapers and the telegraph' (UM II 10).

belonging to a 'Volk' – and the second concerns community in the sense of inter-personal intimacy.

Modernity has ceased to be a people because it has lost the homeland of myth, the unifying ethos which, as we know, is the precondition of being a Volk. Christianity has degenerated to empty ritual, 'hypocrisy and superficiality'; myth in general has lost its 'serious manly nature' and has been debased into the mere 'fairy tale', 'the plaything of women and children' (i.e. less than fully fledged citizens in both Greece and Prussian Germany) (UM III 8).

The reason modernity has lost community in the sense of intimacy is due to the sickness of language. Originating in the expression of 'strong feeling', language has exhausted itself in the attempt to encompass the highest realms of thought. (In the language of *The Birth* it has become 'Socratic'.) Subject to the tyranny of 'universal concepts' man can no longer express his 'simplest needs' and thus 'can no longer really communicate at all'. Subject to the tyranny of 'convention' we have become incapable of speaking 'naively' and dwell in an 'artificial alienation and incomprehension between man and man' (UM IV 5). Remembering that, in *The Birth*, the Dionysian state is described as the 'higher community' of universal 'brotherhood' which comes about through the ecstatic abolition of the 'rigid, hostile barriers established by necessity or caprice' between man and man, we might call this second loss the loss of *Dionysian* community. And recalling the close association between mythic figures and Apollonian art we might call the first loss the loss of *Apollonian* community.

The third major way in which modern culture fails us has to do with death. 'The individual', Nietzsche writes, 'must be freed from the terrible anxiety which death and time evoke' (UM IV 4). But in secular modernity we have lost the world view which, for two millennia, freed us from such anxiety. Hence the underlying mood of modernity is one of anxiety, to overcome which we need the redemptive power of Wagner's art (*ibid.*).

In sum, then, modern culture fails in what Schopenhauer identifies as the two central functions of religion: the provision of ethos and hence community, and a 'solution' to the riddle of death. What it lacks, in a word, is a religion.

Wagnerian redemption

The problems are, then, our 'worldliness', our loss of ethos and community (lack of meaning and loneliness), and our lack of, as one might put it, 'ontological' security, our anxiety about death. What is the 'Wagnerian' remedy? Before answering this question, however, let us attend to the question of just what, for Nietzsche, a Wagnerian music drama *is*.

Obviously a music drama is music and words (plus everything else, action, dance and scenery, that belongs to the world of 'appearance'). It is a music-drama. Though the dichotomy is not explicitly introduced, Nietzsche clearly thinks of the words as the Apollonian (he now tends to say 'poetic') and the music as the Dionysian element. Repeatedly he calls Wagner's music 'dithyrambic' (i.e. Dionysian) and Wagner a 'dithyrambic dramatist' (UM IV 7), which indicates that the conceptual categories to be deployed in analysing Wagner's art remain the same as those *The Birth* employed in analysing Greek tragedy.

So how is the rebirth of Greek tragedy to remedy the ills of modernity? Concerning the 'poetic', Apollonian aspect of Wagner's art Nietzsche emphasises the rebirth of myth. (Wagner's characters are, of course, as in Greek tragedy, nearly always gods and heroes. In Wagner's case they trace their pedigree mainly to the Norse sagas.) Wagner, he asserts, thinks. *Der Ring des Niebelungen*[20] is 'a great system of thought'. It thinks, however, not in 'concepts', as 'theoretical man' thinks, but 'mythically' as the Volk has always thought (UM IV 9). Indeed Wagner's poeticising *is* the Volk poeticising – the Volk being the only true artist (UM IV 8). It is the Volk, as it were recovering, through Wagner, a 'primordial' (UM IV 9) layer of memory buried beneath more recent layers but not entirely extinguished. Although Wagner's art gives no direct instructions for action – the good artist is never an 'educator' in *this* sense – it does produce 'a simpler world, a shorter solution to the riddle of life', an 'abbreviation of the endlessly complicated calculus of human action and desire' (UM IV 4). (Recall *The Birth*'s observation that the mythic figures of Greek tragedy 'abbreviate appearances' (BT 23).)

I take Nietzsche's contrast between mythical and conceptual thought to be a repetition of Schopenhauer's observation (later repeated by Wittgenstein) that what conceptual thought *says* as clearly as possible, art *shows* by 'hold[ing] up to the questioner an image of perception and say[ing], "Look here; this is life (*das ist das Leben*)"' (WR II p. 406). And I take it, too, that the mythic figures (more exactly mythic figures embedded in a narrative), those communal 'educators' who inhabit Wagner's art and provide a 'solution' to the 'riddle' of life, are a reappearance of the role

---

20 *Das Reingold, Die Walküre, Siegfried* and *Götterdämmerung.*

models of the second *Meditation*'s 'monumental' history. Nietzsche discusses some of the particular role models to be found in Wagner: Senta (from *The Flying Dutchman*) is the loving woman become saint through 'a heavenly transformation of *amor* into *caritas*';[21] Tristan and Isolde want to be free from 'separation and dissimulation' (they seek *real* intimacy); Wotan, as he is aware, has become enmeshed through treaties and alliances in 'the curse which lies on all power' and longs for an ending of his power, understanding that the whole (Schopenhauerian) point of existence is the renunciation of power.[22] Finally, Siegfried, as the uncorrupted innocent, is the only one who can redeem the world by breaking up the old Wotanic system (possibly a partial forerunner of the 'lion' and 'child' of *Zarathustra*'s 'Three metamorphoses') (UM IV 11).

There is, then, a morality – a Schopenhauerian ethos of love and renunciation – in Wagner's music dramas. Moreover it is spoken in a language immediately accessible to ordinary people: for Wagner there is no distinction between the cultivated and uncultivated. (Retaining some of the socialism of his youth, Wagner decreed that there should be no boxes at Bayreuth.) Wagner takes away the bad odour of 'common (*gemein*)'[23] (UM IV 10). So what Wagner writes is *Volksmusik* – folk, even 'pop', music, music which is accessible to all. And he does this because the heart of his concern 'collects around the question: how does the Volk come into being? How can it be resurrected?' (UM IV 8).

Nietzsche, then, conceives the Bayreuth Festival as the beginning of a *Volksreligion* in two senses: it is to gather the whole community together in common affirmation of its mythic foundation, thereby resurrecting the Volk as a Volk. And, as a precondition of this, it is to communicate in a simple, 'folksy' way – it is to belong (as Homer and Sophocles did) to *popular* culture – and as such be accessible to the Volk as a whole.

Notice, *en passant*, how close this conception of the redemptive artwork is to that developed by Heidegger in 'The Origin of the Artwork' of 1936 (the year of the Berlin Olympics). Heidegger himself notes the similarity between himself and Wagner. Though criticising the latter for allowing the 'tumult and delirium' of the music to overpower the words,[24] with

---

21 This example is poised uneasily between the Schopenhauerian 'saint' who *rejects* body and sex, and the exceptional person of later Nietzsche who 'spiritualises', sublimates, the sexual in favour of more significant goals. (The former is undoubtedly truer to Wagner.)

22 Nietzsche, of course, will soon assert precisely the opposite of this.

23 As with the English word 'common', '*gemein*' can mean both 'shared' and 'vulgar'.

24 Heidegger objects to the prominence of the music in Wagner on the grounds that 'a solidly grounded and articulated position in the midst of beings' is 'the kind of thing that only great

Wagner's conception of the *Gesamtkunstwerk* he has no quarrel at all. He points out that the music dramas are intended to be 'collective artworks' not only in the sense of collecting together the individual arts but also in the sense of becoming '*the* religion of the people, a religion that would be a celebration of national community' (Heidegger (1979) pp. 85–6).

The tragic effect

So much for the Apollonian aspect of the music drama. What now of the Dionysian element, the 'dithyrambic' music? Nietzsche says that 'to be free of the terrible anxiety which time and death evoke' 'the individual must be consecrated to something higher than himself – that is the meaning of tragedy' (UM IV 4). 'Consecration to (identification with) the higher', in other words, is what one experiences in experiencing the 'tragic effect'.

How does this occur? Immersed in the dithyrambic music of the 'great magician (*Zauberer*)' (UM IV 7),

in an ecstasy we swim in an enigmatic, fiery element, we no longer know ourself, no longer recognize the most familiar things; we no longer possess any standard of measurement, everything fixed and rigid begins to grow fluid . . . For a few hours at least . . . we have returned [from Apollonian constraint] to free nature, to the realm of freedom; from this height we behold as though in immense air-reflections (*Luft-Spiegelungen*), the struggles, victories and defeats of us and our kind as something sublime.

From this vantage point, Nietzsche continues, we experience death as 'the supreme stimulus to life' so that, 'thus transformed into tragic men, we return to life in a strangely consoled mood, with a new feeling of security'. What has previously seemed 'serious and stressful' now appears stressful only as an 'isolated fragment of . . . total experience', since when seen as a part of the whole it becomes no longer stressful but rather 'significant' (UM IV 7). Thanks, then, to the ecstatic moments provided by our 'greatest magician and benefactor' we are able to face life in an immensely 'cheerful' frame of mind (UM IV 9).

Two things seem to be said here. First, that in Dionysian ecstasy, the ecstasy of transcending the 'fixed and rigid' Apollonian world of the

---

poetry and thought can create' (Heidegger (1979) p. 88). But this completely misses the mythic, Apollonian element in Wagner. Unsurprisingly, given his proximity to their source and the fact that he actually knew something about music, the early Nietzsche presents a much more accurate account of Wagnerian music dramas than does Heidegger.

principium individuationis, we overcome individuality, and hence mortality, and hence anxiety about death. Pain and death cease to be 'my' problem because 'I' am 'above' it, removed from the realm in which it happens. For a few moments, that is to say, I realise that my true identity lies with the 'one will' (UM IV 9) that is *above* the realm of 'air-reflections' rather than with anything *in* that realm.

At the same time and for the same reason (this at least seems to be the second point) pain and death cease to be experienced as objections to life – become, in fact, '*stimuli* to life' – since, as we saw in discussing *The Birth*, life viewed as an 'aesthetic phenomenon', as an entertainment for the primordial 'Will', would be unutterably tedious without Heraclitean 'becoming', without the destruction of the old necessitated by lust for the new (see p. 24 above).

In fact, however (though it is not easy to be entirely certain about precisely what is being said in this 'dithyrambically' difficult passage), it seems to me that what is going on in the discussion is not a mere repetition of *The Birth* but rather that the passage occupies an intermediate position between *The Birth*'s account of the tragic effect and that offered in later works such as *Zarathustra*.

The reason it seems to me not a repetition of *The Birth* is that Nietzsche describes the experience of transcendence induced in us by Wagner's music as a 'dream' (UM IV 7). The same point is suggested by the description of Wagner as a 'magician', as someone who deals, now, in tricks rather than in metaphysical insights. According, that is, to the Schopenhauerian metaphysics of *The Birth* it is *everyday life* which is a 'dream', the primal will being the only genuine reality. But here Nietzsche reverses the 'dream'/'reality' labels, which strongly suggests that in the fourth *Meditation* he has finally abandoned Schopenhauerian idealism. What, then, he is doing, in continuing to speak of the tragic effect as transcendence of the world of 'air-reflections' (a less metaphysical term than the Kant-infested 'appearances') to identification with the primal 'will', is, I suggest, not metaphysics but rather *phenomenology*. Schopenhauer's categories continue to be employed because they are useful for describing the content of an *experience*, an experience which, however, is now regarded as without *cognitive* value, as in fact illusion rather than metaphysical insight.

What, then, I think Nietzsche is suggesting is that the death-overcoming transcendence induced by Wagner's music is an illusion. There is *no* 'one Will', nothing at all, beyond the world of appearance – and hence no world of (mere) appearance. None the less, Nietzsche believes, the 'dream' is a *healthy, healing illusion,* something we have a 'metaphysical need' to inhabit from time to time, since, like antidepressants, it allows us to go about the business of living in a reasonably cheerful frame of mind. (Notice that if this reading is correct then, though he has abandoned Schopenhauerian metaphysics, Nietzsche remains, in 1876, a Schopenhauerian pessimist.[25]) *Human* life, he continues to affirm, is actually not worth living. Only *illusion* can overcome the crushing objections to it constituted by pain and death. (Nietzsche, I shall argue, always retains the view that some kind of transcendence of individuality is necessary to human flourishing. But it is not until *Zarathustra,* it seems to me, that he presents an account of transcendence that is genuinely compatible with affirmation of *human* life.)

Transcendence, then, is what overcomes anxiety about death. This makes it clear that the Nietzsche–Wagner solution to the ills of modernity proposed in the fourth *Meditation* remains a religious one. As Nietzsche sees it, that is, the Wagnerian festival fulfils the two central functions of religion. In its Apollonian aspect we are to find, as the Greeks found in their tragic festival, disclosure and affirmation of ethos and so a gathering of community, of Volk. And in the Dionysian aspect we are to find an anxiety-overcoming transcendence of death. In 1876, Nietzsche's solution to the destitution of modernity is, therefore, a religious one. The salvation of modernity lies in a return of 'the Hellenic' (UM IV 4), in the rebirth and refashioning of Greek religion.

This is a relatively unsurprising conclusion. What would be much more startling would be to find Nietzsche continuing to favour a religious solution in the works of his next, 'positivistic', period, to which I now turn.

---

25 This is the truth contained in Nietzsche's claim that it is in 1878, in *Human, All-too-Human,* that he liberates himself for the first time from what '*did not belong to me*' (EH IV 1).

CHAPTER 4

Human, All-too-Human

This chapter will discuss the works of Nietzsche's so-called 'positivist' period: *Human, All-too-Human, Assorted Opinions and Maxims, The Wanderer and His Shadow,* and finally *Daybreak.*

HUMAN, ALL-TOO-HUMAN: A BOOK FOR FREE SPIRITS

Human, All-too-Human (*Menschliches, Allzumenschliches*) was first published in 1878, *Assorted Opinions and Maxims* in 1879 and *The Wanderer and His Shadow* in 1880. They were all republished under the title *Human, All-too-Human* in 1886, with the original work of that title as volume I and the remaining two works, together with a new preface, as volume II. In what follows I shall treat the three works as the unity Nietzsche presented them as being in 1886.

Human appeared after Nietzsche's break with Wagner and covers the time of his abandonment of the life of a university professor (he resigned from Basle with a small pension in 1879). It also marks his break with Schopenhauer whom he now treats as his 'antipode'.[1] In at least three ways, therefore, *Human* is the work of a 'free[d] spirit'.

Here is Nietzsche's own description, in the final days of his creative life, of the circumstances in which he began to write it:

The beginning of this book belongs within the weeks of the first Bayreuth Festival; a profound estrangement from all that surrounded me there is one of its preconditions. Anyone who has any idea what visions had been flitting across my path even at the time can guess how I felt when I one day came to myself in Bayreuth. It was as if I had been dreaming . . . Where was I? I recognised nothing, I hardly recognised Wagner. In vain I scanned my

---

1 In contrast to his later abuse of Wagner, however, throughout his life Nietzsche continues to treat Schopenhauer with great respect and, I think, affection, treats him as a – as *the* – worthy opponent. Still, in the 1886 Preface to volume II of *Human*, he honours him as 'my first and only educator'.

memories. Triebschen [where Nietzsche had first become intimate with Richard and Cosima] a distant isle of the blessed: not the shadow of a resemblance. The incomparable days of the foundation-stone laying, the little band of *initiates* who celebrated it (*sie²*) and did not lack fingers for delicate things: not a shadow of a resemblance. *What had happened?* – Wagner had been translated into German! . . . *German* art! . . . *German* beer!

What this recollection, in *Ecce Homo* (VI 2), says is that the original Bayreuth Circle comprised people of fine ideals and distinguished talents – 'fingers for delicate things'. This raises the possibility that, right to the end of his career, Nietzsche believed that the Wagnerian movement had got *something* right. More specifically it raises the possibility – which is of course the thesis this book is dedicated to arguing – that, right to the end, Nietzsche adhered to the Wagnerian *ideal*, his objection to Wagner being confined to his character and his *music*. What, in other words, he here seems to be accusing Wagner of is *selling out* on his own ideal by giving up on the 'redemption' of modern culture and pandering instead to the demands of a bored and work-weary audience, to its demand for cheap narcotics, for 'beer'-like music.

Nietzsche also records in *Ecce Homo* (VI 5) that on its publication he immediately sent two copies of *Human* to Wagner (one presumably for Cosima). This might seem an act of pointless rudeness, given that, though an honoured guest at the first Bayreuth Festival, he had walked out half-way through, and given that, as we shall shortly see, the content of the work was an 'assassination' of everything Wagner held dear. A more plausible hypothesis, however, is that Nietzsche still retained the naive hope of recalling Wagner to the 'inner truth and greatness' of the Wagnerian ideal, that he was still pursuing the policy of the fourth *Meditation* of contrasting the 'higher' Wagner with the temptations to which his 'lower' self was subject.

If there is any substance to these reflections, then even in the unpromising atmosphere of Nietzsche's 'positivism' we should expect to be able to discover at least a version of the Wagnerian ideal.

Let us call the author of *The Birth* and the *Meditations* the 'romantic' Nietzsche. Most of the themes that figure in this early period, at least in *The Birth*, are now to be the enemy: pessimism, 'metaphysics' (Schopenhauerian idealism) and German nationalism (*The Birth*'s special reverence for *German* music and the *German* Volk). In *Ecce Homo* he says

2 Hollingdale's 'them' makes no sense here.

that *Human* takes an axe to the root of the 'metaphysical need' (VI 6). Under the influence of the empiricist, reductive spirit of his friend Paul Rée, his romantic metaphysics is now replaced by a naturalistic, even materialist outlook. Nietzsche represents himself as continuing the work of the Enlightenment – his new hero is Voltaire, and from time to time one even gets a whiff of Descartes. In general, *Human* favours all things French – the model for its aphoristic style is La Rochefoucauld – and deplores all things German.

Human thus seems to represent a 180 degree turn, a 'paradigm shift', in Nietzsche's thinking. To be more precise, what seems to be going on is that something close to 'Socratism', the position of 'theoretical man', deplored in *The Birth*, has now become Nietzsche's own position. Whereas the idea that human reason, following the 'thread of causality', could know and even 'correct' human existence (BT 15) was treated as an (inferior) 'illusion' in *The Birth*, Nietzsche's position now seems to be that we should give up 'narcoticising' human ills with art and religion since science is well on the way to 'abolishing' the causes of those ills (HH I 108). Scientific 'optimism', deplored in the romantic period, now seems to have become the order of the day. It is no wonder, then, that most of Nietzsche's friends were stunned and appalled when the work appeared (D Preface 2). It was as though the pope, or at least a cardinal, had declared himself an atheist.

The transition in Nietzsche's general outlook was not only radical but also entirely ungrounded. There is, that is to say, no attempt to *refute* the previous outlook. In the 1886 preface to the second volume of *Human* he attempts to *motivate* the change in outlook. He says that the cheerful tone of the work is just a mask covering great suffering: the suffering, he adds in the Preface to *Daybreak*, of a 'subterranean man' – one who has deprived himself of the 'light' of any positive faith by which to live. But, he claims, the suffering was the consequence of a process of self-cure, the process of curing himself of 'romanticism'. What he means by 'romanticism' is 'the whole idealist pack of lies', that which is intimated by 'romantic music', and in particular 'romantic pessimism' (HH II Preface 2–7). So 'romanticism' is (a) belief in another, 'metaphysical' world plus (b) belief that this other world is a 'better' world than our veil of tears.

As Carl Dahlhaus[3] has emphasised, Wagner's and Nietzsche's romanticism was always a *neo*-romanticism, a late reaction against a post-romantic

---

3 See Dahlhaus (1980).

age in which the materialistic, positivistic spirit had long constituted the dominant outlook, at least among educated people. So what is happening, I think, is that Nietzsche has simply decided to try on the *Zeitgeist* for size. (His friend Rhode worried about his conducting his self-education in public.) Given that his fundamental concerns lie always with *life*, 'trying on for size' means asking how positivism stands with regard to the possibility of a healthy humanity.

On the face of it, positivism looks to be a climate unlikely to attach any positive value to religion. And indeed, we will find in *Human* many scathingly anti-religious remarks. But what remains to be decided is whether these remarks are preparations for a life with *no* religion or for a life with a *better* religion.

THE WAY WE ARE NOW

Human repeats many of the criticisms of modernity presented in earlier works. There is, however, a new element which echoes some of Marx's criticisms of modern technology and pre-echoes some of the criticisms of the later Heidegger.

Modern culture, Nietzsche repeats, is a work culture. We live harried, harassed, high-speed lives – which means that we view life 'as from a railway carriage'. There is no time for contemplation, a fact which breeds conformism since no time is available to contemplate alternatives to the status quo. (Well-known trick for manipulating meetings: pack the agenda so full that pressure of time kills dissent.) Another reason for the conformist character of modernity is that it is a *machine* culture: alternatively put, a 'big city' culture (HH II b 218–19).[4]

The machine (which of course includes bureaucratic 'machines') produces mutual co-operation in which each individual performs only one action. Individuals are turned into mere 'instruments', cogs. The machine is extremely efficient and productive. It makes human beings 'active' but 'uniform' in the way that cogs are uniform (HH II b 220).

---

4 Perhaps surprisingly, Nietzsche's 'experimental' embracing of positivism does not diminish his hostility to big-city life. 'We like to live in a small town' (HH II b 219), he says (the 'we' clearly includes himself) and he emphasises the need for a '*country sensibility*': 'if a man has not drawn firm, restful lines along the horizon of his life, like the lines drawn by mountain and forest, his innermost will itself grows restless, distracted and covetous, as is the nature of the city-dweller: he has no happiness himself and [consequently] bestows none on others' (HH I 290). This is one of the passages (for another see p. 81 below) which show that Nietzsche shares the rural nostalgia common to nearly everyone in the Volkish tradition.

The machine culture has two seriously bad effects. First, it militates against 'individual autocracy' (HH II b 218), against creative departure from the norm, against, as *Zarathustra's* discussion of the 'last man' puts it, our culture's ability to 'give birth to a star'. What makes this consequence a bad one is Nietzsche's theory of the 'random mutation' as the agent of cultural growth, a theory already on the way to being developed, as we saw, in the third *Meditation* (see pp. 48–9 above). Second, since it does not engage the individual's creative capacities, it generates both boredom and alienation. HH II b 288 contrasts the modern industrial economy with the craft economy of earlier times. In the latter, purchasing an artefact was (like the purchase of a painting) a 'bestowing of distinction' on the producer. But the machine economy takes away the possibility of taking 'pride' in one's work. Pleasure in work is replaced by 'an anonymous and impersonal slavery'. Certainly the machine generates leisure, but we are too exhausted and (like Charlie Chaplin in *Modern Times*) too engrained by work-habits to do anything significant with it other than seek cheap *Erlebnisse*, thrills.[5]

So things, in modernity, are in a bad way. The question is what to do about it, whether to go forwards or backwards: whether we should attempt a return to our pre-modern culture or to go forward to a post-modern culture. Much of the discussion in *Human* can be seen as a ruling out of the former alternative.

'INDICTING'[6] GOD

Human, All-too-Human contains Nietzsche's first sustained critique of Christianity. Since he views Christianity as the all-dominating fact about the past two millennia of Western culture – the half-hearted continuation of Christian belief, where it still exists, he regards as a dying remnant of the past – the critique can be seen as fitting into the overall argument of the work by providing a negative argument to the question: should we seek a return to the past?

Nietzsche describes the methodology of *Human* as that of 'historical philosophy' (later to be called 'genealogy'). It is an investigation of the *origins* of, *inter alia*, religious belief.

---

5 A flaw in *Human*, a certain shallowness in the work, is that Nietzsche never addresses the question of whether the positivism he embraces might not itself be a manifestation of precisely what he criticises, the question of whether, as Heidegger puts it, the 'essence' of modern technology and the essence of modern science might not be one and the same.
6 HH I Preface 1.

Nietzsche grants that there *could be* a 'metaphysical world'. Kant, that is, could be right that there is a world of the 'thing in itself' utterly different in character from the world as it appears to us. We cannot cut off our heads (cannot, that is, step outside the processing activity of our brains to see what the world is *really* like). But, he claims, only 'error' has made it seem 'valuable, terrible, delightful', in general *interesting*. When one has disclosed these errors that lie at the root of 'all extant religions' one has 'refuted' them (HH I 9).

A word on 'refute'. Nietzsche has his eye on Kant's claim that the point of his metaphysical epistemology of known 'appearance' plus unknowable 'thing in itself' is to 'beat back the bounds of knowledge in order to make room for *faith*' – a remark which he actually quotes at one point (HH II a 27). He knows, of course, that the thing in itself *might* be 'terrible and delightful'. (In section 374 of *The Gay Science* he points out that round the 'corner' we can never look around there might also be many 'ungodly' things.) His point, however, concerns epistemological warrant. To show how we got those beliefs, he claims, is to show that we have actually no right to believe them true. A warranted belief, that is to say, is one that is caused in the *right* way – by exposure to *evidence*. Nietzsche's claim is that our religious beliefs are unwarranted because they are caused in the *wrong* way. How, then, did religious belief arise?

Human contains an interesting account of the origin of animism. Originally, Nietzsche suggests, human beings had no conception of *natural* causality. Everything was understood anthropomorphically: the storm was a god's anger, spring rain a god's benevolence. The way one curries favour with – seeks 'soft power' over – persons is to do them services, offer them gifts. Hence the origin of religious rites and sacrifices lies in a primitive attempt to bring order into nature (HH I III).

This is intuitively compelling. Yet animism is hardly a living phenomenon. So it is not entirely clear what the relevance of this passage is to the refutation of 'all extant religions'. Perhaps Nietzsche's point is that to the extent that one might have a residual belief in divine intervention, in the power of prayer, one is locked into a primitive and *superseded* scientific theory.

In section 30 of volume I Nietzsche observes that religious belief may well make one happy; *happier* at least than himself, a lonely, 'faith'-less 'wanderer' with only his 'shadow' for company, and whose farewell to the 'metaphysical world' contains much sadness and regret. Yet that a belief makes one happy does not, he points out, make it true.

That beneficial psychological consequences are no evidence of the *truth* of a belief seems something to be encountered in logic 101 rather than in a great work of philosophy. But Nietzsche's point, of course, is that wishful thinking (self-hypnosis) *is* a major cause of religious belief: wishful thinking generated by the 'metaphysical need' for a solution to the riddle of pain and death (HH I 26).[7]

A similar point is made in section 15 of volume I. We have 'profound feelings', feelings that seem to take us to the heart of things, seem to be somehow self-certifying. Often these are induced by art. In modern culture, Nietzsche suggests, art's principal function is to be a continuation of religion by other means – a satisfaction of the 'metaphysical need' without one having to subscribe to any dogmas that would be found absurd in a post-Enlightenment climate (HH I 150).[8] So for an enlightened thinker 'art makes the . . . heart heavy';

> How strong the metaphysical need is, and how hard nature makes it to bid it a final farewell, can be seen from the fact that even when the free spirit has divested himself of everything metaphysical, the highest effects of art can easily set the metaphysical strings, which have long been silent or indeed snapped apart, vibrating in sympathy; so it can happen, for example, that a passage in Beethoven's Ninth symphony [in the last movement] will make him feel he is hovering above the earth in a dome of stars with the dream of *immortality* in his heart: all the stars seem to glitter around him and the earth seems to sink further and further away. If he becomes aware of being in this condition he feels a profound stab in the heart and sighs for the man [Wagner] who will lead him back to his lost love, whether she be called religion or metaphysics. (HH I a 153)[9]

Appalled at his own lyricism, Nietzsche pulls himself up short. 'At such moments', he adds sternly, the positivist free spirit's 'intellectual probity is put to the test' (HH I 153). The reason one's 'probity' is challenged is that all such 'profound feelings' consist of is strong feelings plus vague

---

7 A University of Maryland study conducted shortly before the 2004 US presidential election showed that well over half of all habitual Republican voters believed that, following the second Gulf War, weapons of mass destruction *had* been found in Iraq and that Sadam Hussein *was* implicated in the destruction of the Twin Towers. The researchers' explanation appealed to 'cognitive dissonance': since the voters had 'bonded' with President Bush after 9/11 and since their moral convictions told them that it would have been wrong to go to war without these things being true, it followed, for them, that they *must be* true.

8 Notice that, though the perspective is now very different, *Human* retains *The Birth*'s thesis that art and religion are 'necessarily entwined' (see pp. 26–7 above).

9 Nietzsche never, I believe, really abandons the 'dream of immortality'. In *Zarathustra*, as we shall see, he finds a way of preserving it *without* needing to resort to a 'metaphysical world'.

thoughts. And, unfortunately, the *strength* of the feeling has nothing to do with the *truth* of the thought.

It might be wondered why Nietzsche never considers the *arguments* (Aquinas' 'five ways' and so on) for Christian belief. The answer is that Nietzsche holds such arguments to be simply *irrelevant*. No one was ever *argued* into Christian belief, he holds. One is just *born* into it, as someone born in a wine-drinking country becomes a wine drinker (HH 1 226). The geographical clustering of the world's religions testifies to the general truth of this observation.

Though Nietzsche places a great deal of methodological emphasis on the *origins* – historical and psychological – of Christian belief, his main effort, it seems to me, concerns not origins but rather the (unhealthy) *consequences* of such belief. Of course the projects are connected. Particularly in the light of his 'truth-seeker-whatever-the-cost' stance, he needs to destroy the epistemological credentials of Christian belief before he can suggest that it ought to be abandoned on the grounds of its consequences for spiritual health. What, then, are the unhealthy consequences of Christian belief? Nietzsche offers, it seems to me, four lines of criticism.

1. Christ as a model of Christian virtue represents an ideal of perfect 'unegoism (*Unegoismus*)' which we *cannot possibly* match up to since egoism, selfishness, is written into the human condition. This saddles us with a permanent sense of guilt, sin, depression and terror, since the penalty for sin is damnation. The Christian, says Nietzsche, is like Don Quixote who, because his head was so filled with the momentous deeds of the knights of chivalry, underestimated his own courage. In a word, then, Christian belief undermines self-esteem, creates, in Adlerian language, an inferiority complex (HH 1 132–3).

Like the curate's egg, this criticism is good in parts. The point that a role model so perfect as to be beyond even slight emulation has a depressing rather than an inspirational effect is well taken and is even capable of empirical confirmation.[10] It is the point we have met already in *The Birth*, that the Greek gods, unlike the Christian God, are *healthy* role models since they embody not merely virtues but also human, and even

---

10 A study completed in 2005 by Leif Nelson of NYU and Michael Norton of MIT found that fans of (the comic book) Superman unwittingly compare themselves with the superhero and, realising that they can never measure up, are less likely to help others. Asked to donate time to a (fictitious) community project, fans of Superman volunteered much less of their time than did non-fans. (How splendid to be somewhere where projects such as this receive research funding!)

all-too-human characteristics. (Nietzsche would have thoroughly approved the Maori god Maui, a kind of Prometheus-figure who uses trickery, lies and all kinds of deception in order to gain knowledge, science.)

The idea, however, that Christianity demands a kind of unselfishness which it is impossible, physically, psychologically and even logically, for us to fulfil represents two fairly elementary confusions, at least the first of which, I think, Nietzsche *never* overcame.

The reason Nietzsche thinks it physically and psychologically impossible for us to be unselfish is that if

> A man should wish to be, like God, wholly love, and to do and desire everything for others and nothing for himself, then the latter is impossible simply because he has to do a *great deal* for himself if he is to be able to do anything whatever for the sake of others. (HH 1 133).

If, in other words, you fail to eat you are no use to anyone. But here Nietzsche has confused *selfishness* with *self-interestedness* (the wobbly neologism 'unegoism' facilitates this confusion). Eating is not (normally) selfish, just self-interested. Jesus ate – and presumably killed millions of microbes with each footstep he took.

The perfectly sound idea that one cannot take care of others unless one first takes care of oneself is, as we shall see, an important ingredient in the idea of the healthy social leader that emerges in the later texts. Frequently Nietzsche calls it 'healthy selfishness'. But this embodies precisely the above confusion. All he in fact means is '*effective* unselfishness'.

The reason Nietzsche thinks that Christian unselfishness is *logically* impossible is that, though overcoming it later,[11] in *Human*, under the influence of his friend Paul Rée, he affirms the (false) doctrine of psychological egoism, specifically psychological hedonism. Hence 'pity', for example, does not have 'the pleasure of the other as its objective' since 'it conceals within itself at least two (perhaps many more) elements of a personal pleasure and is to that extent self-enjoyment'. The first is akin to the pleasure we derive from weeping over the fate of a tragic hero, the second 'the pleasure of gratification in the exercise of power' (HH 1 103). But this, a consistent habit with Nietzsche, confuses the *object* of a motive with the *side-effects of its satisfaction*. Just because I might derive the pleasure of, let us say, a good conscience from giving the beggar all of the 200 dollars I have just drawn out of the ATM machine does not mean

---

11 'Man does *not* strive after pleasure; only the Englishman does' (TI 1 12).

that I did it *for the sake of* a good conscience. (Yehudi Menuhin once advised violin players to live morally good lives for the sake of the psycho-physical relaxation engendered by a clear conscience and which is essential to good violin-playing. That *is* a case where the side effect plays the role of chief motivation. But not all the virtuous are virtuosi.)

2. Nietzsche makes the point about Christian role models being non- and so anti-human with specific reference to sex, and this time stands on less muddled ground. Christian heroes have always been free of sensual-ity.[12] Christ's was a virgin birth and he, of course, is represented as himself never engaging in the sexual act. Sex as such is stigmatised: as natural beings we are 'begotten in sin'. Christian morality 'crucifies' the human being simply for being human. The aim is not that we should become better but rather to *create the need* for Christian redemption. Like firemen who light fires, or advertisers who manipulate us into wanting things we do not need, Christianity, Nietzsche is suggesting, creates the need *it* needs in order to survive and be powerful. All this is a crazy, self-inflicted thought structure which makes us gloomy, fearful and depressed (HH 1 141–3).

3. 'If thine eye offend thee pluck it out' makes Jesus sound like a bad dentist (HH 11 b 83). This touches on what becomes a key theme in later Nietzsche – that we must not 'exterminate' our 'evil' emotions as Christianity demands because we need them as material for 'spiritualising' (sublimating) into our virtues.

4. When one suffers from something one can either (a) remove the cause or (b) change the effect it has on our sensibility. Religion (and art and 'metaphysical [Schopenhauerian] philosophy') do the latter. So it acts as a momentary amelioration and 'narcoticising'. But this is an unhealthy practice since it diverts us from the much better response of removing the cause of the ill. (In calling religion the 'opium' of the masses Marx, of course, made the same complaint.)

But can we really remove the cause of suffering in those areas of life with which religion is concerned? These days, Nietzsche replies, it is 'a

---

12 Nietzsche remarks that Raphael's life-affirmation means that his Christianity is mere lip service (see p. 167 below). J. M. Coetzee, who calls authentically Christian iconography 'gothic', makes a similar point about Renaissance sensuality. The Mary we see in Correggio is not Christianity's 'shy virgin' but rather 'one who delicately raises her nipple with her fingertips so that her baby can suck; who, secure in her virtue, boldly uncovers herself under the painter's gaze and thence under our gaze./Imagine the scene in Correggio's studio that day . . . With his brush the man points: "Lift it up, so. No not with the hand, just with two fingers". He crosses the floor, shows her. "So." And the woman obeys, doing with her body as he commands. Other men watching all the while from the shadows: apprentices, fellow painters, visitors' (Coetzee (1999) pp. 149–50).

bad lookout for the writers of tragedy – for there is less material for tragedy because the realm of implacable destiny is growing narrower and narrower – [also] a bad lookout for priests' (HH I 108).

This passage is important because, as I have already remarked, it establishes that, at least *pro tem*, Nietzsche really is *inhabiting* something very close to the formerly despised position of Socratism.[13] Being can be known and in its most fundamental aspects 'even corrected'. We have no need any longer for the tragic effect – which, as described in *The Birth*, 'alters out sensibility' with regard to death – since, presumably, modern science will soon render us immortal. (As already remarked, some of the flakier of contemporary scientists can be heard claiming that we now live in an age in which embodied personal immortality is a realistic scientific goal.)

In sum, therefore, even if we could – which we in fact cannot since we have 'burnt our bridges' (HH I 248) – the idea of attempting to make the old Christian culture born again is a very bad idea. Though we may allow ourselves a certain small sadness, the slow death of God is something to be accepted and even celebrated: 'a very high level of culture has been reached when one no longer believes in angels, for example, or in original sin, and has ceased to speak of the salvation of souls' (HH I 20).

So the solution to the ills of modernity must be found in going forward rather than back. But to what? What kind of future should we aspire to? And – to come to our specific concerns – does anything that could be called a religion have a role to play in Nietzsche's conception of a better future?

It seems to me that there are three ingredients in the positivist Nietzsche's vision of the kind of future for which we should strive: what we might call 'science in life', a 'new paganism', and a vision of the globalisation of this combination.

SCIENCE IN LIFE: (I) PERSONAL HYGIENE

Pessimists, Nietzsche observes, think the world a 'veil of tears'. But the reason they see it this way is that they offend against the most elementary

---

13 But not quite the same as. 'Socratism', as we have seen, is the view that all human needs can in principle be satisfied by science. Nietzsche's 'positivism' on the other hand, as we shall see, allows an area of human need where something other than science is required.

laws of body and spirit. This of course is no accident. Since Christianity teaches us to despise both body and earthly happiness it is committed to disregarding such things (HH II b 5–6). (This of course is an aspect of preferring to change our sensibility towards illness rather than remove its cause. At HH I 242 Nietzsche observes that one has to stop believing in miracles to take medicine seriously.)

If we do attend to these things – the articulation and systematic formulation of such laws is an important task for science – then the veil of tears will be dispersed. This process is already in train so that, as we have already seen Nietzsche suggesting, the realm of 'the tragic' is growing 'narrower and narrower'.

What Christianity despises are 'the closest things': eating, housing, clothing, bodily health, sleeping, social intercourse, the balance between work and leisure and climate – an organism can only flourish if it inhabits precisely its right climate.

People just do not know, marvels Nietzsche, that long eggs taste better than short ones, that thunderstorms benefit the bowels, that smells and tastes are quite different in different places, that talking while eating harms the digestion, and so on.

Many of the above examples are, of course, hilarious. But the basic idea – that we could benefit from a science of, as we might call it, 'life coaching' – is entirely sensible. Whether, however, it could possibly dissolve the existential problems which, in the past, have demanded a religious solution is a matter to which I shall return.

SCIENCE IN LIFE: (2) EUGENICS

Nietzsche favours 'the production of a spiritual-physical aristocracy' through the 'physician' acting as 'promoter and preventer of marriages'. This will result in the 'benevolent amputation of all so-called torments of soul and pangs of conscience' (HH I 243). In other words, if only the optimistic, science-affirming, blond and beautiful are allowed to reproduce, if those locked into the old superstitious ways are forbidden to do so, then we will have a scientifically improved culture.

The reason Nietzsche had this strange faith in the power of selective breeding is that he was, like most of his contemporaries, a Lamarckian: he believed in the inheritability of acquired traits, and in particular in traits acquired through education (see p. 168 fn. 11 below). The hypothesis is, of course, as false as the means of employing it are repugnant. The only thing to be said in mitigation of the horrors of this brave new world is that not just the Nazis but just about everyone at the turn of the century thought eugenics a good idea.

SCIENCE IN LIFE: (3) POLITICAL SCIENCE

One objection to state socialism – Nietzsche's lifelong *bête noire* – is that since it desires a comfortable life for all, the achievement of its utopia would destroy the soil out of which the exceptional individual grows (the 'random mutation' in the language I have been using). So it seems that the 'violent', that is competitive, character of life should be preserved (HH 1 235).

We might call this (after the movie, not the Platonic paradox) the 'Third Man argument'. (Italy: five hundred years of war; result: Italian Renaissance. Switzerland: a thousand years of peace; result: the cuckoo-clock.) It goes back to Nietzsche's earliest reflections on the essentially 'agonistic' character of Greek culture and the beneficial effects of envy. Intense competition, though within limits – one never competed with the gods and always competed, ultimately, for the good of one's *polis* and its gods – was, in Greece, the essential ground of every cultural achievement. Every poet, for instance, wanted to step into his predecessor's shoes. (See the unpublished 'Homer on Competition' (GM pp. 187–94).)

Continuing his anti-socialist argument, Nietzsche writes that 'The state is a prudent institution for the protection of individuals; if it is completed and perfected too far it will in the end enfeeble the individual and, indeed, dissolve him – that is to say thwart the original purpose of the state' (HH 1 235).

This makes Nietzsche sound like a classical liberal-conservative (a 'neo-con' in current jargon). This impression is, however, modified by a concession to socialism. Though the communal ownership of wealth will, in general, destroy 'initiative', which is based on 'egoism', so that the moderate accumulation of wealth through work (though not through inheritance) should be allowed, the accumulation of *great* wealth is to be forbidden. The reason is that as a breeder of destructive envy, class warfare, it generates revolution and collapse. (In *The Birth* Nietzsche had predicted the self-immolation of modern capitalism through class warfare (BT 18).) So great businesses and banks must be state owned (HH ii b 285–7). Rather than the USA, therefore, Nietzsche's 'scientifically' organised society looks more like a twentieth-century

Scandinavian social democracy (down to the eugenics) – minus, of course, democracy.[14]

RELIGION IN A POST-MODERN WORLD

Surprisingly, Nietzsche's future world is not based *purely* on science. It contains, too, a kind of religion: we need, he says, a 'double brain' (HH I 251) to accommodate both. Attacking Schopenhauer's notion that religious dogmas are allegorical expressions of profound knowledge, he says that in truth 'there exists between religion and . . . science neither affinity, nor friendship, nor even enmity: they dwell on different stars' (HH I 110). Nietzsche's route, then, to finding a role for religious life within a science-based society is the classic positivist route of treating religion (and morals) as operating in a domain that has nothing to do with the acquisition of knowledge.

In the already discussed passage which discovers the 'origin of the religious cult' in animism (HH I 111), Nietzsche makes a partial exception for the Greek gods. Greek religion (though it, too, surely had its beginnings in animism) incorporated 'nobler ideals' than the attempt to control nature by placating the gods.

In a section entitled 'The Un-Hellenic in Christianity' Nietzsche explains the 'nobility' of the Olympian religion. The Greeks, he says, saw their gods not, on the Christian or Jewish model, as masters but as 'as it were, only the reflection of the most successful exemplars of their own caste'.[15] They saw them as relatives, as an aristocracy that represented 'an ideal, not an antithesis to their own natures' (HH I 114). They saw themselves and the gods as

two castes, living side by side, a nobler and mightier one and one less noble; but both somehow belong together in their origins and are of *one* species, they have no need to be ashamed of one another. That is the element of nobility in Greek religion. (HH I 111)

---

14 Two things are worth noting about this passage. First, Nietzsche's concern for the *preservation* of the social organism, a theme that runs through all his works. Though intensely concerned with society's capacity for change, he is always firmly opposed to *revolutionary* change. Second, as against the claim that Nietzsche had no political ideals, that he had an 'almost anarchistic' attitude to the state (Leiter (2002) p. 296), note that his rejection of the overgrown state is matched by his valuing of the modestly sized state as an essential agent of social stability. In the main, in fact, *Human*'s ideas on the state are surprisingly moderate and sensible. This is a topic to which I shall return in later chapters.

15 Compare chapter 2 footnote 2.

At HH II a 222 Nietzsche observes that the statue in the temple honours man and god together. So what the Olympian religion honours is *man as god*. It is what may be called a 'humanistic' religion: the religion of Michelangelo's big-muscled (as opposed to El Greco's non-muscled) heroes, the religion of Soviet glorifications of soldiers and workers, the religion of Leni Riefenstahl's athletes and blacks.

The theme Nietzsche is picking up here is, of course, once again that of 'monumental' history, the use of partially or wholly mythological figures as 'exemplars of our caste', ideals on which to model one's life.

In section 279 of volume I Nietzsche introduces the well-known 'life as literature' theme, a theme that becomes more prominent in *The Gay Science*. As Goethe knew, he says, one's life will be much more successful if one learns to deploy the subtle techniques of artists to 'idealise' everything that happens in it. (Idealising consists, roughly, in emphasising this and obscuring that so as to narrate one's life into a coherent and estimable whole.) What is usually missed in discussions of 'self-creation', however – missed in particular by Alexander Nehamas who first brought the theme to prominence[16] – is its *communal* context. 'Idealisation', that is to say, requires an *ideal*. And Nietzsche holds, as we have seen, that this is supplied by the cast of role models which embodies the ethos of one's community. One is, remember, to discover the 'fundamental law of one's true self' by selecting from that cast an 'educator' to be one's guiding star (UM III 1; see p. 45 above).

The heroes of Christianity are, of course, *unhealthy* role models. By contrast, section 279 repeats, the Greek gods are *healthy* role models. They are healthy because they are not anti-human but ideally human. Since 'idealising' is what artists do, and idealising involves not seeing everything 'too precisely', Greek artists did not display *every* reality. But they did display *only* reality (HH II a 114). What this means is that the Olympian gods are essentially *natural* beings complete with 'egoistic' and sexual drives; like humans they possess the 'evil' as well as the 'good' emotions.

The Greek religious festivals are, therefore, the opposite of Christian festivals. They are *celebrations* of life and nature (HH I 141, HH II a 160). The '*paganism*' of the Greek festivals consisted in the celebration of *all* the passions, even the evil ones. By channelling the 'animal' and 'barbaric' passions into particular cults and days the 'moral free-mindedness of antiquity' allowed the 'all-too-human' a 'moderate discharge', rather than seeking (like Christianity) its 'total annihilation' (HH II a 220).

16 Nehamas (1985).

This entire system was, Nietzsche continues, built into the constitution of the state – Greek religion was a 'state religion' – which was 'constituted to accommodate not individual people or castes, but the ordinary qualities of mankind'. The construction of the Greek state and religion was determined not by 'a circumscribed priestly or caste-dominated moral code but by the most comprehensive regard *for all human actuality*'.[17] Thanks to this 'wonderful sense for the factual' the Greek religion was able to serve all humanity (HH II a 220).[18] (One might think, here, of Amsterdam's coffee shops and its flourishing though heavily regulated brothels. The Dutch, too, I think, possess a strong, no-nonsense 'sense for the factual'.)

What is the strategic importance of the foregoing discussion of the Greek gods? Speaking of the Greeks, says Nietzsche, is speaking of 'today' as well as 'yesterday'. Their history is a 'polished mirror' in which we can see something of ourselves (HH II a 218). So in experiencing the contrast between the 'noble' health of the Greeks and our own lack of health, we are to feel an impulse towards a particular future. The Greek gods, that is to say, are role models for us, too.

Not, of course, that we should go about in togas and sandals. Rather, we need to

reanimate [figures] . . . from earlier times with our own souls . . . For it is only if we bestow upon them our soul that they can continue to live: it is only *our* blood that constrains them to speak to *us*. A truly 'historical' rendition would be ghosts speaking to ghosts. (HH II a 126)

And speaking about the interpretation of artworks from the past, Nietzsche imagines Beethoven suddenly returning and hearing one of his works being performed in the 'animated and nervous' manner of the present, and wonders how he would react. Probably, he decides, Beethoven would

For a long time stay dumb, undecided whether to raise his hand in a blessing or a curse, but at length say perhaps: 'Well yes! That is neither I nor not-I but some third thing – and if it is not exactly *right*, it is nonetheless right in its own way.'
(HH II a 126)

---

17 This theme of the *naturalness* of the properly constituted state becomes extremely important in Nietzsche's later writings (see pp. 182–7 below).

18 Nietzsche goes on to suggest that the Greeks derived their 'sense of the actual' from Homer and the poets who were the 'instructors and pathfinders' for the state builders, which calls to mind Heidegger's ideal of a state created by, in descending order of importance, 'poet, thinker (interpreter of the poet), and state-founder' (Heidegger (1977–) vol. 39 p. 144).

What Nietzsche is talking about here is, in Gadamer's phrase, 'fusion of horizons'. Religions die, we have seen him observing, when 'orthodox dogmatism' corrals myth into the 'narrow confines' of historical fact. They die because this destroys the natural tendency within myths 'to go on living and to throw out new shoots' (BT 10; see p. 26 above). Modernity is to transform its ethical horizon through the inclusion of role models inspired by Greek antiquity but in the process to translate them into a form that speaks to modernity in a living way. The present borrows from the past and the past from the present so that the result (as Nietzsche puts it with a concision not emulated by Gadamer) is 'some third thing'.

ART AND THE GREEK REVIVAL

As compared with the 'art deification' of earlier works, *Human* adopts a generally antipathetic stance towards art. Nietzsche calls it obscurantist, a lure back to the old metaphysics, a narcotic, emotional power without intellectual responsibility, and so on. And in a section entitled 'The evening twilight of art', sounding like a cross between Plato and Hegel, he says that

the artist will soon be regarded as a glorious relic, and we shall bestow on him, as a marvellous stranger, upon whose strength and beauty the happiness of former times depended, honours such as we do not grant to others. (HH 1 223)

The reason why art is a relic is that 'the scientific man is the further evolution of the artistic' (HH 1 222).

Yet actually it is only Christian and quasi-Christian art (the bulk of the art of the post-classical Western tradition, of course) to which we are to bid farewell. For it turns out that there is still a vital role for art to perform – a role that strikingly resembles the role of the Homeric, Apollonian artist as described in *The Birth*.

The crucial passage is the following. Art, says Nietzsche, ought to be dedicated to 'signposting the future'. Not by, like a futurist, drawing up a blueprint for a society in which we would 'prosper better', but rather by emulating

The artists of earlier [Greek] times who imaginatively developed the existing images of the gods and *imaginatively develop* a beautiful image of man: he will scent out those cases in which, in the *midst* of our modern world and reality and without any artificial withdrawal from or warding off of this world, the great and beautiful soul is still possible, still able to embody itself in the harmonious and well-proportioned and thus acquire visibility, duration and the status of a model, and in so doing through the excitation of envy and emulation, help create the future. (HH II a 99)

And then Nietzsche gives some general directives as to what it is that constitutes (in Aristotle's words) a model of a 'great-souled' human being:

> The poems of such poets will be distinguished by the fact that they appear to be secluded and secured against the fire and breath of the *passions* . . . everything tragic and comic in the old customary sense will be experienced as tedious . . . Strength, goodness, mildness, purity and an inbuilt moderation in the characters and their actions: a level ground which it is repose and joy to the feet to walk upon: countenances and events mirroring a luminous sky [Raphael]: knowledge and art blended in a new unity: the spirit dwelling together with its sister, the soul, without presumptuousness or jealousy . . . all this would make up the general all-embracing golden ground upon which alone the tender *distinctions* between different embodied ideals would then constitute the actual *painting*. (HH II a 99)

Notice that this art of the future is Apollonian in two senses. First, it glamorises, raises to a state of glory, 'transfigures', certain models of the 'great soul' in order to give them charismatic and so motivating power. And second, the 'golden ground' on which all the particular images of the great soul are to be constructed is constituted by the *Apollonian* virtues of balance, proportion, harmony, moderation, control, justice, science, and so on.

Notice, too, that Nietzsche does not say that the great-souled person *is* 'secured' against the passions, only that he must 'appear' so. As has often been observed, by emphasising the Dionysian, 'Asiatic', undercurrent to Greek 'cheerfulness', *The Birth* placed a revolutionary question mark against the portrait of Greeks as *effortlessly* serene and rational painted by the Weimar classicism of Goethe and Winkelmann. But what I think Nietzsche is doing here is demanding that, when it comes to creating role models, those models, as models, *should* accord with the constructions of Weimar classicism. Though an historical falsification, such classicism is precisely what we need as the 'golden ground' on which role models are to be constructed.

This generates an anti-Wagnerian critique. In *Wagner at Bayreuth* the great 'magician' is celebrated as a reviver of Dionysian passion, a creator of the intimacy of naked, soul-to-soul exposure. But now, in a section called 'Poets no longer teachers', Nietzsche says that today's artists are 'unchainers of the will' which – here he gestures towards his earlier esteem for Wagner – can indeed sometimes liberate us from the straitjacket of convention. But what we need to build a post-modern future is not this, but rather artists who, like earlier ones, are 'tamers of the will, creators of life' (HH II a 172).[19]

The immediately following section continues the theme:

An art such as *issues forth* from Homer, Sophocles, Theocritus, Calderón, Racine, Goethe, as the *surplus* of a wise and harmonious conduct of life – this is the art we finally learn to reach out for when we ourselves have grown wiser and more harmonious: not that barbaric, if enthralling, spluttering out of hot and motley things from a chaotic, unruly [Wagnerian] soul which as youths we [i.e. Nietzsche] in earlier years understood to be art. (HH II a 173)

The reason we need this kind of art is that civilised life in society depends on that which 'constrains us and keeps us within bounds, creates social forms, imposes on the unmannerly rules of decency, cleanliness, politeness, of speaking and staying silent at the proper times' (HH II a 174). The essence of what Nietzsche is saying here – a reflection later repeated by Freud in *Civilisation and Its Discontents* – is that Dionysian community (see p. 52 above) is all very well, but what is ultimately essential to life itself is Apollonian community so that the art we need is, above all, art which valorises the Apollonian.

So what Nietzsche wants is a *classical* revival, a revival of, as the later texts call it, 'the classical ideal', a revival which will replace the anti-humanism of Christianity with the 'noble' humanism of Greek religion. This is why he calls the Renaissance (of classical antiquity), for all its blemishes and vices, the 'golden age of the present millennium' (HH I 237). Christian iconography of course continued to dominate the Renaissance. But as Nietzsche stresses in later works, Christian form becomes filled with humanistic meaning, so that what the works glorify is man not God. ('Let us not be childish . . . Raphael said Yes, Raphael *did* Yes, consequently Raphael was no Christian' (TI ix 9).)

The foregoing does not, as yet, quite establish my claim that religion plays a central role in Nietzsche's vision of a post-modern future, since religion

---

19 This is essentially the criticism of Wagner embodied in Heidegger's remark that what we need is not Wagner's 'tumult' of feeling, but rather 'a solidly grounded and articulated position in the midst of beings' (see chapter 3 footnote 24). And it has the appearance of being similarly unfair, since it now ignores Nietzsche's earlier observation that Wagnerian music drama is an elaborate system of 'mythic thinking'. What Nietzsche *needs* now to claim, as Heidegger does, is that the music is allowed to dominate the words to such an extent that the thought-content of the work becomes fatally obscured, the work becoming, in essence, 'absolute music'.

as both he and Schopenhauer understand it is a *communal* phenomenon.
(He often distinguishes between a religion and a mere 'sect'.) Yet it might
be that the new ethos of nobility embodied in its Apollonian role models
is intended as a purely private morality offered by an 'individualistic'
philosopher whose interest is entirely confined to *individual* flourishing
and self-creation.

The key question is this: does Nietzsche envisage his Apollonian role
models merely as private 'educators' or as objects of *communal* celebration? Can we discover any continuity in the positivist Nietzsche with the
romantic Nietzsche's valuing of the *communal festival*?

There are in *Human* two passages (I shall call them the 'Foucaultian'
passages) which might seem to suggest that Nietzsche really is, after all, a
Greta Garbo individualist, that for him social constraints are always a
form of oppression, that being-in-society can never promote, only frus-
trate, the only thing that matters, namely individual flourishing. HH II a
98 suggests that customary morality is an arrangement by which the
community benefits but the individual 'languishes', and HH II b 31
suggests that community is a matter of individuals huddling together
for security, the reluctance of which is demonstrated by the appearance of
'new shoots' of individualism once security is achieved. (This is somewhat
reminiscent of Schopenhauer's parable of the two porcupines living
together in a cold climate: they are drawn together for warmth, but when
they get too close they spring back, pricked by each other's spines (PP II
pp. 651–2).)

Though these themes become more strident in later works, in *Human*
they are by no means the main current of opinion. An important discussion is headed 'Ennoblement through degeneration':

History teaches that the branch of a people (*Volk*) that preserves itself best is the
one in which most men have, as a consequence of sharing undiscussable
principles (*undiscutirbaren Grundsätze*), that is to say as a consequence of their
common belief, a living sense of community (*Gemeinsinn*). Here good, sound
custom grows strong, here the subordination of the individual is learned, and
firmness imparted to character as a gift at birth and subsequently augmented.
The danger facing these strong communities founded on similarly constituted,
firm-charactered individuals is that of the gradually increasing inherited stupidity
such as haunts all stability like its shadow. It is the more unfettered, uncertain
and morally weaker individuals upon whom *spiritual progress* depends in such
communities: it is the men who attempt new things and, in general, many
things. Countless numbers of this kind perish on account of their weakness
without producing any visible effect; but in general, and especially when they

leave posterity, they effect a loosening up and from time to time inflict an injury on the stable element of a community. It is precisely at this injured and weakened spot that the whole body is, as it were, *inoculated* with something new; its strength must, however, be, as a whole, sufficient to receive this new thing into its blood and to assimilate it. Degenerate natures are of the highest significance wherever progress is to be effected. Every progress of the whole has to be preceded by a partial weakening. The strongest natures *preserve* the type, the weaker help it to *evolve.* (HH 1 224)

This of course is a much more developed account of the 'random muta-tion' theory of social evolution we have seen intimated in earlier works (see pp. 48–9 above).[20] Social development depends on the No-sayer, the 'free spirit', where the latter is defined as one

who thinks differently from what, on the basis of his origin, environment, his class and profession, or on the basis of the dominant views of the age, would have been expected of him. He is the exception, the fettered spirits are the rule.

(HH 1 225)

But it does not *just* depend on the free spirit. It depends, too, on the capacity of the community to bend without breaking, to accommodate itself to and assimilate this 'new blood'. *Two* things are necessary, there-fore, to social growth: a living sense of community and 'degenerate' natures which help it to evolve. And they are of *equal* value: 'only when there is securely founded and guaranteed long duration is a steady evolu-tion [as opposed to the revolutionary chaos which we have seen Nietzsche rejecting] and ennobling inoculation at all possible' (HH 1 224).[21] And

---

20 Nietzsche, given his account of evolution through 'degeneration', thinks he has refuted Darwin, has shown that 'the celebrated struggle for existence' is not the only theory that can explain 'the strengthening of a . . . race' (HH 1 224). But what matters for Darwin, of course, is simply adaptive *difference*. Evaluative terms such as 'degeneration' have no place in his theory. (It is, in fact, probable that Nietzsche never read Darwin, that his knowledge was entirely second-hand.) One might note, moreover, the extreme perverseness of calling the No-sayer – the 'free spirit' – 'degenerate', 'sick' or 'weak'. More naturally one would call him 'strong'. He is only 'degenerate' *from the point of view of the mores of the society of his day.* Later on, Nietzsche is somewhat more careful and deploys scare-quotes round 'degenerate', 'immoral' and so on. This whole attempt to refute Darwin with puns does Nietzsche no credit at all.
21 In the previous chapter we found Nietzsche emphasising the importance of a community's 'plastic powers' (UM 11 1, 9, 10; see p. 41 above), its ability to update the ethos-embodying role models inherited from the past so they play a meaningful and effective role in the current context. A crucial question is: is it the essential task of the 'degenerate', free-spirited No-sayer to perform this task of updating, or is it something more radical? In other words, does the free spirit say 'No' just to the current manifestation of communal ethos, or does he say No to the entire ethical tradition of his community? At present we are not in a position to answer this question. A crucial first step to doing so involves seeing – as we will in the next chapter – that there is more than one type of No-sayer, more than one type of free spirit.

what guarantees such steady evolution is that the great majority of souls remain fettered spirits, since 'all states and orderings within society – classes, marriage, education, law – derive their force and endurance solely from the faith the fettered spirits have in them' (HH I 227). So what Nietzsche will later call 'the herd' is a vital necessity. The fettered spirit (the 'camel' of *Zarathustra*'s 'Three Metamorphoses') must always remain the 'rule', the free spirit (very roughly, *Zarathustra*'s 'lion') the 'exception'.

The way to make this line of thought consistent with the 'Foucaultian' remarks mentioned earlier is, I think, to take note of the already mentioned fact that Nietzsche's target audience is by no means everybody but rather only those who are, as it were, free-spirits-in-waiting. The book is, after all, subtitled 'A Book for Free Spirits [alone]', which can be taken as an, as it were, R 18 warning. From this point of view one can understand Nietzsche's point to be, not that *every* individual languishes under the constraints of community and longs to escape, but only that the rare individual, the genuinely free spirit, so longs. Only to the potential free spirit are the 'fetters' fetters; the average individual hardly notices them at all. That this, psychologically much more realistic, account of the relation between individual and community is in fact Nietzsche's position will become increasingly clear in later works.

THE FESTIVAL

So, in *Human* at least, Nietzsche is not the rabid, community-hating individualist of popular repute. Of course, he himself is a free spirit. But a great deal of pain and nostalgia is involved in acknowledging this to be his destiny. Being, as a critic, unable to accept current social norms makes one *lonely* (HH II Preface 3), turns one into a 'homeless' (HH II b Introduction) 'wanderer' – not even a *traveller*, since as a mere destroyer[22] one has no *destination*, no alternative norm. As a man of science, committed to the coldly forensic use of truth, one wanders in the 'desert' (HH II a 31; see too HH I 635–8) far from human habitation, with only one's 'shadow' as companion (a somewhat melancholy companion since, as GS 278 makes clear, one's 'shadow' is in fact death). It is a brave and necessary life (Nietzsche's own life by this time was that of a wanderer from one

---

22 This, as intimated in the previous footnote, is merely a crude and provisional conception of the free spirit.

cheap *pension* to another) but involves the immense sacrifice of what Nietzsche clearly recognises as a *natural* desire for community.[23]

It is in recognition of this fundamental need, I think, that religion has an essential place in Nietzsche's post-modern future. The reason is that the 'undiscussable principles' on which any community depends are contained in the 'monumentalised' figures of its 'gods'.

This is made explicit in a section entitled 'Art in the age of work' (HH II b 170). In an age such as ours, Nietzsche repeats, art is mere recreation to which we devote only the *remnants* of our time. It has to be the art of 'narcotics, intoxicants, convulsives, paroxysms' – Wagnerian *Erlebnisse* – since the work-weary are incapable of attending to anything else. But one day, authentically 'grand' art will return, an art which 'shall one day bring back *true* festivals of joy and freedom' (my emphasis). Such a future age will have no use for our (Wagner's) art any more.

'Grand' art is, presumably, art in the 'grand style', which Nietzsche defines as art in which 'the beautiful carries off victory over the monstrous' (HH II b 96). But that, fairly clearly, is just another name for Apollonian art, the art which glorifies 'great-souled' individuals, individuals in whom 'strength, goodness, mildness, purity and an inbuilt moderation' *appear* to make them secure against 'fire and breath of the passions' (see p. 75 above).

Perhaps surprisingly, then, the festival, conceived as the celebration of exemplary figures constructed on the 'all-embracing golden ground' of the classical ideal – that is to say, the Bayreuth *ideal* of the rebirth of 'the Hellenic' – seems to be preserved in *Human*. The decisive divergence

---

23 Nietzsche expressed his own yearning for community in a 1884 Schubert-like poem for which he envisaged 'The Free Spirit', 'Departure' and 'Isolated (*Vereinsamt*)' as possible titles. It reads (in my own prose translation) as follows:

The crows screech/and make their whirring flight to the town:/soon it will snow/fortunate is he who still has a homeland (*Heimat*)!//Now you stand stiffly,/looking backwards. Oh! How long already?/ What are you, fool,/fled into the world before winter?//The world – a gate/ to a thousand deserts, mute and cold!/ Who has lost/what you have lost will find no resting place.// Now you stand there, pale/condemned to winter-wandering/that like smoke/ always seeks cold skies.//Fly bird, croak/your song in desert-bird tones!/ Hide, you fool,/your bleeding heart in ice and scorn.//The crows screech/and make their whirring flight to the town:/soon it will snow/woe to him who has no homeland! (*Die Krähen schrei'n/Und ziehen schwirren Flugs zur Stadt:/Bald wird es schnei'n – /Wohl dem, der jetzt noch – Heimat hat! //Nun stehst du starr,/ Schaust rückwärts, ach! wie lange schon!/Was bist du Narr/ Vor Winters in die Welt – entflohn?// Die Welt – ein Thor/Zu tausend Wüsten stumm und kalt!/ Wer das verlor,/ Was du verlorst, macht nirgends Halt.//Nun stehst du bleich,/ Zur Winter-Wanderschaft verflucht,/Dem Rauche gleich,/Der stets nach kältern Himmeln sucht.// Flieg', Vogel, schnarr/ Dein Lied im Wüstenvogel-Ton! – /Versteck, du Narr,/ Dein blutend Herz in Eis und Hohn!/// Die Krähen schrei'n/ Und ziehen schwirren Flugs zur Stadt:/ Bald wird es schnei'n, /Weh dem, der keine Heimat hat!* (KSA II 28 [64]).)

from *The Birth*, however, is that Wagner's music is no longer regarded as living up to the inner truth and greatness of his own ideal.

Scattered remarks attempt further development of the idea of the festival of the future, that is, a 'temple of joy' where, once more, like the ancients, we will find 'occasions for happiness and celebration' (HH II a 187). *Assorted Opinions and Maxims* offers 'A vision' of the festive setting:

> Lectures and hours of meditation for adults [to counteract the speed of modern life], and these daily, without compulsion but attended by everyone as a command of custom: the churches as the worthiest venues for them [a *new* 'reformation'!] because richest in memories: every day as it were a festival of attained and attainable dignity of human reason: a new and fuller efflorescence of the ideal of the teacher, in which the priest, the artist and the physician, the man of knowledge and the man of wisdom [i.e. Nietzsche] are fused with one another . . . this is my vision: it returns to me again and again, and I firmly believe that it lifts a corner of the veil of the future. (HH II a 180)

Recalling Nietzsche's persistent hostility to the big city and its machine culture, '*Et in Arcadia ego*' adds a bucolic setting to this new 'temple of joy': his idea of paradise, he says, is Poussin populated by Hellenic heroes (HH II b 295).

Nietzsche's attempt to construct the details of the new festival may strike one as over-earnest, stilted, and short on the Dionysian (more like a Workers's Education Club than a genuine 'festival of joy'). The main conclusion, however, is unmistakable. In *Human*, Nietzsche's highest value is the flourishing of the community as a whole and this, even within the positivistic framework of the work, leads him to endorse a rebirth of a humanistic religion modelled on that of Greece.

COSMOPOLITANISM

More specifically, Nietzsche's highest value is *global* community. The greatest fact in the civilisation of Greece, he says, is the fact that Homer became pan-Hellenic so early. Of course there was a price to pay for this: by centralising, levelling 'dissolv[ing] the more serious instincts for independence' all great spiritual forces have a 'repressive' effect. But, he adds, it makes all the difference whether it is Homer (with his natural morality) or the Bible (with its anti-natural morality) that 'tyrannises' (HH I 262).

Section 23 of volume I deals with the same theme. We live – here Nietzsche returns to the 'motley cow' theme (see p. 40 above) – in an 'age of comparisons'. We are surrounded by a 'restless polyphony' of possible life options on account of being less and less bound by tradition and place. Now, however, Nietzsche sees a certain upside to the motley cow. Though the current situation involves suffering (the suffering of 'homelessness'), there will be a (Darwinian?) 'selecting out' among 'the forms and customs of higher morality', the end product of which will be a culture which transports us beyond both the national cultures of earlier times and the age of comparisons.

So it seems that what Nietzsche wants is a return to the kind of cosmopolitanism that unified the many diverse 'nations' that had previously occupied Greece. HH II b 87 says this quite explicitly: we must learn to write and think well, he says, 'to *prepare the way* for that still distant state of things in which the good Europeans will come into possession of their great task, the direction and supervision of the total culture of the earth'.[24] HH II b 189 adds a further dimension to Nietzsche's affirmation of cosmopolitanism:

That which in senile short-sightedness you call the overpopulation of the earth is precisely what proffers the more hopeful their greatest task: mankind shall one day become a tree that overshadows the whole earth bearing many milliards of blossoms that shall all become fruit one beside the other, and the earth itself shall be prepared for the nourishment of this tree.

(Given this, in Heidegger's pejorative sense, 'humanistic' ambition, it becomes rather opaque as to where the Poussinesque landscapes are to be found in which one can avoid the horrors of the big city.)

What is it that makes Nietzsche so keen on *global* community? The answer seems to be the obvious one that only through the consequent demilitarisation (HH II b 284) can there come into being an age when everyone has transcended animal aggression and can genuinely say: 'peace all around me and goodwill to all things closest to me'. Christianity said this too early, Nietzsche adds:

The time has, it seems, still *not yet come* when *all* men are to share the experience of those shepherds who saw the heavens brighten above them and heard the words: 'on earth peace, good will toward men'. – It is still *the age of the individual* [a difficult remark for the 'individualist' interpreter to accommodate].

(HH II b 350)

This cosmopolitan ideal – which is what, in my judgment, reappears as the 'one yoke' needed to 'carry into one' *Zarathustra's* 'Thousand and one

---

24 Substituting 'good Americans' for 'good Europeans' one begins to see why Nietzsche occupies an important place in the canon of the neo-Leo-Straussians.

Goals' – feeds into some reasonably crazy remarks about fashion. Only the ignorant, Nietzsche claims, wear national costume. The opposite is 'fashion', which is a reflection of *European* virtues. Simple, plain and uniform, it makes the statement 'I wish to cut a figure neither as individual nor as member of class or nation' (HH II b 215).[25]

These remarks conjure up the image of a brave new world full of Mao jackets and Nietzschean moustaches, which suggests that Nietzsche wants not merely to embrace local differences within an overarching ethical umbrella but to *eliminate* such differences. But this, I think, would be a misreading. What he is talking about here is merely the uniform of the avant-garde of the new world order. Nietzsche does not want to eliminate difference. For, remember, when he talks about the Apollonian role models of the future, Apollonianism is said to constitute only the 'general golden ground' upon which 'tender *distinctions* between different embodied ideals' are constructed (see p. 75 above.) Nietzsche's is the classical ideal of unity and plurality in harmonious combination, of 'unity in multiplicity' (BGE 212).

CRITICISMS

In *The Birth*, tragedy was seen as the highest expression of Greek culture, and tragedy was defined as the 'fraternal union' of the Apollonian and the Dionysian, a union, however, in which 'the Dionysian predominates'. This Dionysian-dominated union was said to be 'the highest goal of tragedy and of all art' (BT 21, 24). In *Human*, however, the classical ideal is transformed into something much more severe. And this means that the Dionysian is no longer seen in a 'fraternal' way but rather as an *enemy*, as something dangerous in the extreme and requiring rigorous suppression. Thus, as we have seen, any role model that embodies the ethic of a future society must be, *qua* role model, 'secured against the fire and breath of the passions' (see p. 75 above). And, to borrow the words of *The Birth*, the 'highest goal of all art' is now the 'grand style' which is the '*victory*' of the beautiful (i.e. the Apollonian) over the monstrous (i.e. the Dionysian) (see p. 80 above). This is a return to the Doric conception of the classical ideal according to which the Dionysian is simply a barbaric, 'hostile principle' (BT 4), a conception *The Birth* had regarded as a lower form of culture

---

25 In other words, neither as an individual nor as a national ego. As Heidegger remarks, both individual and national selfishness are forms of 'egoism'.

than the tragic culture of the fourth century which synthesised the two principles.

There are three difficulties with this return. The first is that it involves Nietzsche in contradiction (always a danger, of course, with the aphoristic style). For as we have seen (p. 17 above), what he admires about Greek morality, in contrast to that of Christianity, is its deification of *all* human impulses, even the evil ones which it guides into safe forms of expression. But Nietzsche's return to the Doric is his own form of rejectionism, his own refusal to 'deify' all things human.

The second difficulty is that the endorsement of the Doric ideal ignores the validity of the remarks in the fourth *Meditation* about the repression of true feeling and communication in a purely Apollonian world. Nietzsche describes great art as 'dancing in chains' (HH II b 140). But it is hard to see anything but the 'chains' in *Human*'s brave new world, hard to see how there can be much dancing going on.

The most serious difficulty, however, with *Human*'s declaration of war on the Dionysian is that it renders it incapable of dealing with what, remember, Schopenhauer points to as the central topic of any kind of religious thinking, the certainty of death.

DEATH

Discussions of death in *Human* are few and far between. And when they do occur they are shallow and inadequate.

So, for example, HH II a 88 says that it is merely superstitious to think of death as 'a very important thing', as crossing a bridge of tremendous significance. This simply confuses 'death is important' with 'death is going somewhere'. (How much more profound are Henry James' last, murmured words: 'So this is the distinguished thing.')

HH II b 322 suggests that death introduces a 'precious, sweet-smelling drop of levity (*Leichtsinn*)' into life, so it is a bad mistake to make it 'an ill-tasting drop of poison through which all life is made repulsive'.

Leichtsinn suggests 'not taking it all too seriously'. In other words we are simply to accept that life is absurd, pointless. But then why should we take any of the things Nietzsche cares about, community, the exceptional individual, the overcoming of the sickness of modernity, seriously either? The remark also seems the kind of thing one could only say to someone *else*. The problem of *my death* remains unaddressed, evaded even.

'The desire to live for ever and inability to die is . . . a sign of senility of the faculties: the more fully and ably one lives, the readier one is to

relinquish one's life for a single good sensation' (HH II b 187). A clue to
the meaning of this is provided by a passage entitled 'Of rational death'
(HH II b 185) which says that it is silly to let the 'machine' run on after
it has completed its task and that the 'wise regulation and disposal of
death' will belong to the morality of the future. (The idea appears more
clearly in *Zarathustra*'s discussion of the 'Free Death', where we are
advised to die 'at the right time', and not hang on to the tree like a
wizened apple.)

There is something seductive about the idea that just as one should
finish a novel one is writing 'at the right time', so one should finish one's
life. The difficulty with the analogy, however, is that, except for cases of
extreme and terminal physical or mental decrepitude, one can only ever
know *in retrospect* that 'the right time' really was the right time. One
cannot know what possibilities the future may throw up, possibilities
which may dramatically alter the story-line of one's life as a whole.

But even if one could determine 'the right time' the remark pays no
attention at all to the elemental nature of our fear of death. Nietzsche
writes as if choosing to die were as trivial a matter as choosing to
terminate one's subscription to *Time* magazine. He writes, that is to
say, evasively, inauthentically. And notably, when his own 'machine'
could no longer perform its task, he failed to take his own advice,
spending eleven years in what at least seems to have been a 'wizened' state.

Human's remarks on death are tritely inhuman. The 'all-too-human' is
precisely what is *not* allowed to appear. Perhaps Nietzsche recognised this
in the 1886 preface to volume II (section 5), where he says that it is only a
fake 'cheerfulness' that covers over the 'wanderer's' misery.

A final piece of triteness concerns the 'metaphysical need'. Schopenhauer
holds, recall, that the 'need' which religious metaphysics tries to satisfy is
above all the need for consolation in the face of death. Nietzsche's
response is to suggest that the 'metaphysical need' is not 'immutable',
that it can be 'weakened' and eventually 'exterminated'. Since the decline
of organised religion, he suggests, philosophers have tried to satisfy the
'need' philosophically. But this is a mistake. The need is 'time bound' and
rests on 'presuppositions that contradict those of science' (HH I 27).

The underlying idea, here, is the one we met earlier (p. 67 above), that
like advertisers who *create* needs where none existed previously in order to
generate a market for their products, so the 'metaphysical need' is a
Christian *creation*, and hence, as one might seek to 'de-programme'
someone brainwashed by Scientology, something that should and can

be eliminated. But this is surely absurd. As Schopenhauer and Francis Bacon observe, anxiety about death is a human *universal.* The history of *every* culture exhibits structures designed to assure one of the non-finality of death.

It might be thought that what generates *Human's* inability to confront the 'riddle' of death is generated by its naturalism. Of course, it might be said, if one denies the existence of all metaphysical worlds one can have nothing comforting to say about death. This, however, seems to me mistaken. For one does not, I believe, need *two worlds* to overcome anxiety about death. Rather, all one needs is the possibility of *two perspectives* on this world. Nietzsche, that is to say, should have explored the possibility of *naturalistic* consolations for death, should have taken more seriously the possibility of a naturalistic realisation of Beethoven's dream of immortality among the stars (see p. 64 above). What prevents him from doing this is not naturalism but positivism – the assumption that the world is, and is *only,* the way natural science says it is.

By the time he came to write *Zarathustra* Nietzsche had indeed discovered a naturalistic solution to the riddle of death. But before he could do that, before he could discover a perspective on life that allows one to rise above mortality, he had to overcome positivism, something he first accomplishes in *The Gay Science's* doctrine of 'perspectivism'. (In *The Will to Power* the first thing he says about perspectivism is that it is 'against positivism' (WP 481).)

DAYBREAK

Published in 1881, *Daybreak* is the final work of the positivistic period. The general spirit, much like *Human,* is rationalistic, materialistic, and hostile to 'metaphysics', to religion and to the effects of community, custom and 'morality' on the individual – on, at least, those individuals who have the potential to become 'free spirits'. Section 272, however, provides an important corrective to the impression one might otherwise receive.

It is called, somewhat ominously, 'The purification of the race (*Die Reinigung der Rasse*)'. 'Mixed' or 'crossed' races are, it says, bad news. God, he reports someone as wisely saying, 'created white and black men but the devil created half-breeds'. With their 'disharmony of habits and value-concepts', mixed races are 'more evil, crueller, more restless'. (Cruel, presumably, in the first instance, to each other.) *Becoming* 'pure' is what is required. Pure races are 'stronger and more beautiful': more beautiful because beauty is a matter of harmony and proportion, stronger because (an early intimation of the 'will to power') 'all the energy formerly expended in the struggle of the dissonant qualities with one another[26] will stand at the command of the total organism'. The Greeks offer us a model of a 'race and culture' that has become pure. And 'hopefully we shall one day achieve a pure European race and culture'.

Given Nietzsche's Lamarckianism (see p. 168 fn. 11), it would, I think, be a mistake to read this passage as supposing that cultural unity *presupposes* biological unity. Rather, Nietzsche holds that, via the inheritance of culturally acquired characteristics, cultural unity *produces* biological unity. For present purposes, however, the main point to notice in the above passage is that cultural 'purification' just means the replacement of a 'motley cow' chaos of dissonant values by a community-creating common ethos, and that Nietzsche retains the hope for the coming into being of a 'European' (and ultimately global) community. So it seems likely that, as in *Human*, the production of flourishing community rather than a few flourishing individuals remains Nietzsche's highest goal.

In section 551 Nietzsche expresses his yearning that artists should be 'again what they were once supposed to have been: – *seers* . . . who let us feel in advance something of the *virtues of the future*', his yearning that they become, once again, 'astronomers of the ideal'. Since this exactly repeats *Human*'s demand that artists should become 'signposters of the future' (see p. 74 above) one can assume that the embodiment of communal ethos in artistically glorified role models who form the revered and inspirational objects of a humanistic religion remains, for Nietzsche, an essential prerequisite of authentic and healthy community.

26 Plato's description of democracy and of the 'democratic soul'.

CHAPTER 5

The Gay Science

Books I–IV of *The Gay Science* were published in 1882. Book V was added in 1887, the year in which *The Genealogy of Morals* also appeared. The work is thus interrupted by both *Zarathustra* and *Beyond Good and Evil*. In the main, however, I shall treat it as the unity Nietzsche intended. Though the work is a wonderfully rich discussion of everything under the sun I shall confine my attention to what it has to say that bears on my topics of community and religion.

Bernard Williams, in his introduction to the Cambridge translation of the work, claims that 'This book, like all his others [*The Birth*?], makes it clear that any life worth living must involve daring, individuality and creative bloody-mindedness' (GS p. xiv). This is the familiar Nietzsche: the 'aristocratic individualist' who, concerned only for the flourishing of the exceptional type, takes society – the 'herd' – to be at best a footstool for, and at worst a serious impediment to, the flourishing of a creative elite.

If this were the whole story about *The Gay Science* – if all Nietzsche valued was the masterful individual hammering society's 'idols' to smithereens in the interests of 'doing his own thing' – then religion, as a society-bonding 'fetter', could be expected to appear as nothing but an oppressive force and as such a prime target for deconstruction. 'Antichrist' would then be the long and the short of *The Gay Science*'s philosophy of religion.

What I want to show in this chapter, however, is that this familiar Nietzsche is only half the story. That in fact Nietzsche values, continues to value, social stability and cohesion at least as much as he values individual creativity, and that his real interest lies in promoting neither the one nor the other but rather in resolving the *tension* between the two. I want to show, in other words, that the author of *The Gay Science* is a much more *interesting* thinker than the 'ranting-elitist' reading makes him out to be. And I want also to show that because he values communal stability he also values religion – of the right kind. I want to show that, as in earlier works, religion still figures as the essential agent of the existence and health of community.

In a word – and in spite of the negative rhetoric to which I shall attend in due course – Nietzsche values both the 'free spirit' *and* the 'herd type'. Neither, however, is his ultimate value. His ultimate value is the flourishing of communal 'life' which, as we shall see, consists in a dialectical interplay between the two.

So what I am going to do is to present, first, the familiar, individualistic Nietzsche – his validation of the 'bloody-minded creative individual' – second, his validation of the herd type and the forces of social conservatism in general, and finally, his reconciliation of the two sets of values.

THE FAMILIAR NIETZSCHE: THE BLOODY-MINDED, CREATIVE INDIVIDUALIST

The qualities of character praised by society and conditioned into the individual through education are, says Nietzsche, those that are useful to *it*. Selflessness, diligence and industriousness, for example, promote the good of the social whole but – particularly in the degree promoted by society – 'victimise' the individual, are to his private disadvantage. Arguments that society's morality makes the individual happy are just 'propaganda', part of the conditioning process. This harming of the individual is, however, of no concern to society at large: its aim is to turn him into a mere 'function' of the whole (GS 21).

Again: the evaluations of morality always express the needs of 'the community or herd'. (That these vary according to time and place is the reason there are many moralities.) Morality instructs the individual to value himself only as a function of the herd. 'Morality [i.e. the 'voice of conscience', or 'super-ego'] is the herd-instinct in the individual' (GS 116).

So 'morality' is a kind of confidence trick to which, it seems, Nietzsche is alerting us. Those who go along with the trick, it appears, are objects of contempt, 'herd animals'. They lack the courage to be self-sufficient. What they really fear is the 'cold look', the 'sneer', 'growing solitary', in short the social ostracism which is the penalty for departing from social norms (GS 50). Conversely, 'nobility' belongs precisely to those who defy convention, who 'create themselves' as 'new, unique, incomparable, who *give themselves laws*'. We must, says Nietzsche (sounding like Sartre), commit ourselves to the 'purification of our opinions and value judgements and to the *creation of tables of what is good that are new and all our own*' (GS 335). Nietzsche asks (for neither the first nor last time): what makes a person 'noble'? It is, he answers, 'the use of a rare and singular standard and almost a madness; the feeling of heat in things that feel cold to everyone else; a hitting upon values for which the scale has not yet been invented; a sacrifice on altars made for an unknown god' (GS 55). In Williams' term, 'bloody-mindedness'.

In short, then, Nietzsche seems to be employing the by now familiar rhetoric of 'authenticity' to tell us to have the intelligence and courage to see through the machinations of, in Heidegger's language, 'the They' and to achieve authentic selfhood. One is, it seems, to become *eigentlich*, one's own (*eigen*) person, a '*free* spirit' rather than a 'herd animal'.

THE UNFAMILIAR NIETZSCHE: CONSERVATISM AND COMMUNITARIANISM

In fact, however, one does not have to look very hard in *The Gay Science* to find a great many things seriously at odds with the above picture. Section 10, for example, praises 'atavistic' people, those rare spirits who feel old powers and values which were once common but now seem extraordinary (Nietzsche's moustache, for example, a legacy of an already antiquated military style). If they avoid becoming mad or eccentric, such people are 'great human beings'. Their ancient practices they must 'nurse, honour and defend'. Such people (surely related to the 'antiquarian spirits' of the second *Meditation* and the 'slow-willed' of *Twilight of the Idols*) are valuable because what is absolutely necessary to the 'development of a people' is *andante*, 'the tempo of a passionate and slow spirit', the spirit characteristic of 'conservative generations'. While there is a suggestion here of *andante* as, as it were, the 'goldilocks' speed for social change (not too fast and not too slow), the emphasis is on the need for relative slowness. Change that is too fast, the implication is, defeats the 'plastic power' (see p. 37 above) of a culture to assimilate the new while preserving its unity and identity.

There is, to be sure, a certain 'bloody-mindedness' involved in this conception of the noble human being: a stubborn resistance, extreme suspicion, towards the flux of fashion, towards current political correctnesses. But rather than forging a new and unique personal morality the nobility of the 'passionate, slow spirit' consists in its fidelity to *past* cultural practices, to, in the language of the second *Meditation*, 'memorialized history'. It consists in *backwards* bloody-mindedness, in resistance to, rather than promotion of, change.[1]

What is interesting about this section is its indication that, contrary to the 'rabid individualist' interpretation, (a) the survival and thriving of a Volk remains, as in *The Birth*, something Nietzsche values and (b) such preservation – whatever else it might require – requires the 'antiquarian' spirit of conservatism as conservation.

Another important passage is the remainder of section 55 (the 'feeling heat where everyone else feels cold' passage quoted on p. 90 above) which I earlier suppressed. What Nietzsche actually goes on to say – the question, remember, is 'What is noble?' – is that

Hitherto . . . it was rarity . . . that made noble. Note, however, that by means of this standard everything usual, near, and indispensable, in short, that which most preserved the species, and in general the *rule* of humanity hitherto, was inequitably judged and on the whole slandered in favour of the exceptions. To become the advocate (*Anwalt*) of the rule – that could perhaps be the ultimate (*letzte*) form and refinement in which noble-mindedness manifested itself on earth.

So, properly read, the sense of this section is actually the opposite of the bloody-minded individualist reading; it is, in fact, an *attack* on knee-jerk abasement before 'the hero' (possibly Nietzsche's consistent dislike of Carlyle is based on this). Given that the 'rule' genuinely promotes the health of the community (as, in Nietzsche's view, it did at certain times in ancient Greece and during the Italian Renaissance), the section says, nobility consists precisely in *commitment to and defence of* the ethos of one's community rather than in opposition to it. (When we come to discussing *The Antichrist* in chapter 11 we will find Nietzsche expanding on precisely this possibility.)

This thought is elaborated in section 356, which contrasts the stability of the Middle Ages where a man's profession was his character, with the modern, 'democratic', 'American faith'[2] according to which one's profession is just a role one acts for a time before moving on to some other that takes one's fancy. The great advantage of the 'broad based pyramid' of the Middle Ages was, says Neitzsche, 'durability (and durability is a first-rank

---

1 Notice, in reference to the remark that the worthwhile life must be one of 'creative bloody-mindedness', that while the 'atavistic' form of nobility is bloody-minded, it is not creative. 'Bloody-mindedness' is necessary but not sufficient for creativity, a point to which I shall return in discussing the development of the concept of the 'free spirit' in *The Gay Science*.

2 Actually a 'New World' faith in general. The highest rate of small-business creation per head of population in the world is in New Zealand. (Most fail.)

value on earth)'. And the disadvantage of modern fluidity is that the strength of great social 'architects' to build for future generations is 'paralysed'. What is dying out, that is, is

> that fundamental faith on the basis of which someone could calculate, promise, anticipate the future in a plan on a grand scale . . . namely, the basic faith that man has worth and sense only insofar as he is *a stone in a great edifice*, to this end he must be *firm* above all, a 'stone'.

A similar point is pursued in section 76. Without pride in the discipline of the herd on the part of 'the majority of men', without the majority being friends of 'healthy common sense', humanity would have perished long ago. The 'greatest danger that hovered and still hovers over humanity' is 'madness', that is, 'an outbreak of arbitrariness in feeling, seeing, and hearing', something that is so prevalent in the modern age that 'it is with little confidence that one may speak of the future of humanity'. The opposite of 'madness', Nietzsche continues, is not 'truth' but rather 'the non-arbitrary in judgment', a 'law of agreement', a 'universally binding faith' which holds 'regardless of whether [the things agreed on] . . . are true or false'.[3]

'Universally binding faith' is, of course, the 'undiscussable principles' (HH I 224), the community-creating ethos, which, according to all the texts so far discussed, is inseparable from a religion which provides its exposition and empowerment. Religion is the 'discipline' (GS 76) which, so far, has 'preserved humanity'. This view is repeated in section 353: religion, Nietzsche says, binds together people who have not yet recognised each other as allies. The establishment of a religion turns into 'a long festival of recognition' – observe how this repeats, almost exactly, the 'Wagnerianism' of *The Birth*.

Notice that community-fragmenting 'arbitrariness' is the '*greatest* danger', not just to 'the herd' but to '*humanity*' *as such*. This surely implies, contrary once again to the radical individualist interpretation, that for Nietzsche, in the penultimate year of his creative life,[4] the *highest* value is the existence and 'duration' (GS 356) of (of course thriving) community.

---

3 This remark connects up, I suspect, with the numerous references to 'error' as a condition of existence and with section 111's account of epistemological caution, 'scepticism', as a non-adaptive trait. Though most obviously thinking about the conceptualisation of experience in terms of 'objects' – 'fictions', Nietzsche suggests – he also, I think, has value-beliefs in mind. His point is that moral absolutism, anti-relativism – the chauvinist conviction that the morality of one's own time and place is *the* one and only true morality (the moral equivalent of monotheism (GS 143)) – is a condition of the survival of society.

4 Sections 355 and 356 come from Book v which, as already noted, was added to *The Gay Science's* first four books in 1887.

Section 76 applies these thoughts to the present situation. As already noted, we cannot be confident about the future of humanity because contemporary counter-drives to communal ethos are so strong. There are, that is, *too many* 'free spirits' about. What is needed is not them but rather a

virtuous stupidity; what are needed are unwavering beat-keepers of the *slow* spirit ['tick-tock' people, *Zarathustra* calls them] so that the believers of the great common faith stay together and go on dancing their dance; it is an exigency of the first order which commands and demands. *We others* [we 'free spirits'] *are the exception and the danger* – we stand eternally in need of defence! – Now there is certainly something to be said for the exception *provided exceptionality never wants to become the rule.*

(I shall return shortly to the question of just what there is to be said for the free spirit.)

An issue that needs to be touched upon at this point is the question of whether the 'virtuously stupid' are not, for Nietzsche, mere cannon-fodder, mere 'functions', as he puts it, of the social organism, and as such condemned to a life of slavery and misery? This is equivalent to the question of Nietzsche's so-called 'immoralism' concerning which there is a great deal of secondary literature. In later works, that is, Nietzsche calls himself, in a polemical way, an 'immoralist' – meaning merely that he rejects *Christian* morality. Many people have argued, however, that he *really is* an immoral thinker on the grounds that it is a condition of any morality that everyone's well-being counts equally – or at least *counts* – whereas for Nietzsche only the well-being of the exceptional few is accorded any moral significance at all.

As far as *The Gay Science* goes, however, this is clearly a misreading. Nietzsche certainly believes in a society of hierarchy, rank, and disciplined obedience. In a metaphorical sense it could be said that he believes in the 'enslavement' of the many (especially women.) But this is not because he is indifferent to their well-being but because, as everyone recognises with regard to children, he believes that most people best flourish in positions of subordination. Many people, he says, exercise a 'surplus of strength and pleasure' in becoming the 'function' of another. Especially women (he probably has Cosima Wagner in mind here) who pick on an aspect of a man that is necessary but weakly developed and 'become his purse or his politics or his sociability' (GS 119). Of course, if you are a potential creator of the future you should not make yourself a 'function' of anyone else. Goethe should write poetry, Maria bear him healthy children and run his household. Both can live satisfying, meaningful lives but in quite different ways. (It is this stratified view of human well-being that leads to the hatred of moral universalism which we will meet in later texts. Different virtues are appropriate to different forms of life – 'herd' virtues are appropriate to 'herd' types, other virtues to free spirits.)

These are not, of course, to put it mildly, fashionable views. But they are utterly standard for the period in which Nietzsche was writing. The fact of the matter is that Nietzsche is not an immoralist at all. What he is, rather, is a *paternalist.* Paternalism may well be based on factual *mistakes* – about female psychology, for example – but it is clearly a form of *moral* thinking, indeed the standard form for nearly all of human history. If Nietzsche is an immoralist then so has been nearly everyone else. (There is more to be said about Nietzsche's alleged immoralism: I shall return to the issue in chapter 7.)

THE FREE SPIRIT AS THE AGENT OF GROWTH: RECONCILIATION OF INDIVIDUALISM AND COMMUNITARIANISM

Seemingly, then, there are two utterly different sides to Nietzsche: the 'bloody-minded' individualist and the communitarian, the one honouring the 'exception', the other honouring the 'rule'. Is this one of Nietzsche's celebrated contradictions, or is there a reconciliation of the two sides? The answer, for which the earlier works have prepared us, is that there is a reconciliation.

To understand this, the first important matter is to understand for whom *The Gay Science* is written for – a question Bernard Williams conspicuously fails to address.

Nietzsche says – in defence of what he calls 'obscurity' – that he does not want to be understood by just anybody. (This, as already noted, is an oft-repeated assertion: *The Antichrist*, for example, 'belongs to the very few' and *Zarathustra* belongs, perhaps, to 'no one'.) 'Every nobler spirit and taste selects his audience . . . [and] erects barriers against "the others".' Being an 'immoralist', he says, he needs to be careful not to corrupt 'old maids' (i.e. the 'virtuously stupid') to whom life offers nothing but their 'innocence' (GS 381). His books, that is to say, are 'dangerous' (GS 76).[5] On the other hand he hopes that nothing will impede his comprehensibility to '*you* my friends' (GS 381).

---

5 This is another of Nietzsche's many affinities with Plato, who observes in the *Phaedrus* that one of the disadvantages of books as opposed to conversation is that they can easily fall into the wrong

Who are Nietzsche's 'friends'? What is his target audience? He tells us explicitly in the subtitle to *Human, All-too-Human*: it is a book 'for [potentially] free spirits'. *Zarathustra* is subtitled 'A Book for Everyone and No One' because, I think, while it is written for free spirits, Nietzsche thinks that the 'democratic' dumbing-down of modernity has reached such a pitch that, quite possibly, there are none left. A recurrent theme in the work is Zarathustra's disillusionment with modernity's so-called 'higher men' who most of the time turn out to be nothing but cheap 'actors' pandering to the degenerate masses.

'Erecting barriers' to keep out unwanted readers helps explain the general tenor of Nietzsche's rhetoric, its demeaning of the 'herd'. But there is another, and more important reason for the rhetoric. As section 29 explains, human beings are essentially conservative, in a certain sense, lazy. We are creatures of habit, innately resistant to changing those habits. (As we now know, this has a neurological basis: travelling established neural pathways is effortless, forming new ones increasingly difficult and stressful.) So something is needed to overcome the innate laziness of the potential free spirit, to chivvy him along into preferring the difficult to the easy.

Throughout his career Nietzsche thinks of envy, pride and contempt as dynamic forces in human affairs. In the Prologue to *Zarathustra*, Zarathustra precedes his speech about 'the last man' with the reflection that people

Dislike hearing the word 'contempt' spoke of them. So I shall speak to their pride.

So I shall speak to them of the most contemptible man: and that is the last man. (Z Prologue 5)

This, it seems to me, is the point of the regular abuse of 'the herd', 'the mob' and 'the rabble' throughout Nietzsche's later writings.[6] The point is, by appealing to his envy, ambition, pride and contempt, to make the potential free spirit become an actual one.

hands. The contemporary influence of Leo Strauss – who, as a supporter of the social democrats of the Weimar Republic, has almost certainly been massively misunderstood by his unfortunately influential American disciples – reminds us how right they both were.

6 But never, as noted in the Introduction, of '*Volk*' (in the sense of 'nation'). I suspect that the level of Nietzsche's invective against the herd is directly proportional to the level of his anxiety concerning the dearth of genuine free spirits in modernity.

But why does Nietzsche want there to be *any* free spirits, given that they are 'the greatest danger'? Would we not be better off if there were none of these disturbers of the peace?

Nietzsche's answer is that we would not be, since it is the most 'evil' who contribute most to the 'preservation of the species' (GS 1). (Here, as almost always with Nietzsche, 'evil' is an abbreviation of 'regarded as evil'.) Why should this be so?

When 'corruption' sets in, he says, 'free-spiritedness of the second rank' takes over and 'the previous common faith is powerless against it'. The proliferation of individual lifestyles leads defenders of 'the old religion and religiosity' to speak of 'corruption' and 'moral laxity'.[7] But actually, among these newly individual individuals will be found a few who are the 'seed-bearers of the future, the spiritual colonisers and shapers of new states and communities. Corruption is just another name for the *autumn* of a people' (GS 23).

Notice that these few are, by implication, 'free spirits of the *first* rank'. In other words, the *real* free spirits – the target audience for Nietzsche's books – are not those who *merely* ridicule and destroy an old 'faith'. 'Only as creators can (*können*) we destroy', writes Nietzsche (GS 58).[8] Only, that is, as a creator, a 'spiritual coloniser' of the future – the future, note, of a *people* – does one count as a genuine free spirit.

Why should the future well-being, indeed existence, of the Volk be entrusted to the free spirit? Because, as already noted, 'to become the advocate of the rule . . . might be the ultimate form and refinement in which noble-mindedness manifests itself',[9] the ultimate apotheosis of the free spirit. The ultimate goal of the free spirit, that is to say, is, through 'overflow[ing] and communicat[ing] to men and things', to become the new rule (GS 55).

---

7 Nietzsche has in mind here the dying days of the Roman Republic, which he sees as an historical parallel to the present. It is worth remembering that Nietzsche is an exact contemporary of the self-declared 'decadent' Oscar Wilde, and that the 'decadence' of modernity is much complained of in his later works.

8 Notice, too, the double meaning given to Nietzsche's pregnant affirmation by the careful choice of 'can' as opposed to 'may'. It is capable of meaning both 'Only as creators *may we set out to* destroy' but also 'Only as creators *can we succeed in* destroying.' The idea behind the latter meaning (one that often seems to pass the deconstructionists by) is that criticism alone is waste of time; without the creation of an alternative to the criticised, people will simply slither back into the old ways.

9 Notice that there is a studied ambiguity in this already quoted remark. The 'rule' in question might be the already existing rule, in which case its 'advocate' is *merely* noble-minded, or it might be what is to become the *new* rule, in which case the advocate is *both* noble *and* creatively free-spirited.

Nietzsche emphasises that the conditions of the preservation of a society vary over time and from place to place (GS 116), so that to survive – communal 'durability' is, remember, 'a first-rank value on earth' (GS 356) – it has got to 'mutate'. Change or die is the (Darwinian) law. But because of our already discussed natural conservatism, our attachment to the habitual (see p. 95 above), 'monotheism' (the enforcement of 'one norm, *the* human being') threatens stagnation. Hence 'polytheism', 'the invention of gods, heroes, and supermen of all kinds', the flourishing of a 'plurality of norms', is, says Nietzsche, necessary to overcome the stagnation and threat of extinction faced by most other species (GS 143). Societies, that is to say, tend to ossification. Only – as we have already seen – the 'random mutation', the free spirit (of the first rank), promotes the growth of a community that is necessary to its continued survival. It is because Europe has so far done this, because of its continual generation of 'malcontents (*Unzufriedenen*)', that it possesses its 'celebrated capacity for constant *transformation*' (GS 24). And it is because of its pre-eminence in this that it[10] appears to be in the process of achieving global hegemony (compare HH 11 b 189).

So the natural history of a successful Volk might be: its birth through the acceptance of a 'common faith', a shared ethos expounded and endowed with authority by religion, followed by (after, perhaps, a period of stability and 'perfection' (see pp. 181–2 below)) ossification and stagnation which coincides with a change in the conditions of survival (for example, perhaps, the introduction of new technology). This is followed by disintegration, 'corruption', together with the rise of 'free spirits' of at least the 'second rank', a few of whom prove to be free spirits of the first rank who 'colonise the future' by teaching what eventually becomes the new 'rule'. Provided the period of disintegration has not been too long or too radical – provided there have been no *revolutions* – the identity of the Volk will have been preserved throughout this life-history.

In sum, then, what *The Gay Science* is *ultimately* concerned with is not the exceptional individual but rather the continual growth – that is to say, survival – of the community as a whole. As a *type* the exceptional individual is of no greater value than the 'herd' type, since the 'virtuously

---

10 'Europe comprises much more territory than geographical Europe . . . America especially belongs to it, insofar as it is the daughter-land of our culture. On the other hand the cultural concept "Europe" does not include all of geographical Europe. It includes only those peoples and ethnic minorities (*Völker und Völkertheile*) who possess Greek, Roman, Jewish and Christian culture as their common past' (HH 11 b 215).

stupid' and the 'free spirit' are equally necessary to a flourishing community. As *individuals*, however, Nietzsche would certainly want to add, free spirits are of infinitely greater value, since while they are few and far between, herd-individuals are everywhere.

ASPIRATIONS FOR THE FUTURE

This account of *The Gay Science*'s fundamental concern as communal rather than individual is confirmed by Nietzsche's account of the state of contemporary society and his aspirations for the future.

The 'monotheistic' God of Christianity is, of course, 'dead', his death being for the first time officially announced in section 125. There are terrible consequences of this yet to be lived through, such as the collapse of the whole of European morality (GS 343). Yet, as we have seen, there are also tremendous possibilities in our 'polytheistic' age in which everyone creates his own 'god' (GS 143; see p. 97 above). As at the end of the Roman Republic, the 'corruption' of our age is just the autumn of our culture in which the seeds of spring are already present. We live in a 'time of transition' (GS 377).

Obviously Nietzsche sees himself as an agent of transition, of *beneficial* transition, sees himself as a free spirit (of the 'first rank'), as a 'coloniser of the future'. Only as creators, to repeat, can we destroy. And we, Nietzsche insists, are creators. We – Nietzsche and his perhaps imaginary friends – have a 'positive faith' (GS 377), are 'argonauts of the ideal', heralds of 'the great health' (GS 382). But what is the 'ideal' Nietzsche has in view? What is the 'great health' towards which he yearns to move us?

One of the themes we noticed in earlier texts (see p. 44 above) was Nietzsche's admiration for the medieval Church, and a corresponding dislike of Luther and the Reformation. This reappears particularly forcefully in *The Gay Science*. Here the Reformation is called a 'peasant rebellion of the spirit'. The medieval Church was a magnificent *Roman*[11] construction which Luther's plebeian mind destroyed by allowing priests to marry. By taking away chastity as a mark of exceptionality and destroying the mystery of the confessional, he destroyed the *general*

---

11 Nietzsche often emphasises the 'Roman' in 'Roman Catholic Church', partly, I think, to avert his gaze from the fact that it is a *Christian* institution and partly to portray it as the heir to the Roman Empire.

exceptionality, the apartness, of the priest. Luther destroyed the Church, in other words, by destroying the idea of a spiritual aristocracy:

> Let us not forget what a church is, specifically as opposed to any 'state'. A church is above all a structure for ruling that secures the highest rank to the *more spiritual* human beings [Zarathustra admits that he is 'of the same blood' as the priests] and that believes in the power of spirituality to the extent of forbidding itself the use of all cruder instruments of force and on that score alone the Church is under all circumstances a *nobler* institute than the state. (GS 358)[12]

The same theme appears in section 350. The Reformation was a victory of the superficial over the profound. It and the French Revolution made 'the sheep, the donkey, the goose, and everything that is incurably shallow and loudmouthed [newspapers?]' into 'the good people'. It destroyed, in other words, respect for the noble, 'spiritual' type of person.

None of this, of course, is inconsistent with Nietzsche's critique of the *content* of Christianity. What Nietzsche admires is the institutional *structure* of the Church, the fact, as we saw earlier (p. 44 above), that it created and preserved unity out of warring diversity. Luther, Nietzsche complains, saw only corruption in the Church. What he missed was its '*victory*' (GS 358), its victory over fractious division.

What this strongly suggests is that Nietzsche's 'ideal' for the future includes the rebirth of something resembling the hierarchical structure of the medieval Church, the rebirth of a society unified by the discipline of a common ethos, a discipline expounded and given effect through respect for the spiritual authority of those who occupy the role once occupied by priests. It goes without saying, of course, that the content of the new 'church's' message will be naturalistic rather than transcendentalist, will be moulded by 'physics' (GS 290) rather than metaphysics. It will be a life-affirming rather than life-denying church, a humanistic religion whose gods are modelled on the Greek gods in the manner described in *Human, All-too-Human* (see pp. 71–4 above).

This new church is to be, like the medieval Church, Europe-wide (and so world-wide) in extent – the 'cosmopolitanism' theme met with in

---

12 This is clearly an idealisation. Nietzsche is of course aware of Schopenhauer's observation that the Church's ultimate argument is 'the stake'. What he is really talking about is his 'Church' of the future. Note that this passage is written in 1887, only one year before *The Antichrist*, where the idea of a spiritual aristocracy reappears. Some scholars have argued, as we shall see, that the latter discussion is not to be taken as an affirmation of the idea. But its appearance in Book v of *The Gay Science* makes this harder to maintain.

earlier texts. The promotion of this ideal of globalised neo-classicism is what accounts for Nietzsche's admiration for Napoleon:

Napoleon should be credited one day for having enabled *man* to become master of the businessman and the philistine – perhaps even over 'woman', who had been spoiled by Christianity . . . Napoleon . . . proved to be one of the greatest continuators of the Renaissance: he brought back a whole piece, a block of granite, perhaps the decisive one, of antiquity's essence . . . Napoleon – who wanted one Europe, as is known, and wanted it as mistress of the earth. (GS 362)

Notice, here, the theme of *continuity*. The death of God does not mean the end of European culture. Rather, it means returning to its more authentic beginning. We 'untimely ones' are, of course, says Nietzsche, 'homeless' in the present – we suffer the self-isolation of the radical cultural critic, of one who breaks the already thin ice on which people are standing. We live (like Zarathustra) on mountain tops. We particularly loathe the cant of nationalism. We are

In a word – and let this be our word of honour – *good Europeans*, Europe's heirs, the rich, superabundant, but also superabundantly obligated heirs of two millennia of the European spirit. As such we have outgrown Christianity and are averse to it. (GS 377)

In other words, unlike Hölderlin or Heidegger who look for a synthesis between the Christian and the Greek, Christianity is, for Nietzsche (as it is for J. M. Coetzee[13]), a long aberration, and what he wants is a return to the true, Graeco-Roman essence of the 'European'. Specifically, he wants a return to Greek religion. Nietzsche himself is in part an 'atavistic' spirit (see pp. 90–1 above).

Not of course – a point on which we have seen him several times insisting – that he wants a literal return to Greek religion. Nietzsche says, apropos translation, that the French of Corneille's age[14] – whom he greatly admires – were not lumbered with 'antiquarian' reverence for the past (see p. 38 above). As self-conceived new Romans, they conquered by translating: by deleting historical detail, by adding allusions to the present, by, in general, 'crossing out' past names and replacing them with their own, they created something that was a 'Roman present', something 'contemporary and Roman' (GS 83).

---

13 See Coetzee (1999) pp. 116–55. Coetzee's philosophical, and philosophically literate, work (thinly disguised as a novel) often sounds Nietzschean without ever mentioning Nietzsche by name.
14 Corneille lived from 1606 until 1684.

This is a reappearance of the coming into being of a 'third thing', the 'fusion of horizons' theme (see pp. 73–4 above). Applying this to Nietzsche's desire for a revival of Greek religion, we can infer that what he wants is something that is 'contemporary and Greek', something that shares the essential characteristics of Greek religion but at the same time makes living sense in the current context.

This becomes clear through *The Gay Science*'s discussion of the religious festival which according to the Wagnerianism of *The Birth*, it will be remembered, is the focal event of any flourishing community.

Significantly, right after he announces the death of God, the 'madman' cries out (*de profundis*, as Heidegger comments):

what festivals of atonement, what holy games will we have to invent for ourselves? Is the magnitude of this deed ['murdering' God] not too great for us? Do we not ourselves have to become gods merely to appear worthy of it? (GS 125)

'Holy games' is, of course, a reference to the Olympic games (a holy festival dedicated to Zeus) and the idea of ourselves 'becoming gods' is simply *The Birth*'s observation that in their gods the Greeks constructed 'an ideal image of their own existence' (BT 3), honouring man and god as one (HH II a 222). So the 'madman' calls for a return of the Greek festival.

About festivals in general, *The Gay Science* says quite a lot. The trouble with our contemporary, Americanised, workaholic society in which the 'true virtue' is simply 'doing something in less time than someone else', is that there is no time for non-productive activity, neither the time nor the energy for, in particular, ceremony (GS 329). But time for 'stepping aside' from the noise of the 'big city' is essential to both communal and individual health (GS 280).[15] Individuals in a more thriving society than today's will have 'their own working days, their own periods of mourning' and 'their own festivals' (GS 283). (Part of what Nietzsche sees here is that even though God is dead, we still need – and indeed use – the rites of passage traditionally supplied by Christian baptisms, weddings, funerals.)

The point of the festival and the stepping aside from the *vita activa*, is not, however, simple stress relief. It is also religious. For as we have already seen, religion in general is a 'long festival of recognition', of

---

15 Nietzsche now thinks that churches have too many Christian memories to be suitable places for 'our' contemplation (GS 280), thus reversing the opinion of HH II a 180 that the rededicated church would be a suitable site for the future festival (see p. 81 above).

affirming the being-in-community with others that is conferred by a shared ethos (GS 353).

That *The Gay Science* attaches essentially the same importance to the festival as did *The Birth* is even more obvious when we turn to its discussion of art. Artists, says Nietzsche ('art' is again, clearly, a synonym for 'Apollonian art'), do nothing but 'glorify' (GS 85). Since 'niggardly' nature does not allow great individuals to 'shine' by themselves (GS 339), this is their only worthwhile function. This deployment of art is explicitly linked to the festival in section 89:

What do all our art or artworks matter if we lose the higher art, the art of festivals! Formerly, all artworks were displayed on the great festival road of humanity, as commemorations and memorials of high and happy moments.

And so they must become once more. In short, 'Art and nation, myth and morality' (BT 23) are to be as 'necessarily intertwined' as *The Birth* saw them, as being at the birth of the European in ancient Greece.

DEATH

In sum, then, the exposition and empowerment of community-creating ethos, one of the two main functions of religion identified by Schopenhauer, remains, in *The Gay Science*, an essential part of Nietzsche's ideal for the future. What, now, of the second essential function of religion, that of providing a solution to the 'riddle' of death?

Death is little discussed in *The Gay Science*. Section 278 suggests why:

The thought of death. – it gives me a melancholy happiness to live in the midst of . . . thirsty life . . . And yet things will soon be so silent for all these noisy, living, life-thirsty ones! How even now everyone's shadow stands behind him as his dark fellow traveller! . . . everyone takes the past to be little or nothing . . . Everyone wants to be first into th[e] future – and yet death and deathly silence are the only things common to all in this future . . . It makes me happy to see that people do not at all want to think the thought of death. I would very much like to make the thought of life even a hundred times more *worth being thought* to them.

The rhetoric of this passage takes death to be the *summum malum*, the deprivation of that for which we most 'thirst', namely, life. But since Nietzsche has nothing to offer by way of consolation, since death is just 'silence', it is better not to think about it. We are to focus on living life to the full and as far as possible not think about death. And so Nietzsche takes his own advice and avoids – evades – the subject.

But what, one might wonder, has happened to the Dionysian and the tragic outlook which, up until the end of the *Meditations did* provide a 'metaphysical consolation' for death?

As far as the first four books go, Dionysus is as absent from *The Gay Science* as he is from the works of the positivist period.[16] And though tragedy makes an appearance it is treated in an entirely novel way. Thus section 80 says that what we, and especially the Greeks, enjoy in tragedy is people speaking well in stressful situations, a '*deviation from nature*' which is 'perhaps the most pleasant meal for human pride'. (This might be called the 'anti-Method' method of acting.) And section 135 says that what the Greeks found satisfying in tragedy, as in the case of Prometheus or Ajax, was the discovery of 'dignity' even in 'sacrilege'.

Common to both these accounts of tragedy is the idea that the appeal of tragedy is defiance in the face of death (or worse); as with Camus' Sisyphus, we are to admire defiance in the face of the *summum malum*. This is of a piece with the idea that death is absolute 'silence'. If that is all there is to say about it, then the 'good' death can consist only in heroic defiance.

But this is inadequate. If death is the *summum malum*, then, since it is impossible fully to suppress knowledge of its inevitability, it is impossible to live life with whole-hearted exuberance; underlying anxiety – 'melancholy' – will always be with us. To live well, to repeat, one has to know how to die. Nietzsche's aim of making life worth living requires that he provides a compelling solution to the problem of death. Trying not to think about it, emphatically, will not do.

As mentioned at the beginning of this chapter, the fifth book of *The Gay Science* was added to the first four books five years after their publication, during which interval Nietzsche had written *Zarathustra*. The greatest contrast between the fifth and the first four books is that in the fifth Dionysus *does* appear – his first significant appearance since *Wagner at Bayreuth*, eleven years earlier.

In section 370 Nietzsche compares those with a 'superabundance (*Überfülle*) of life' who need 'a Dionysian art as well as a tragic outlook' with those who suffer an 'impoverishment of life' and so need the sick

---

16 The only exception to this is section 43, which says that the Romans feared the 'Dionysian cult' because under its influence women were incapable of saying 'No'.

'romanticism' of Wagner and Schopenhauer. The former, the 'Dionysian god or man', 'can allow himself the sight of what is terrible and question-able . . . and every luxury of destruction, decomposition, negation' because he is 'pregnant with future', full of 'procreating, fertilizing forces capable of turning any desert into bountiful farmland'.

The metaphorical character of this passage makes it difficult to de-cipher. But it contains a strong echo of the outlook of *The Birth* and of *Wagner at Bayreuth* where death is the great 'stimulus to life' since, as I irreverently put it, you can't make an omelette without breaking eggs (see p. 24 fn. 8 above). This idea, of course, does nothing to solve the problem of *my* death, unless it is accompanied, as it was in those early texts, by the idea of the Dionysian state as one in which I achieve some kind of transcendence of the mortality that is the price of individuality. To see whether this idea, too, has returned to Nietzsche's thinking, we need to look at that which comes between Books i–iv and Book v: *Thus Spoke Zarathustra*.

CHAPTER 6

Thus Spoke Zarathustra

One of the benefits of coming to *Thus Spoke Zarathustra* (1883–5) with a good grasp of the concerns and continuities of the previous texts under one's belt is that the utterances of its eponymous hero, in themselves often biblical, oracular ink-blots on which to project one's favourite philosophy, become, in most cases, clear and unambiguous. I shall attend to four themes in the work: the critique of Christianity, death, Volk, and the festival. Finally I shall make some comments on 'the child', the last of the 'Three metamorphoses' of the spirit.

CHRISTIANITY

Christianity, of course, together with such 'shadows' as 'metaphysical' – i.e. Schopenhauerian – transcendentalism ('afterworldliness') from which Nietzsche/Zarathustra is now 'convalescing', comes out badly in the work. Section 3 of Part I makes three points. First, 'suffering and impotence . . . created all afterworlds', 'the sick and dying . . . invented the things of heaven and the redeeming drop of blood'. Second, such world-'weariness' wants to reach the ultimate at 'a single leap'. And third, that the 'other world' is an 'inhuman . . . heavenly nothing' since 'the belly of being does not speak to man except as man'.

The last of these observations makes the same point as appears later in section 374 of (the final book of) *The Gay Science*. This section observes, first, that existence has a 'perspectival character'. Access to the real is always mediated by a 'horizon of knowledge' (WP 482) (a 'conceptual scheme'), and to the number of potential horizons – 'perspectives' – there is no limit. Moreover, we can never step outside the constitution of our own intellects, our own perspective, can never 'look around our corner'. Hence there are more things in heaven and earth than can be dreamt of in our philosophy: there really is an 'unknown world' (or worlds) – the infinite richness of all those aspects of reality which are beyond our ken since they are disclosed by horizons utterly different from our own.

Nietzsche is perfectly aware that this 'beating back of knowledge' is the move Kant made in order to make room for (Christian) 'faith'. And it is to Kant that he responds with the simple tautology that the unknown other world really is unknown. Epistemologically it is 'nothing' to us. From the point of view of the search for the 'heavenly' it is 'nothing'. (*The Gay Science* rubs the point home by pointing out that the unknown contains just as many 'ungodly possibilities' – e.g. Schopenhauer's evil 'Will' – as 'godly' ones.) So Christian belief is radically unjustified, an infringement against the rules of rational belief, an 'error'.

This, however, is hardly a crushing objection. For Nietzsche asserts many times, of course, that 'error' is a condition of human existence, that certain 'errors', that is, 'faiths' (moral chauvinism, for instance), are necessary, beneficial errors. And he also asserts, many times, that religious belief is not formed on the basis of rational argument. So what, then, is the objection?

If one does not believe Christian doctrine on the basis of evidence then one believes it because it makes one happy – or at any rate happier. This is the point made by the observation that 'suffering and impotence' created all transcendent worlds. One believes not on the basis of evidence for the belief but on the basis of the psychological consequences of believing. But why should that be problematic?

In *Human, All-too-Human* we saw Nietzsche objecting that by 'narcoticising' us against suffering, Christianity destroys the will to deal with its causes (see pp. 67–8 above). This, I think, is the point behind the objection to the impatience that wants to reach the ultimate with 'one leap' (As R. J. Hollingdale points out (Z p. 339) this is probably a reference to Kierkegaard's 'leap of faith'.) With patient attention to little things like diet, climate and so on (see pp. 68–9 above) we would, Nietzsche thinks, be able to remove the causes.

With regard to pain, spiritual and a great deal of physical pain, Nietzsche is quite possibly right; his science of spiritual and physical 'hygiene' ought, in principle, to be able to do away with a great deal of it. But (the objection I raised to *Human*'s idea that the 'metaphysical need' could in principal be abolished (p. 85 above)) with regard to death it is surely absurd to suppose that we can remove *its* causes. It is indeed true, as Nietzsche claims (repeating Schopenhauer's observation), that 'impotence' in the face of death is the principal source of belief in an 'afterworld'. But the point is, surely, that, when it comes to death, we *really are* 'impotent'.

It seems to me, however, that (though it requires some reflection to recognise it as such) there in fact *is* a prescription of a way of overcoming fear of death in *Zarathustra*, a radical extension of the techniques of spiritual 'hygiene' which consists in a revisiting and recasting of the Dionysian overcoming of death as described in *The Birth*. Arguably this is the single most significant advance made in *Zarathustra* over its positivist predecessors. In the positivist works Nietzsche could not, I think, see how to retain the Dionysian given his abandonment of Kantian–Schopenhauerian idealism. But in *Zarathustra*, as I read the work, he finally sees how to avoid throwing the baby out with the bathwater. He sees, that is, how it is possible for there to be a non-'metaphysical', *naturalistic* Dionysianism.

The motto at the beginning of Part III of the work – and as such of considerable significance – is: 'He who climbs the highest mountains laughs at all tragedies real and imaginary (*Trauer-Spiele und Trauer-Ernste*).' '*Trauer-Spiel*' refers specifically to the theatre, so this takes us back to the tragic effect discussed in *The Birth*, a discussion whose import is summed up in the fourth *Meditation*'s 'to be free from the anxiety which time and death evoke the individual must be consecrated to something higher than himself – that is the meaning of tragedy' (see p. 52 above). In other words, it takes us back to the idea of identifying with something other than our mortal individuality. Important, here, is the fact that the motto that begins Part III is actually a quotation from section 7 of Part I where it is used to describe Zarathustra's state of '*Erhebung*' – exaltation, sublimity, in other words transcendence.

This idea of 'exaltation' is continued in section 4 of Part III which is entitled 'Before sunrise' – a time, it is important to notice, when, though there is illumination, day has not yet arrived. Zarathustra speaks to the sky:

O pure deep sky! You abyss of light! Gazing into you I tremble with divine desires. To cast myself into your height – that is my depth. The god is veiled by his beauty: thus you hide your stars ... Together we learnt everything; together we learnt to mount above ourselves and smile uncloudedly – to smile uncloudedly down from bright eyes and from miles away when under us

compulsion and purpose and guilt stream like rain ... This however is my
blessing; to stand over everything as its own sky, as its round roof, its azure bell
and eternal certainty: and happy is he who thus blesses. For all things are blessed
in the fount of eternity and are beyond good and evil ... The world is deep:
deeper than day has ever comprehended. But day is coming: so let us part!

There are, it seems to me, four ideas contained in this wonderful,
poetic passage – poetic, as we will see, for a particular reason.

1. The soul's ascension from its mortal shell (as in Plato's *Phaedrus*)
so that it *becomes* the all-embracing starry sky, that is, the totality of things –
you are '*my* depth', Zarathustra says to it. (In *Twilight of the Idols*
Nietzsche speaks of the insight that 'one belongs to the whole, one *is*
the whole' (TI vi 8).) The same metaphor of transcendence to the stars
appears in Hermann Hesse's poem which Richard Strauss set as the third
of his 'Four Last Songs': 'And the spirit unguarded/longs to soar on free
wings/so that in the magic circle of the night/it may live deeply and a
thousandfold.' It also appears in *Human, All-too-Human*'s description of
Beethoven's 'dream of *immortality*': 'all the stars seem to glitter around
him and the earth seems to sink further and further away'. (Being at
the time, however, in his anti-Dionysian phase, Nietzsche tries to debunk
the 'dream' (see p. 64 above).) And it appears, elusively, in section 3
of *Zarathustra*'s first part where it is said that the 'afterworldly' 'wanted
to escape from their misery' into another world because 'the stars were
too far for them'. The afterworldly look, in other words, for other-
worldly transcendence because they miss the possibility of *this-worldly*
transcendence.

2. The idea that through becoming the totality of things one enters,
becomes, the 'fount of eternity', an 'eternal certainty'; in other words, that
one transcends mortality.

3. The idea that one *smiles* down on the earth because once one has
entered this perspective things are 'beyond good and evil'. This is somewhat tricky to interpret. The temptation is to read backwards from *The
Genealogy of Morals*, from, in particular, its insistence that 'beyond good
and evil' does not at all mean 'beyond good and bad'. But, for three
reasons, this will not, I think, do. First, because reading backwards is a
bad idea – the distinction between good/evil and good/bad still lies some
way into the future. Second, because what is important about the world's
being beyond good and evil is that if it is to be the object of the kind of
ecstatic identification Nietzsche is talking about there must be nothing
questionable about its nature at all. But, in fact, if it is, in some measure,
'bad', this blocks identification just as much as would its being, in some

measure, 'evil'. And third, because the 'smile' of ecstatic transcendence is 'unclouded', and because Nietzsche says that '*all things* are blessed'. (Note that this phrase is strongly reminiscent of the quotation from Emerson on the title page of the first edition of *The Gay Science*: 'to the poet, to the philosopher, to the saint, *all* things are friendly and sacred, *all* events profitable, *all* days holy, *all* men divine' – my emphases.) So what Nietzsche means is not that the world is beyond good/evil because it is good/bad but rather it is beyond the contrast between good and evil *because all things are good* – and are in some sense *necessarily* so.

How could there possibly be a perspective from which that were the case? To answer this question we need to return, I think, to section 370 of *The Gay Science*.[1] There it is said that the 'Dionysian god or man' accepts, indeed desires, the 'terrible and questionable . . . every luxury of destruction, decomposition, negation', the reason being that he feels himself to be surfing a wave of 'fertilizing forces' that are capable of 'turning any desert into bountiful farmland'. In ecstatic transcendence, in other words, one performs a kind of theodicy: the world is divine because one is sublimely confident that everything contributes to some greater good. This is of course the state in which one can will the 'eternal recurrence', in which one says 'never have I heard anything more divine' (GS 341), to the idea of the exact and eternal recurrence of the history of the world to date. It is also the state in which 'all "it was"' finds its 'redemption' in a 'thus I willed it . . . thus I will it' (Z II 42). (Notice that, since the individual self cannot possibly have 'will*ed*' 'all "it was"', 'redemption' is something that can only occur from a transcendent point of view.)

4. 'The world', Zarathustra says to the sky, 'is deep: deeper than day can comprehend.' This same refrain appears at the very end of *Zarathustra* (Z IV 19.6) where Nietzsche talks about an 'ancient [i.e. Greek] happiness . . . intoxicated midnight's dying happiness which sings: the world is deep: deeper than day can comprehend'. Joyfully deep, he adds. 'For though woe be deep: *joy is deeper than the heart's agony.*'

'Intoxication' takes us back to *The Birth* and the Dionysian. There are perspectives on the world, Nietzsche, I think, is saying, other than the 'sober', ordinary perspective of the 'day'. As extra-ordinary they can of

---

1 It may be protested that *this* is reading Nietzsche backwards, too, since the section was written after *Zarathustra*. But this is not entirely so, since the basic idea of the section – what I have called the 'you-can't-make-an-omelette-without-breaking-eggs' principle – appears already, in embryonic form, in *The Birth* and in the fourth *Meditation* (see pp. 24, 56 above).

course only be reached, evoked, in extra-ordinary language – hence the magnificent poetry of 'Before sunrise'. Specifically, there is the 'sky's' perspective, the perspective of identification with 'the god who is veiled by his beauty', the _causa sui_, the divine totality and 'fount' of things. This is the perspective of 'being God',[2] a perspective which guarantees not only that one inhabits – is – a perfect world but also that one is _ontologically_ secure, that one is immune to harm and death; in Wittgenstein's words, that one is 'safe, _whatever_ happens'.

Nietzsche's view, I think, is that there is no right or wrong about these different perspectives.[3] There is no epistemological reason to privilege the everyday mortal-individual perspective over that of poetic, Dionysian pantheism or vice versa, just as there is no reason, in the famously ambiguous drawing, to privilege the 'duck' over the 'rabbit' or vice versa. 'Intoxication' is no closer to truth than sobriety nor sobriety than intoxication. But intoxication is what we _need_ when we confront fear of death, so that if we can revisit it from time to time, and carry it always at the back of our minds, we will have learnt how to overcome that fear. Having learnt how to die we will have learnt how to live; how to live the life of exuberant, unqualified affirmation Nietzsche wants us to live.

It seems, then, that _Zarathustra_ contains a reappearance of _The Birth_'s solution to the problem of death, modulated by and rendered compatible with the later Nietzsche's naturalism. Instead of this world being an 'illusion' and the 'primal unity', the real 'in itself' of things, we have instead two different perspectives on a natural world affirmed as real, neither being truer than the other, but each useful for different purposes.

So for the first time since the 'romantic' period, Nietzsche presents a serious solution to the problem of death, a solution that consists in

---

2 At the time of his mental collapse, Nietzsche made various remarks effectively claiming to be God. These are generally taken to be expressions of megalomaniac lunacy. Once one sees, however, the centrality of Dionysian pantheism to his deepest thinking they present themselves as continuous with his 'sane' thought. A happy interpretation of Nietzsche's madness would be to see it as an entry into the Dionysian state and a refusal to re-emerge. This is not an original interpretation. Something like it occurred _inter alios_ to Heidegger (like Hölderlin, Nietzsche experienced, he suggests, 'too much light'), August Horneffer, Rudolf Steiner and Isadora Duncan, who wrote in 1917: 'How do we know that what seems to us insanity was not a vision of transcendental truth?' (quoted in Aschheim (1992) p. 27).

3 'Perspectives', here, should not be fully identified with the perspectives of 'perspectivism'. The latter – conceptual schemes, horizons of disclosure – disclose _different worlds_. Here, however, we are talking about different perspectives on _one and the same world_; or, better, different modes of self-location with respect to that world. The ordinary 'daytime' individual identifies himself with something _in_ that world. The Dionysian pantheist, on the other hand, identifies with its totality.

becoming the god hidden in his beauty, in habitation of the perspective of Dionysian pantheism. There is, therefore, an at least private religiosity in *Zarathustra*.

In fact, however, it is not merely private. In 'On the free death' (Z I 21) Nietzsche advises us to 'die at the right time' and not hang on, a shrivelled apple on the tree.[4] In other words, we should die (or perhaps go mad) when we have completed our life-defining mission, whatever that might be. And then Nietzsche complains that 'death is not yet a festival'. We must, he says, 'learn to consecrate the fairest of festivals'. In other words, funerals should be celebrations of *life*, 'a spur and promise to the living'. They should be, like Greek tragedies, occasions when, communally, we inhabit the perspective of Dionysian pantheism, when we 'climb the highest mountains' and, looking down, realise that the death of the loved one, and our own future death, is not really a tragedy at all.

What, however, of the other function of religion – the expounding and empowering of community-creating ethos? Before this question can be answered we need to ask whether the topic of community, of Volk, appears in *Zarathustra* and, if so, how it fares.

VOLK

Section 14 of Part II takes up the theme that no genuine Volk exists today. It repeats the 'motley cow' critique that we have seen running through earlier texts. This so-called 'land of culture (*Bildung*)' is 'spotted', nothing but 'blotches', 'mirrors' (of past cultures), 'scraps of paper glued together'. It is gutless, has no virility, only sterility. It prides itself on its lack of 'faith (*Glauben*)' but this merely makes a virtue out of necessity since, in reality, its sterility makes it *incapable* of faith. This is the 'nihilism of post-modernity' critique we have already encountered: comparisons, an excess of 'history' (see pp. 39–42 above), breed spectatorship, ironic detachment, 'scepticism', as *Beyond Good and Evil* calls it (BGE 208). It makes commitment impossible, paralyses action. The highest values devalue themselves; nihilism arrives.

'Faith', communal ethos, and the religion which supports and expounds it, we know from the earlier texts, is the precondition of there being a Volk. This is repeated in *Zarathustra*. A 'people' is something which 'has a faith and a love hung over [it]' (Z I 11). And again: 'no people

---

4 Compare HH II b 185, discussed on p. 85 above.

could live without evaluating', evaluating differently from its neighbours, no people could live without a 'table of values', a table of what is both 'hard' and 'indispensable'.[5] Such a table is the 'voice of their will to power' (this is the first appearance of the concept in Nietzsche's published works), the voice of their will to 'rule and conquer and glitter, to the dread and envy of its neighbour' (Z I 15).

So what emerges is that Volk is (a) something absent from modernity and (b) desirable. This point becomes even clearer in III 12.21. Modernity, Nietzsche writes, is the age in which 'shopkeepers rule', the age in which 'everything that glitters is shopkeepers' gold'.

The age of kings[6] [Nietzsche continues] is past: what today calls itself Volk deserves no king.[7] Just see how these people themselves now behave like shopkeepers: they glean the smallest advantage from sweepings of every kind. They lie in wait for one another – they call it 'good neighbourliness'. Oh blessed, distant time when a Volk said to itself: 'I want to be *master* over peoples. For my brothers, the best shall rule, they shall *want* to rule.'

Various Nietzschean themes are mixed together here. Anti-democracy, anti-materialism, and the will of a people to mastery over its neighbours (through, I would suggest – in the light of the above talk of 'glitter' and 'envy' – the 'soft' power of cultural charisma, rather than the 'hard' power of arms.)

---

5 'Hard' because there is no point in elevating something to the status of a virtue which everyone does anyway – breathing, for example – and 'indispensable' because, from Nietzsche's quasi-Darwinian point of view, a society selects as its virtues those practices which enable it to survive and thrive.

6 'The age of kings is past because the peoples are no longer worthy of them: they do not *want* to see the ur-symbol of their ideal (*Urbild ihres Ideals*) in kings, but a means for their profit' (WP 725). According to this interesting and plausible account of monarchy, the function of a king is to be his Volk's primary role model. Thus the Queen of England, for example, is required to embody all that is best about being English. This, perhaps, is part of the reason for the widespread dismay at the prospect of Charles becoming king: lacking the capacity for 'fusion of horizons', he seems to many a museum-piece from the 1950s rather than a living exemplar of how the British could and should live now.

7 Compare the following poem written some twenty years later by Rilke. It begins:

> The kings of the world are old,
> and they will have no heirs.
> The sons are dying as boys,
> and their pale daughters gave
> all the sickly crowns to force.
> The rabble grinds them into specie;
> the time-serving lord of the world.
> (quoted in Heidegger (2002) p. 218)

The point I want to attend to, however, is that, in *Zarathustra*, 'Volk' – for all of Nietzsche's continual emphasis on the restrictions it places on the free creativity of the individual – is a noble, even sacred word. (This, to repeat, is true of all of Nietzsche's published writings.) Modernity – German modernity – 'calls' itself a Volk, but is not *worthy* of the title. Its claim to be a 'people' is entirely spurious.

'On the new idol' (Z 1 11) similarly treats Volk as a desirable state of affairs.[8] It complains of the hijacking of the word by the 'new idol', the state (Bismarck's in particular, of course). The state says, 'I the state am the people' (*'das Volk in seinem Staat'* was a favourite piece of Nazi jargon) but it lies. Peoples 'serve life'. But the state, as an object of reverence, represents 'the death of peoples'. It turns individuals into 'nimble apes', robots. 'Only there, where the state ceases, does the man . . . [who is not a robot] begin.'

This passage is sometimes appealed to by those eager to clear Nietzsche of the charge of fascist totalitarianism. It shows that far from glorifying the state, it is suggested, Nietzsche was in fact 'anti-political' (Kaufmann (1959) p. 119), something approaching an anarchist (Leiter (2002) p. 296), that he would have preferred there to be no state at all. But this is overkill. Though Nietzsche is indeed, as Kaufmann suggests (*ibid.*), attacking the proto-totalitarianism he sees in the modern state (the transformation of individuals into *nothing but* its robotic functionaries), the premise on which he does so is not anarchism but rather what I called in the Introduction the thesis of the 'priority of Volk to state'. As I there pointed out, this is a thesis that runs through German anti-Enlightenment thinking going back to Herder, Hegel and Fichte (see further the Epilogue below). According to the thesis, to repeat, the just state is a nation-state, and its laws are just only in so far as they (partially) articulate the ethos of the nation/Volk. State laws are subordinate to the grounding 'faith' of the Volk; the legitimate state is the vehicle and expression of the Volk. What Nietzsche objects to in the above passage is not *the state*, but rather the state that has turned from servant into master of the Volk, the state which claims to *be* the Volk, which no longer looks to Volk and its higher source of legitimacy.

In sum, then, community, Volk, together with its grounding ethos, is, in *Zarathustra*, something to be prized and achieved. This would

---

8 While denigrating 'the state', what the section actually elevates is 'peoples and herds'. As I have emphasised before, 'herd', unlike 'mob' or 'rabble', is not a term of unmitigated abuse. A *healthy* herd is something to be valued.

lead us to expect that religion and the religious festival will be similarly prized.

The most prominent appearance of the theme of the festival is in sections 17 and 18 of Part IV which disclose the 'higher men' celebrating what the title of section 18 calls 'The Ass Festival'. Zarathustra returns to his cave to discover the sound of giggles, the smell of incense, and the higher men worshipping an ass. The high point of the festival is the sudden descent of a mood of (either actual or mock) solemnity and the singing of a 'litany' in praise of the ass, a song which begins: 'Amen: And praise and honour and wisdom and thanks and glory and strength be to our God for ever and ever' (Z IV 18.2).

Historically, the Ass Festival, otherwise known as the Feast of Fools, was a carnivalesque letting-off of steam that took place in medieval Europe, especially in France, usually in December or at New Year. A central role in the festival was played by the ass, to whom, in various forms, a hymn of praise, 'the song of the ass', was sung. In *Beyond Good and Evil* (section 8) Nietzsche quotes the words of 'an ancient mystery': *adventavit asinus/pulcher et fortissimus* (In came the ass, beautiful and very strong)'. Since this is virtually a direct quotation from the version of the Ass's Song sung at Sens in the fifteenth century[9] there can be very little doubt that it is the historical Ass Festival that is before Nietzsche's mind in the final part of *Zarathustra*. And since, as I have frequently emphasised, Nietzsche writes for an audience of highly educated people much like himself, there can be little doubt, either, that we are expected to be aware of the allusion.

The medieval festival, condemned – though in a somewhat half-hearted way – by the Church hierarchy, was usually performed in a cathedral by members of clergy. The ass was often led up the aisle covered in a golden cloth, the four corners held by the cathedral's four most eminent canons. It involved such things as playing dice and eating 'black' (i.e. blood) pudding at the altar (a parody, of course, of the Eucharist), wearing masks, dressing up as women or animals, and, after the ceremony, raging round town, in a generally riotous manner. Not infrequently the day ended in minor bloodshed.

---

9 See Backman (1952) p. 54. Other useful references are Chambers (1903) pp. 274–335, and Gilhus (1990) pp. 24–52.

The presentation of the Ass Festival in Part IV of *Zarathustra* is a deconstructionist's delight. The fundamental uncertainty concerns Nietzsche's attitude to the higher men – whether he is laughing with or at them. In a long, detailed and scholarly essay, Jörg Salaquarda opts for the latter view.[10] Noting that in Nietzsche's writings in general (as in everyday metaphor) the ass stands for a kind of stupidity, namely, the holding of 'convictions',[11] and furthermore that Nietzsche describes himself as 'anti-ass' (EH III 2), he concludes that in part IV Nietzsche is making fun of the kowtowing to the convictions of the Volk by modernity's supposedly (but not actually) 'higher men'.

This seems to me wrong on several counts. First, as we have seen, Nietzsche is not against the holding of 'convictions': on the contrary, as we have repeatedly seen, 'virtuous stupidity' (see p. 93 above) is essential to communal life. Of course, Nietzsche himself – the critic of 'convictions' such as Christianity, and 'modern ideas' such as feminism, socialism, democracy, Utilitarianism, the Bismarckian state, and so on – is 'anti-ass' in relation to the present. But that by no means entails that the higher type cannot be the 'advocate' (see p. 96 above) of a current 'rule' where it is a vibrant and healthy rule (see further chapter 11). The main thing wrong with Salaquarda's reading, however, is that, given the historical allusion to the medieval festival, the higher men are *themselves* laughing at 'convictions' – *those very 'convictions' they themselves profess*, during, as it were, 'office hours'. (Note that *temporary release from* the 'sober' world of 'convictions' is not at all the same as *abandonment of* those 'convictions'. With the necessary return to the 'office', its 'convictions' will return, too.) This cancels the possibility of Nietzsche's laughing at their kowtowing to convictions: one cannot laugh at someone who is laughing at himself. In what follows, therefore, I shall suggest that Nietzsche is laughing *with* the higher men, i.e. that, at least for the moment, they have become *genuinely* higher spirits.

Two elements of the historical Festival are of particular importance. First, it is astonishingly blasphemous, quite at odds with the 'age-of-gloomy-piety' stereotyping of the Middle Ages.

---

10 Salaquarda (1973), pp. 203–38.
11 Section 8 of *Beyond Good and Evil* reads in full: 'In every philosophy there is a point where the philosopher's "conviction" steps onto the stage: or to use the language of an ancient Mystery: in came the ass/ beautiful and very strong.'

Second, it recalls the Saturnalia of the ancient world, in being a day of quasi-sanctioned disorder. In Nietzsche's language, that is, it recalls a day of release from the Apollonian, a day devoted to Dionysus. (Remember that in *The Birth* he talks about the dancing, singing throngs roaming the streets on the day of St John or St Vitus as the 'Dionysian enthusiasts' of the Middle Ages (see p. 20 above).)

Both these aspects of the historical Festival seem to me relevant to Nietzsche's festival. That a blasphemous burlesque on Christianity would appeal to the self-styled 'Antichrist' is obvious. But that the Ass Festival represents the subterranean survival of pagan Dionysianism into the Christian era is, I think, what is really important. For, discovered celebrating the Ass Festival, the 'higher men' who had previously disappointed Zarathustra on account of their lack of true 'highness' now give him genuine pleasure. 'Oh my new friends', he says,

you Higher Men, how well you please me now since you became joyful again! Truly, you have all blossomed forth: for such flowers as you, I think, *new festivals* are needed, a little brave nonsense, some divine service . . . a blustering wind to blow your souls bright. (Z IV 18.3)

'Brave nonsense' means here, I suggest, a stepping out of the Apollonian sobriety of everydayness and into the Dionysian perspective on life and death, a perspective which 'blows the soul bright' because it leads to joyous affirmation of life and (a necessary condition of such affirmation) overcomes anxiety about death.

In the next section (Z IV 19.1), 'The somnambulist (*Nachtwandler*[12]) song', the 'ugliest man' is moved by the festival to will the eternal recurrence – '"Was *that* life?" I will say to death. "Very well! Once more!"' – which confirms that it is the view of 'the Dionysian god or man' (GS 370) that has been inhabited. And he adds that what he has experienced and what we need is a festival which teaches us to 'love the earth' – rather than hate it as in the Christian festival. That this is Nietzsche himself speaking is confirmed by the already quoted passage in which he says that funerals, especially, should be celebrations of life (Z I 21).

Zarathustra deplores the festivals of the present as fake: 'I do not like your festivals . . . I have found too many actors there and the audience behaving like actors.' For the time being, therefore, 'may your friend be

---

12 This is translated as 'intoxicated' by Hollingdale and 'drunken' by Kaufmann. Both these radical departures from the ordinary meaning of '*Nachtwandler*' seem to me mistaken. Admittedly 'intoxication' figures prominently in the song, but so, about equally, does 'night'.

to you a festival of the earth' (Z I 16). 'Actor' here, of course, means Wagner and 'festival' means Bayreuth. And the complaint about the audience, rather than the usual one that, work-weary, they are incapacitated for anything but cheap thrills, seems to be that they go to the opera to show off their ball gowns and tiaras. They are, in any case, incapable of genuine festivity, which is why, at present, the best one can do is engage in the mini-festival, the festival *à deux*, as it were.

The main point, however, that emerges from all these discussions is that the festival, the rebirth of the life-affirming Greek festival, remains at the centre of Nietzsche's thinking. Though Wagner *qua* man and artist is rejected, 'the inner truth and greatness' of the Wagnerian ideal remains.

GODS

'Of old and new law-tables' (Z III 12) is about 'gods' – i.e. role models – and so, too, about festivity. 'A *new nobility* is needed', writes Nietzsche,

to oppose all mob-rule and all despotism and to write anew upon new law-tables the word: 'Noble'. For many noblemen are needed, and noblemen of many kinds, *for nobility to exist*! Or, as I once said, in a parable: 'Precisely this is godliness, that there are gods but no God!' (Z III 12.11)

'Mob rule' is Nietzsche's word for democratic modernity, and 'despotism' is what he – presciently – predicts will arise out of it. In place of this threatening state of affairs we need a new idealism, a new ethos. But this will be a 'polytheistic' rather than a 'monotheistic' ethos (compare GS 143) – an ethos of gods, not of God, as he quickly adds. This is an affirmation of what I shall call the 'stratification of the virtues' thesis, the anti-universalism which is part and parcel of Nietzsche's Volkish thinking. Since, as I pointed out in the Introduction, the Volkish tradition holds that the individual is subordinate to the community as a whole, the virtues appropriate to a particular kind of individual are relative to his or her 'station' in life – the role he or she is supposed to play in promoting the well-being of the organic, communal whole – rather in the way in which the 'virtues' of a bodily organ are relative to what organ it is, i.e. what role it is supposed to play in promoting the life of the body as a whole.

It is important not to confuse the 'polytheism' of normative stratification with the 'polytheism' of moral chaos. As *Antigone* illustrates, it would not, for example, do for unrestricted loyalty to family to be an absolutely unqualified virtue for women and unconditional loyalty to

the state to be an unconditional virtue for men. For there to be a genuine
Volk, the different 'gods' must accommodate each other so as to form a
coherent whole.[13]

This distinction is crucial to understanding Nietzsche's view of the
history of morality. Everything, he says, quoting Heraclitus' dictum, is 'in
flux' (Z III 12.8). At Z III 12.3 he applies his fundamentally Heraclitean
outlook (compare BGE 208 and GM II 16) to the history of morals:

All becoming seem[s] to me the dancing of gods and the wantonness of gods,
and the world unrestrained and abandoned and fleeing back into itself – as many
gods blissfully self-contradicting, communing again and belonging again to
one another . . .

In other words social history consists in an old set of ethos-embodying
gods, then new ones mingling with them and creating a 'self-contradicting'
'motley cow', and finally a new unity where the gods 'commune and belong again' to each other which they must do for *us* to 'commune and
belong' to each other, for there to be genuine community.

This is what Nietzsche longs for above all: to 'carry into one' what is
'fragment, riddle and terrible accident' (Z III 12.2), to create a new neo-
classical unity. He yearns, he says, for 'a warmer South than artists have
ever dreamed of, there where gods, dancing, are ashamed of all clothes'
(Z III 12.8). He yearns, in other words, for a new Greece.[14]

THE CHILD

As in the earlier texts, then, Volk, community, and hence a unifying ethos
and religion, represents Nietzsche's conception of thriving social – and so
human – existence. What, however, appears out of line with earlier texts
is *Zarathustra*'s conception of the way in which Volk is to be achieved.

The crux of this lies in Zarathustra's conception of the 'child' of the
'Three metamorphoses' (Z I 1). The incarnation of 'the spirit' which

---

13 Section 28 of *The Antichrist* makes the claim that the philological attempt to resolve the
'contradictions' in Christian tradition is a waste of time since the stories of the Christian saints are
too 'ambiguous' to constitute a genuine ethical tradition at all.

14 This passage is strongly reminiscent of Hölderlin's poem 'Remembrance', in which 'the South' is
always, more or less directly, Greece. Though 'Remembrance' is ostensibly a remembrance of his
time in Provence, the poet wrote to his friend Böhlendorf that 'the athleticism of the Southern
[French] people in the [in fact Roman] ruins of the antique spirit made me more familiar with the
authentic essence of the Greeks. I came to know their nature and their wisdom, their bodies, the
way in which they grew in their climate' (quoted in Heidegger (1977–) vol. 52, pp. 80–1). From
early schooldays, Nietzsche was passionately devoted to Hölderlin. Like Hölderlin, I believe, he is
strongly inclined to identify 'the South' with 'Greece'.

precedes that of the child, 'the lion' who says 'No' to old values but cannot create new ones, appears to be equivalent to *The Gay Science*'s 'free spirit of the second rank' (see p. 96 above). The child who can create new values seems to be the 'free spirit of the first rank'.

The creativity of the child is conceived as its being 'innocence and forgetfulness, a new beginning, a sport (*Spiel*), a self-propelling wheel, a first motion'. This theme is continued in other parts of *Zarathustra*. Section 17 of Part I specifically builds into the 'way of the creator' that the creator is a 'self-propelling wheel'. And section 12.25 of Part III says that 'he who has grown wise concerning old origins . . . will seek new springs of the future and new origins'. If this happens, it says, 'it will not be long before *new peoples* [Nietzsche's emphasis] shall arise and new springs rush down to new depths'. What we need, he continues, is 'the earthquake' which, while it 'blocks many wells and causes much thirst . . . reveals new springs'. So creation in *Zarathustra* seems to be, like that of the Christian God, *ex nihilo*. It appears to constitute an absolute rupture with the past, not a modulation or re-creation of the past but a beginning – as the Germans described the first moments after the catastrophe of the Second World War – at *Stunde Null* (hour zero).

This account of creation comes as a considerable shock to the reader of the pre-*Zarathustra* texts. What has happened, one wonders, to Nietzsche's hatred of Rousseau, of 1789 and of revolution in general? What has happened to his insistence on an '*andante*' speed in the 'development of a *Volk*' (GS 10), a gradualness of change which preserves that 'first-rank' value, the 'duration' of the identity of a people (see pp. 91–2 above)? What has happened to the idea that 'arbitrariness of seeing and feeling', too many radical departures from a 'universally binding faith', constitutes 'the greatest danger that hovers and still hovers over humanity' (GS 76)?

What has happened is that it is no longer 'arbitrariness' but rather 'the good and just' who now represent the 'greatest danger for the whole human future' (Z III 12.26). Not the destruction of communal life by fragmentation but destruction by ossification has now become the greatest danger: 'whatever harm the wicked [the "wicked"] may do, the harm the good [the "good"] do is the most harmful' (*ibid.*). This is why he says, of the one who creates 'one heart for many who long, one will for many instruments', that 'around him assembles a *people* [Nietzsche's emphasis], that is to say, many experimenters' (Z III 12.25). The idea, here, I think, is that in a Heraclitean world there can be no *rest*. Since external conditions are always in flux, there must be *constant* experiment with new 'faiths', new social groupings. (There is an echo, here, of Marx's prediction of eternal restlessness as the condition of capitalism generated by the fact that profits *always* need to be increased.)

To my mind this impatient demand for discontinuous change, 'new origins', for the repeated experimenting with new and 'experimental' social forms, is quite inhuman and very close to totalitarianism. (Indeed the idea of a 'people' as an experiment with a new 'faith' sounds like nothing so much as Elizabeth Förster Nietzsche's attempt, together with her rabidly anti-Semitic husband, to found a fascist colony in Paraguay.) The demand for an 'earthquake' that will create 'new origins' is what led to Hitler, Mao, Stalin and Pol Pot, all of whom were imbued with the *tabula rasa* idea of social creation.

It is a relief, therefore, that in the post-*Zarathustra* part of *The Gay Science* Nietzsche reinstates the theme of continuity. In Book v, as we saw, we are to be '*good Europeans*' (Nietzsche's emphasis), to cherish the fact that we are 'the rich heirs of millennia of European spirit' (GS 377). We are, that is, to use the resources of our European heritage to restore an authentic *European* culture – *not* a post-European one. In other words, Nietzsche has returned to the idea adumbrated in section 83 of *The Gay Science*, for example, of, not an *abandonment* of old 'origins', but a 'fusion' between them and the new. 'New' origins are to be updated versions of the old.

It is also a relief (see pp. 181–2 below) that in *The Antichrist* Nietzsche explicitly rejects the idea of social life as *always* one of 'experiment'.

In a word, *Zarathustra*'s 'child' is an aberration.

CHAPTER 7

Beyond Good and Evil

As with most of Nietzsche's works, the 'medical' procedure of diagnosis of disease followed by prescription of a cure provides the overall shape of *Beyond Good and Evil* (1886). Its motivating force, that is to say, is once again cultural criticism. Indeed Nietzsche now makes cultural criticism into something approaching a defining condition of authentic philosophy: the philosopher is, he says, the 'bad conscience' of his age (BGE 212).

Two themes dominate the critique of modernity: the 'motley' critique, once again, and the critique of Christianity together with its 'shadows'.

CULTURAL CRITICISM: (1) THE 'MOTLEY COW'

We denizens of modernity are, says Nietzsche, 'hybrid', mixed men. We need history as a storage closet of costumes, but nothing looks right on us. Thanks to our 'historical sense' (the critique from the second *Meditation* reappears) part of every past way of life radiates in us, making us a kind of chaos (BGE 223–4). Section 215 applies this to modern morality in particular. Our actions come under the aegis of a variety of moralities and so present themselves ambiguously. We attempt to negotiate between moralities but rarely succeed. The result is ethical confusion both between people and within the individual soul (BGE 260). In every aspect of cultural life modernity is 'chaos' (BGE 224).

But what is actually so wrong with this state of affairs? Nietzsche calls us 'half-barbarian'. We have a taste for everything (one might call to mind, here, the nineteenth century's raiding of past styles of architecture or our own taste for each and every ethnic cuisine). Such lack of discrimination is, however, 'ignoble'. Noble cultures distrust everything new and foreign. What modernity has no feeling for are those moments in which human life is 'transfigured', when art and culture reach a genuinely 'noble' moment of 'smooth seas and halcyon self-sufficiency', when a culture has 'perfected' itself and undergoes a 'sudden harnessing and fossilizing' in 'settling down . . . on ground that is still shaking'. Instead of being able to take pleasure in this moment of perfect stasis,[1] our pleasure is in 'the thrill of the infinite, the unmeasured' (the Internet, for example) (BGE 224).

The point Nietzsche is really making here is that we have *no* culture (*Kultur*). In that sense we are 'barbarians'. We are only 'half' barbarians because we do have 'civilisation (*Civilization*)' – police and plumbing.[2] What we lack is a shared, meaning-giving conception of the good life.

Anticipating the post-modernists' earnest insistence that we regard everything as 'play',[3] Nietzsche says that the only way to survive *in* the modern world is to make it all a motley carnival of mocking laughter. If, that is, we live in ironic detachment we may be able to take some pleasure in the 'infinite and unmeasured': in surfing from one Internet chat-room to another, 'morphing' from one personality to another, in chameleon-like role-playing, 'costume' changing, in being, as Nietzsche often puts it, an 'actor'.

The trouble with modernity is then, in a word, that we are not in Nietzsche's sense a Volk. We lack the 'hardness, uniformity and simplicity of form' (BGE 266) of a genuine community, the shared understanding of world and ethos which produces 'something that "understands itself"' – a people' (BGE 268). In a word, whereas a healthy culture/people/community needs structured unity, modernity is simply 'chaos'.

CULTURAL CRITICISM: (2) CHRISTIANITY AND ITS 'SHADOWS'

Christian morality – inseparable, in Nietzsche's view, from Christian metaphysics – was the first great 'revaluation of values'. It revalued all of the values of antiquity (BGE 46). For two main reasons it has been a 'disaster' for the West. First, it turns the human being into a 'sublime abortion' (BGE 62): a natural being deeply conflicted about its naturalness

---

1 This idea of the moment of perfect stasis, the moment when, as it were, the wave is fully formed but has not yet broken, is an important corrective to the understanding of Nietzsche's Heracliteanism as *nothing but* 'flux'. As we shall see in chapter 11, it becomes particularly important in *The Antichrist*.

2 As pointed out in the Introduction, Volkish thinkers drew a contrast between the Anglo-Saxons' shopkeeper *Civilization* and authentic German *Kultur*. Though Nietzsche has a low opinion of modern Germany's claim to *Kultur* his consistent hostility to everything English (even when English thinking seems close to his own) – his hostility to Utilitarianism, Darwin, Carlyle, George Eliot, the English Sunday, the bourgeois character of English life, the English concept of happiness, English Christianity, English alcoholism, the Anglicised thought-processes of his friend Paul Rée after they had fallen out, and so on – is, I think, a partial manifestation of this polarity.

3 The trouble with this insistence is that if everything is play then nothing is, since there is nothing serious to take time out from.

and at the same time somehow transcending the natural. (Notice that the combination of 'sublime' with 'abortion' suggests that there is a certain upside to Christianity, that Nietzsche's attitude is not one of *unmitigated* hostility.) Second, the doctrine of 'equality before God' weakens the strong and preserves the failures (BGE 62). Democracy, feminism, socialism and anarchism are continuations of Christianity, of the ethics of equality, in another form (BGE 202).

A prima facie problem with Nietzsche's cultural criticism is that its two strands appear to be incompatible with each other, since while the first pictures modernity as 'chaos', the second seems to find a unifying (if unhealthy) order. One way of resolving the conflict would be to read the 'motley' critique as concerned with the educated, the 'Christianity' critique as concerned with the masses. But this seems implausible given that democracy, feminism and socialism belong to the 'modern ideas' of educated people that Nietzsche consistently attacks (for example at BGE 203).

The real solution, I think, is that democracy, feminism, socialism and anarchism are, for Nietzsche, essentially *negative* or destructive values. In the language that comes more into its own in the *Genealogy of Morals*, they are 'slave' values. Nietzsche says that a 'noble' culture create values by 'honour[ing] everything [it] . . . sees in itself'. (The Greeks, remember, in the creation of their gods constructed ideal self-portraits.) 'Slave' cultures, on the other hand, create only derivatively – by reacting against, negating, the values of the nobles (BGE 260). Whereas there could be noble cultures without slave cultures, the reverse is not the case. So Christian morality and its 'equal-rights-for-all' heirs are nothing more than a vengeful destruction of the 'rank-ordering' of society by the older morality, nothing but, as one might put it, the 'ethics of envy'. In short, therefore, these 'modern ideas' do nothing to overcome the 'chaos' of modernity because they offer no *positive* ideal, no positive ethos.

These two aspects of Nietzsche's modernity critique add up to the charge of 'nihilism' (BGE 10, 208), which is defined simply as the failure to possess any ultimate answer to the questions of 'Where to (*Wohin*)?' and 'What for (*Wozu*)?', an answer that can only be provided by an ultimate ethos and which is necessary to any healthy existence (BGE 211).[4] As the well-known definition in the *Will to Power* puts it, nihilism

---

4 Nietzsche thinks that positivism has a particular propensity to nihilism since such 'puritanical fanatic[ism] of conscience . . . would rather lie dying on the assured nothing than an uncertain

is a matter of the highest values 'devaluing' themselves (WP 2) and nothing taking their place – save the negative, non-values of slave morality.

It is worth pressing the question of just what is so terribly wrong with nihilism? Nietzsche's answer is effectively given, I think, in section 259. 'Life', it says, is the 'will power', that is to say, to 'growth': a 'self-overcoming' which may (as in the Greek *agon*) involve the 'overcoming' of others too. But without a 'what for', without an 'ideal' (see p. 45 above) for the sake of which one acts, there can be no 'growth', since growth is essentially growth-*towards*. So nihilism is the frustration of, in Nietzsche's view, the most fundamental of all human impulses.

Nietzsche makes clear that the predicament of nihilism is not just Germany's but that of Europe as a whole, that is, of the entire West (see chapter 5 footnote 10). Behind the foreground of petty nationalisms a *European* type of person is in the process of becoming the norm: 'nomadic', undetermined by local environments, a function of 'artifice' (art, media and technology) rather than nature (BGE 242). This raises the stakes. The task before us is the rescue of the West as a whole. And since the next century will be the struggle for *world* domination (between the West in one corner and Islam, India and China in the other, presumably), it is time to give up the petty politics of nationalism for the sake of 'grand' (*grosse*) politics (BGE 208).[5] What is at stake – this is the appearance of the 'globalisation' theme once again – is the future of humanity as a whole.

OVERCOMING DISEASED MODERNITY: THE 'FÜHRER' PRINCIPLE

'Every enhancement of the type "man"', writes Nietzsche, in a much quoted passage,

has been the work of an aristocratic society – and that is how it will be, again and again, since this sort of society believes in a long ladder of rank order and value distinctions between men, and in some sense needs slavery. Without the *pathos of distance* as it grows out of an ingrained difference between stations, out of . . . the ruling caste's . . . continuous exercise in obeying [communal ethos] and

---

something' (BGE 10): 'dying', of course, since, as Nietzsche never tires of repeating, 'untruth is a condition of life' (BGE 4). Commitment to communal ethos – this is *the* way to live – as he explains many times, Nietzsche regards as a 'faith', not the discovery of an evidence-based fact. So the evidence-obsessed are condemned to nihilism.

5 The theme of 'grand' politics reappears in *Ecce Homo*, see pp. 193–4 below.

commanding, in keeping away and below, that *other*, more mysterious pathos could not have grown at all,

that 'mysterious pathos' which leads to 'expansions of distance within the soul', to 'self-overcoming' (BGE 257). Unless, runs this dubious argument, one's social environment places one *between* the higher and lower (unless it places one on the *midway* point of *Zarathustra*'s tight-rope walker's rope) one will not spiritually position oneself between the higher and the lower, and hence will not engage in the self-overcoming which constitutes striving towards an ideal.[6]

In understanding this argument it is important to remember that much of Nietzsche's Europe – the Prussian *Reich*, for example – was still fundamentally aristocratic. Democracy and other such 'modern ideas' were, for Nietzsche, an advancing threat rather than contemporary reality. So what he regards as the social environment out of which the spiritually ambitious soul grows was, in his day, more or less in place (albeit under threat). It follows that what the 'enhancement of the type "man"' really stands in need of is the second, 'more mysterious' pathos of distance, that which constitutes the 'noble' soul. Nietzsche says that what (inner) nobility amounts to today is an unshakeable 'faith' in one's own spiritual rank and 'reverence' for oneself (BGE 287). So what is needed are those who stand out above the mediocrity of the majority, those who are self-consciously confident of their own spiritual exceptionality.

What we need, in short, is a new spiritual aristocracy, exceptional types who are 'sent out ahead' and are 'strong and original enough to give impetus to opposed valuations and initiate a revaluation and reversal of [what are wrongly, but necessarily, taken to be] "eternal values"' (BGE 203). This, of course, is a reappearance of the 'random mutation' thesis: only the exceptional type, the creative free spirit, the one who can 'give birth to a [new] star' in the firmament, can rescue from decay and disintegration a culture whose 'eternal values' have become non-adaptive.

Nietzsche says that there is a terrible danger that these new spiritual 'leaders (*Führer*)' will not appear. If they do not, then we can expect that

---

6 The argument is dubious, first, because it assumes that an hierarchical society must involve slavery 'in some sense'. A string quartet and a rugby team involve order-givers and order-takers but the order-takers do not, unless something has gone seriously wrong, *serve* the order-givers. Second, it is dubious because the hypothesis that hierarchy in the soul can only develop in a context of social hierarchy is pretty obviously false. All that is needed to generate the notion of higher and lower states is an 'Olympic', *competitive* society in which there are not 'castes' but simply winners and losers.

the process of the 'total degeneration (*Gesammt-Entartung*) of humanity' into 'stunted little animals' will complete itself (BGE 203).

We can call this Nietzsche's 'death of man' nightmare. (*Zarathustra*'s 'last man' is so-called, of course, because he stands at the brink of the death of man.) To understand why the non-appearance of a new communal ethos, of a new ideal that can command and commit in the current context, means, quite literally, the 'brutalisation' (BGE 203), the '*Entartung*',[7] of man, we need to say something about the will to power.

The reduction of man to a mere 'brute' entails the loss of some distinguishing feature, something unique to man. Mostly, in *Beyond Good and Evil*, when Nietzsche says that 'life is the will to power' – in for example the crucial section 259 – his interest is clearly confined to *human* life. So the reduction of man to animal would entail the loss of the will to power. Unfortunately, however, Nietzsche sometimes succumbs to the temptation to provide a speculative biology intended to outdo Darwin. 'Organic life' *as a whole* is, he claims, 'will to power'. What Darwin's focus on survival missed, he claims, is that 'self preservation is only one of the indirect and most frequent *consequences* of this' (BGE 13). (I call this temptation to dabble in a field in which he was at best an amateur 'unfortunate', since, applied to animal life, Nietzsche's thesis is obviously false: with rare exceptions animal species do not attempt to colonise each other.)

Given, however, that the will to power is thus universalised, it cannot be said to be unique to man. What, however, Nietzsche would hold to be unique is what we may call the 'intentional' will to power: that is, 'self-overcoming' (which, as observed, may or may not involve the 'overcoming' of others) that is guided by the *conscious* (or at least intentional) pursuit of an ideal or goal. At the level of – certainly the lower – animals Nietzsche must conceive the will to power as, in Schopenhauer's terminology, 'blind', not guided by any conscious goal. Acting in a way that increases power – such must be his view – is something animals just *do*, and speaking of this as being the result of a 'willing' is just a metaphorical, anthropomorphic shorthand for describing behavioural dispositions that are underpinned by no intentional structures at all.

So Nietzsche's view, it is reasonable to suppose, is that the *intentional* will to power *is* unique to human beings. Thus modified, the connexion

---

7 '*Ent-artung*', degeneration, means, literally, falling out of the type (*Art*) 'man'.

between nihilism and the death of man becomes clear: if man loses his ultimate goal – if there is no longer a 'where to' and 'what for' that commands his obedience – then he cannot exercise his unique form of the will to power and will slowly lose all that distinguishes him from the (other) animals.

Before exploring the question of who the new leaders are to be I should like to return briefly to the topic of Nietzsche's intended readership.

In section 203 he says that 'the image of such [new] leaders hovers before *our* eyes'. So here, at least, Nietzsche is casting himself in the role of John the Baptist, the herald – or maybe the midwife – of the new leaders. And in some sections he addresses himself directly to 'you free spirits' (BGE 203) and 'you new philosophers who are approaching' (BGE 44). This makes clear the truth of the thesis I have been defending for some time, that, all along, Nietzsche writes not for everyone but for a very special target audience.

Beyond Good and Evil, in fact, contains a strong and explicit endorsement of this thesis. Affirming what I have called his 'stratification of the virtues' thesis – 'the virtues of a common (*gemein*) person could indicate vice and weakness in a philosopher' – he infers a corresponding 'stratification of books' thesis:

There are books which have inverse values for soul and for health, depending on whether they are used by lower souls . . . or by higher and more powerful ones. In the first case they are dangerous and can cause deterioration and dissolution: in the second case . . . they summon the most courageous to *their* [particular type of] courage. Books for the general public always smell foul,

since they have to be dumbed down to the lowest common denominator (BGE 30) of the airport bookstore. Section 192 repeats (see p. 95 above) the thesis of our innate resistance to change – 'we greet everything novel with reluctance and hostility' – and section 199 indicates that even the potential free spirit has an inherited instinct to take the easy path of following rather than leading. As I have argued, it is this (and *not* 'aristocratic' individualism[8]) that explains the violence and hyperbole of Nietzsche's anti-'herd' rhetoric.

---

8 Section 126 reads: 'A Volk is nature's roundabout way of getting six or seven great men. – Yes: and then of getting around them', i.e. assimilating the exception so that it becomes the new norm. This is an explicit rejection of 'aristocratic individualism', and an explicit warning against taking the 'great man' as an end in himself.

So what Nietzsche is doing, I believe, is something redolent of the nineteenth century, something, in fact, not too far in fundamental conception from the works of contemporaries such as Baden-Powell and Cecil Rhodes. His works are conceived as *training manuals* addressed to the select few who are destined to positions of leadership – those, in the main, who have, like himself, attended the top schools and universities. They are addressed either to those who will become or, more immediately – since spiritual leaders need to be 'bred' over many generations (BGE 213) – to those who will prepare the way for those who will become, our new spiritual 'leaders': those who will rescue the West from contemporary nihilism by instituting a 'revaluation of all values' that will provide us with a new ethos.

I want now to return to the question of who these 'new leaders' are that we need. What will they be like? Nietzsche calls them 'philosophers of the future (*Philosophen der Zukunft*)' (BGE 44).[9] Who are these philosophers of the future and what do they do?

The first thing to note is the phrase's ambiguous genitive. It can mean either 'philosophers who – literally – inhabit the future' (a 'subjective' genitive) or 'philosophers who philosophise *towards* the future' (an 'objective' genitive). Section 212 speaks of the philosopher as being out of step with his time because he is '*necessarily* of tomorrow and the day after tomorrow'. So one could say that the second kind of philosopher inhabits the future, too: but only metaphorically. A philosopher of the first kind I shall call 'the philosopher triumphant'. A philosopher of the second kind – who is, of course, just the free spirit (of the first rank) – is what I have called the 'random mutation'.

The ambiguity as to which kind of philosopher Nietzsche is talking about centres on the notion of the philosopher as 'commander' or 'legislator' (BGE 211). Sometimes such talk is an unmistakable resurrection of Plato's philosopher-king. In these contexts Nietzsche is talking about the philosopher triumphant, the philosopher as the literal inhabitant of an ideal (or at least better) future and as literally 'commanding' and 'legislating', as in Plato's *Republic*. (As we will see in chapter 11, this role for the 'philosopher' becomes even more prominent in *The Antichrist*.)

So, for example, section 208 seems to envisage philosophers as Europe's new ruling 'caste', a caste that will overcome its petty nationalisms and

9 Wagner's music was called *Zukunftsmusik*. Nietzsche's phrase is surely coined with Wagner in mind.

endow it with a single 'will'. Again, section 61 talks about the philosopher as 'making use of religion for his breeding and education work' and for 'selection' which, it would seem, only the philosopher triumphant is in a position to do.

It is important to the understanding of this kind of talk to bear in mind that Nietzsche's conception of 'the philosopher as *we* understand him' is the concept of someone 'who bears the weight of the overall development of mankind' (BGE 61) on his shoulders, a concept that is 'miles away from a concept which includes in it even a Kant, not to speak of the academic "ruminants" and other professors of philosophy' (EH v 3). As we shall shortly see, the essential attribute of 'the philosopher' in Nietzsche's sense is that he 'creates values'. Thus while Kant, a mere codifier of *current* values, is excluded, Napoleon – the heir to antiquity and the Renaissance, the reviver of classical values, the best moment in modern European history (BGE 199) – counts as a 'philosopher' *par excellence*. Hegel thought of Napoleon as history on horseback. Nietzsche thinks of him as 'philosophy' in action.

As I have already mentioned, section 224 talks about modernity's blindness to those instants when, for a brief and 'perfect' moment, a culture 'hardens' into a perfect, 'noble', state (see pp. 121–2 above). As we shall see in chapter 11, in *The Antichrist* Nietzsche holds that the philosophical ruler quite rightly 'legislates' so as to 'harden' and preserve a society that has reached a state of perfection for as long as possible. That is the job of the philosopher triumphant, the philosopher-king. We others, we free spirits, are to work as best we can for the coming into being of the philosopher triumphant – though in the full knowledge that, in our Heraclitean world, the moment of perfection will be (in world-historical terms) only a brief pause in the eternal flux of things.

Most often, however, the talk about 'new' philosophers is about those who are to prepare the way for the philosopher triumphant. Though, as we will see shortly, these philosophers 'command and legislate' too, here the phrase is not a 'success verb'. (One can command and legislate without, at present, anyone taking a blind bit of notice.) Rather than being philosopher-kings, these philosophers are their forerunners and heralds.[10]

---

10 The situation becomes somewhat confusing in section 44, which says that 'we free spirits' are the 'heralds' of the new philosophers. I take it that 'free spirit' here is free spirit of the 'second rank', that the new philosophers are free spirits of the first rank who prepare the way for the philosopher triumphant.

So how are these forerunning, objective genitive, 'philosophers of the future' portrayed in *Beyond Good and Evil*? (For the remainder of this chapter I shall use the phrase to refer to them alone.) Why are they 'new' – new, at least, in relation to philosophy as currently practised?

First of all, they will not be, like Kant and Hegel, mere codifiers of current, that is Christian, values (BGE 211).[11] Rather than affirming accepted norms they will be 'very free spirits', will deconstruct, *à la* Foucault, Christian thought-structures. They will, that is to say, actively focus on such structures. Though disgust at the state of contemporary society may tempt the 'exceptional' spirit to seek a Spinoza-like solitude, tempt him to withdraw into icy intellectual heights far removed from the actuality of human society, the temptation will be resisted. The 'average man', the 'norm', will become, for the exceptional person, an object of 'long and serious study' (BGE 25–6). Like Nietzsche himself, in other words, the new philosopher will engage in cultural criticism, will (like Zarathustra) 'wend his way *downwards*' (BGE 26).

He will, that is, learn to oppose majority opinion (BGE 43). But he will not be a *mere* sceptic, will not, like the 'positivists', represent debunking, 'scepticism', as 'philosophy's master task and authority' (BGE 204).[12] And neither will he be a merely 'critical' philosopher, concerned, like Kant, solely with emphasising the limits to human knowledge. All this 'under-labouring' is indeed valuable (Nietzsche's own positivist phase is being validated), but merely as a preparatory stage on the path to authentic philosophy. The real philosophers will be 'free, *very* free spirits' but 'they certainly will not *just* be free spirits [of the second rank] but rather something more, higher, greater, and fundamentally different' (BGE 44). They will undergo *Zarathustra*'s final 'Metamorphosis of the spirit'

---

11 The philosopher triumphant is of course a codifier (as will become even clearer in the discussion of *The Antichrist*). Nietzsche is by no means against codifying as such. His objection is only against codifying *current*, Christian, values. Codifying *healthy* values he thoroughly approves of.

12 It is sometimes said that Nietzsche regarded 'convictions' as the asinine (see BGE 8 and p. 115 above) province of the herd mentality and that he prided himself on being 'free spirited' in the sense of being entirely without 'convictions'. In fact, however, he regarded 'the spider of scepticism' (BGE 209) (or scepticism about everything save that impoverished set of beliefs acceptable to a 'positivist') as a *disease*. As a culture-wide phenomenon it is equivalent to nihilism: 'Scepticism is the most spiritual expression of a certain complex physiological condition which in layman's terms is called weak nerves or a sickly constitution. It originates whenever races or classes that have been separated for a long time are suddenly and decisively interbred. The different standards and values, as it were, get passed down through the bloodline to the next generation where everything is in a state of restlessness, disorder, doubt, experimentation', the result of which is 'paralysis of the will' (BGE 208). 'Scepticism' is, in short, just another name for the ethical 'chaos' of modernity, its lack of community-creating 'conviction'.

and become 'creators' (BGE 211). They will, that is, observe *The Gay Science*'s injunction that 'only as creators can we destroy'. But what is it that they create?

Though not a *mere* critic, the authentic philosopher *is*, as we have seen, a critic. As a belonging to the future he is necessarily the 'bad conscience' of his age. He even *enjoys* taking a scalpel to the chest of current values, in vivisecting the virtues of the age. He enjoys showing 'how much hypocrisy and laziness [compare p. 95 above] . . . [is] hidden beneath the most honoured type of . . . present-day morality, and how much virtue is *out of date*' (BGE 212). ('Out of date', one might interpolate here, in the way in which, for example, the values of free-market capitalism are out of date in the age of ecological crisis.) A morality of humility and self-abnegation was just fine (or at least had a strong upside) amidst the 'most savage floods and storm tides of egoism' that raged in the sixteenth century, but in these days of (as Nietzsche sees it) flabby will-lessness something like the opposite ethos is needed: 'strength of will and the hardness and capacity for long-term resolutions must belong to the concept of "greatness" ' (BGE 211).

What the 'true philosophers' create, then, are 'new values'. They are '*commanders and legislators* [who] . . . say "That is how it *should* be!"' They are the ones who first determine the 'where to?' and 'what for?' of a community, a new ethos that enables it to thrive in the current context.

As long as he is talking about the philosopher as herald, this imperious language – borrowed from and more appropriate to the image of the philosopher-king – is in fact somewhat misleading. For though Nietzsche says that the philosopher of today will disagree with current majority opinion (BGE 43), will initiate a revaluation and give impetus to opposing values (BGE 203), he will not do so 'dogmatically' (BGE 43). Rather, he will be an 'experimenter', an 'attempter (*Versucher*)' (BGE 42, 210). And he will exhibit the attempt at new values by example: rather than taking life 'philosophically' he will 'put *himself* at risk, . . . play . . . *the rough game*' (BGE 205).

The foregoing confirms that the 'new philosophers' are what I have been calling the 'random mutations', those *creative* No-sayers who enable a culture or people constantly to reinvent itself so as to survive and flourish in an ever-changing environment. Thinking in Darwinian fashion, Nietzsche anticipates that many of the 'attempts' at a new 'where to' and 'what for' for a people will fail. With luck, however, one of the value experiments will succeed and a new age of stability will replace the age of experiment (see pp. 181–2 below). In this new age the philosopher as codifier will replace the philosopher as experimenter. Each experimenter has before his eyes this ideal of his own superfluity (BGE 212).

NIETZSCHE'S 'REPUBLIC'

What will the new age, the age in which the philosopher-king replaces the philosopher-experimenter, look like? Nietzsche, of course, cannot say in any detail. Partly because the new ethos grows out of empirical experiments whose results cannot be anticipated in advance, partly because of the paradox of creativity, the paradox that the attempt to teach creativity appears destined to stifle creativity. (This, of course, is why Zarathustra tells his disciples to stop being disciples. (See, further, pp. 192–3 below.)) Nietzsche's description of the new age is, therefore, highly abstract, formal in character.

The 'image of greatness' that hovers before the eyes of any authentic philosopher will be one, he says, that (in opposition to the levelled out, mass culture of today) 'will locate the concept of greatness in the very scope and variety of human society, its unity in multiplicity (*Ganzheit im Vielen*)' (BGE 212). The looked-for future will be one that belongs to a culture or people unified as such by a shared ethos (containing all of humanity according to the 'globalisation' theme (BGE 208)). Secondly, unlike the levelled, mass culture of today, it will be a culture of 'rank ordering': like Plato's Republic, an aristocracy. In fact, like Plato's Republic, it will contain exactly three classes: the spiritual leaders, an educated and self-disciplined class who aspire to 'higher spirituality' and from whom, one day, future rulers might arise, and, finally, 'common people, the great majority' (BGE 61). Since rank excludes 'equality and equal rights', and since, like virtues, rights and duties are relative to one's station in the social hierarchy, *Beyond Good and Evil*'s future society will, as we have seen, contain slavery 'in some sense' (BGE 257).

Since this proposed structure is identical with the 'pyramid' explicitly borrowed from Plato in the unpublished essay of 1871/2 entitled 'The Greek State' (see especially, GM pp. 184–5), one can say that Nietzsche's ideas on the *structure* of society (and the need for the state as the 'iron hand' that enforces that structure) have altered not at all since the period of the writing of *The Birth*.

The reaffirmation of the necessity of 'slavery' returns us to the 'immoralism' issue briefly touched on in connexion with *The Gay Science* (pp. 93–4 above). What makes this an issue of importance to this book is that its interpretative thesis – that Nietzsche is (always) a religious communitarian – would not have the *philosophical* interest I take it to have if Nietzsche's communitarianism did not represent a serious challenge to the elevation, in contemporary thought, of secular liberal democracy (plus free-market capitalism) to the status of an 'eternal value'. If, however, Nietzsche's communitarianism is *genuinely* immoral it immediately follows that there is no possibility of it representing such a challenge.

Nietzsche is, I take it, not just a polemical 'immoralist' – an opponent of Christian morality – but the proponent of a genuinely immoral position if he holds that only the higher types of human being have a claim to well-being. If he holds that the 'mediocre' masses have *no* such claim, that they are *just* a support system for the lives of the elite, then his thought is immoral. If, in a word, Nietzsche treats the majority as mere *things*, if he infringes Kant's imperative never to treat human beings as *mere* means, then he really is an immoral thinker.

John Rawls thinks that both of these things are true: that Nietzsche believes in an elite consisting of the likes of Socrates[13] and Goethe whose eliteness consists in their doing art and science, which alone constitutes the justification of humanity and, further, that he has no independent concern for the well-being of the 'mediocre'. This, he suggests, is an immoral attitude which elevates a taste for aesthetic 'perfection' above the claims of 'justice'. For Nietzsche, he claims, Greek philosophy justified Greek slavery (Rawls (1971) section 50).[14]

---

13 That Rawls can think that the castigator of 'Socratism' could possibly be admitted to Nietzsche's highest elite suggests that he has read too much Kaufmann and not enough Nietzsche.

14 Another conspicuous defender of the 'immoralist' reading is Philippa Foot. Nietzsche, she claims (see 'Nietzsche: The Revaluation of Values' in Richardson and Leiter (2001) pp. 210–20), was a genuinely 'immoral' thinker because he 'was prepared to throw out the rules of justice in the interests of producing a stronger and more splendid type of man' (pp. 218–19), one to whom we attribute value 'in the way we attribute value (aesthetic value) to art objects' (p. 216). In evidence of her reading, Foot quotes (on p. 216) Nietzsche as affirming, in section 6 of the Preface to *The Genealogy of Morals*, that his fundamental aim is to realise 'the highest power and splendour actually possible to the type man'. But this is a Walter Kaufmann mistranslation. What Nietzsche desires is the 'highest power and splendour *of* the type man (*höchste Mächtigkeit und Pracht des Typus Mensch*)'. (Though 'species' is a little free, Carol Diethe gets the sense of the passage exactly right in rendering it as desiring that 'man as a species' should reach '*his highest potential power and splendour*' (GM Preface 6).) Given this translation, it clearly makes no more sense to think of *the species* 'man' achieving splendour through the production of a few beautiful individuals than to think of a vegetable garden full of weeds and rotting potatoes achieving 'splendour' on account of the thriving of a couple of freak tomato plants. In general, it seems to me, when Nietzsche speaks of the flourishing of the 'species' or 'type' 'man' he is speaking of the flourishing of an *organic whole*. A withered community inhabited by a freak 'genius' would resemble the 'inverse cripple' – a tiny stunted body with a huge ear (Wagner), for example – who arouses Zarathustra's

The first part of this claim is clearly wrong and based on a very shallow acquaintance with Nietzsche. Exceptional individuals, 'philosophers', are, we know, important because they enable the community to mutate so as to continue to thrive and grow. (Or else, in the case of the 'philosopher triumphant', rule wisely for the good of the community as a whole.) And the idea that great artists might be ends in themselves is directly contradicted by Nietzsche's repeatedly expressed contempt for '*l'art pour l'art*' (a contempt shared with and inherited from Wagner) which he regards as a 'disease': a 'dressed up scepticism and paralysis of the will', a symptom of 'weak nerves and a sickly constitution' (BGE 208). But the second part of Rawls' claim – that as Bertrand Russell puts it, 'the happiness of common people is no part of the good *per se*', that 'what happens to the . . . [non-elite] is of no [moral] account'[15] might still be true.

What seems to support this attribution of genuine immoralism to *Beyond Good and Evil* is section 258, in which Nietzsche says that, unlike the pre-Revolutionary French aristocracy which had 'throw[n] away its privileges with a sublime disgust and sacrifice[d] itself to an excess of its moral feeling' thereby entering a state of 'corruption', a healthy aristocracy 'does *not* feel that it is a function (whether of the kingdom or the community) but instead feels itself to be the *meaning* and highest justification (of the kingdom or community)'. Only thus can it accept

in good conscience the sacrifice of countless people who have to be pushed down and shrunk into incomplete human beings, into slaves, into tools, all *for the sake of the aristocracy*. Its fundamental belief must be that society *cannot* exist for the sake of society, but only as the substructure and framework for raising the exceptional type up to its . . . higher state of *being*. In the same way the sun-seeking, Javanese climbing plant called *Sippo matador* will wrap its arms around the oak tree so often and for such a long time that finally, high above the oak, although still supported by it, the plant will be able to unfold its highest crown of foliage and show its happiness in the full, clear light.

This passage is invariably taken to support the claim of Nietzsche's immoral elitism, is taken to show that his concern for the flourishing of 'humanity' boils down to 'aristocratic individualism', to the production of a couple of Goethes per millennium. The 'immoralism' charge amounts to the claim that *nothing else* has any value for him. But let us notice, first

disgust (Z II 20). Even if, for Nietzsche as for both Aristotle and Wittgenstein, the good and the beautiful do ultimately coincide, beauty requires a beautiful society, not just a few beautiful individuals.
15 Russell (1957) p. 796.

of all, that *if* this is the correct reading of the passage then it is inconsistent with almost everything else Nietzsche says about social elites.

Thus, as we have seen, if the elite person in question is the 'random mutation', the experimental herald of the future, then it is certainly not Nietzsche's view, as we have so far discovered it, that such a person is the 'meaning and justification' of society. Rather *the opposite*: the significance of the random mutation is his contribution to the survival and flourishing of society as a whole. If, on the other hand, the person in question is the philosopher triumphant then, as in Plato – this will become absolutely clear in the discussion of *The Antichrist* (see especially, pp. 179–85 below) – his elite position is based on the fact that he is best equipped to rule in the interests of the good of society as a whole. In both cases, therefore, rather than the exceptional type being the 'meaning and justification' of society as a whole, precisely the opposite is the case: the exceptional type is valuable only as a means to the flourishing of the social organism in its totality.

This provides a motive for trying to read section 258 in something other than the standard way. And in fact it is not at all hard to see that something is almost certainly wrong with the standard reading. The crucial point to notice is that Nietzsche does not say '*my* fundamental belief' is that the 'aristocrats' are the 'meaning and justification' of everything else. He is reporting, rather, the way *the aristocrats* feel, reporting the fundamental 'faith' of a healthy aristocracy, something that may well be, from his point of view, false: as he repeatedly emphasises, 'false judgments', 'untruths', are a 'condition of life' (BGE 4).

What Nietzsche is doing in section 258, I think, is simply surveying the past, in his anthropological manner, and noting that in healthy aristocratic societies the aristocrats have a sublime arrogance which, when it collapses, leads to the decay, 'corruption', of that aristocracy and hence of that society. The passage *does not even commit Nietzsche to the view that aristocracy is the best ordering of society* – though this is something he in fact believes, provided that the aristocracy is of the correct, 'spiritual' kind. The passage no more commits Nietzsche to endorsing the arrogance of the aristocrats than his treatment of 'master morality' societies as healthier than 'slave morality' societies – the distinction receives its first airing two sections later in section 260 – commits him to endorsing every aspect of the former.

Still, the question remains: what about the 'slaves'? Slavery 'in some sense', Nietzsche asserts, in his own voice, is the condition of any higher culture (BGE 239, 257). If he himself believes in slavery is he not reducing a large section of the population to mere scaffolding so that he really does have to be adjudged an immoral thinker?

Nietzsche displays some unclarity on the issue. Section 258, as we have seen, talks of slaves as having been 'shrunk into incomplete human beings' out of the necessity to support the aristocracy, though it is unclear whether this is how the healthy aristocrats see them or how Nietzsche does. And section 61 speaks of the masses as only existing for 'general utility', though again is it unclear whether this is Nietzsche the anthropologist reporting on how things generally are or Nietzsche the normative philosopher talking about how things ought to be.

Nietzsche recognises that the traditional position assigned to women is one of 'slavery' (BGE 239). Since his views on women are emphatically his own, the best point of entry into his views on slavery is, I believe, via his views on women.

Beyond Good and Evil's account of women is an elaboration of *The Gay Science*'s view that women exercise a 'surplus of strength and pleasure' in being the 'function' of a man (GS 119): that they are 'both predestined to servitude *and fulfilled by it*' (BGE 238: my emphasis). In our increasingly democratic age with its lack of respect for rank and difference, he says, women are being accorded equal rights with men (BGE 238–9). But this 'de-feminising' of women is in no one's interest. When it comes to the intellect, women cannot compete – 'enlightenment' is a man's business (BGE 232), as is cooking (BGE 234) – so that equality simply deprived them of the satisfaction of their will to power, a satisfaction they used to derive by working with 'cunning humility'. The 'orientals' have it right – it is best for everyone if a woman remains a man's property: '*how* logical', comments Nietzsche, '*how* humanly desirable' is 'Asia's [Islam's?] enormous rationality' in this regard (BGE 238). The first and last duty of women remains the bearing of strong children. This by no means implies that, in their proper role, women are not accorded respect. On the contrary,

what inspires respect and, often enough, fear of women is their *nature* (which is 'more natural' than that of men), their truly predatory and cunning agility, their tiger's claws inside their glove, the naivety of their egoism, their inner wildness and inability to be trained, the incomprehensibility, expanse and rambling character of their desires and virtues.

What inspires genuine respect for women, concludes Nietzsche (anticipating the eponymous movie), is 'the dangerous and beautiful cat "woman"'. What is depriving her of respect is the 'demystification' of the feminine (BGE 239).

Beyond Good and Evil's account of the proper role of women is unlikely to make Nietzsche many friends in the feminist movement (except among those who are particularly bad 'philologists'). But, once again (see pp. 93–4 above), it is clearly a *paternal* or *patriarchal* rather than an *immoral* position. Rightly or wrongly, it holds (as the majority of the earth's population still does) that women's best interests are served by their subordination to men. And this, as I have suggested, represents the main tenor of Nietzsche's views on slavery in general.

Since *Beyond Good and Evil*'s views on slavery are remarkably unchanged from the early discussion in 'The Greek State' it is worth noting that in that work, taking note of the 'misery' of slavery in the ancient world, Nietzsche expresses a clear preference for the medieval form of 'slavery':

What an elevating effect on us is produced by the sight of a medieval serf, whose legal and ethical relationship with his superior was internally sturdy and sensitive, whose narrow existence was profoundly cocooned – how elevating – and how reproachful [to 'rank'-less modernity]! (GM p. 180)

Though this is no doubt rose-tinted romance, it clearly represents, once again, paternalism rather than immoralism. The serf, as Nietzsche represents him, far from being reduced to a mere thing, is provided with security by an elaborate network of reciprocal rights and duties.

To conclude this discussion of the immoralism charge, let me widen the context to show why paternalism rather than immoralism really *has* to be Nietzsche's position.

I referred, earlier, to what I called Nietzsche's 'stratification of the virtues' thesis (p. 117 above). But a better title would be the 'stratification of the good' thesis, since there are in fact two aspects to Nietzsche's anti-universalism, both of which can be comprehended under this second title. The first aspect is the already mentioned thesis that virtues are 'rank' (or, as Christine Swanton calls it, 'role'[16]) specific – that the virtues of a worker (or a woman, of course) could well turn out to be vices in a philosopher (BGE 30: see p. 127 above). The second, its natural partner, concerns 'the good' in the sense of well-being or happiness. Nietzsche holds that in this sense, too, there is no universal good.

16 See Swanton (2005).

'Human diversity', he says, in a passage of Sartrean insight, is apparent not only in the variety of human beings' 'table of goods' – in, for example, their different ranking of commonly acknowledged goods – but also in what they take to count as 'possession of a good'. One man, for example, counts mere sexual availability as possessing a woman. Another wants the total sacrifice of the woman's will to his own. A third wants the sacrifice of her independence to a *correctly perceived* image of himself (BGE 194).

In general, Nietzsche affirms the commonplace wisdom that one man's meat is another man's poison. Some, for example, have an unconditional need for obedience, others (though they need to overcome the disposition to laziness) are born to command (BGE 199). The utilitarians do not really aim at the 'happiness of the majority' but at 'English happiness' – 'comfort and fashion (and, at the highest level, a seat in parliament)' (BGE 228). As a social mission, that is, utilitarianism (hand in hand with British imperialism) projects onto others what is in fact its own, highly parochial conception of happiness.

In sum, then, there are two reasons why the healthy society must be above all a society of 'rank'. The first is the rank-specificity of happiness. And the second is the rank-specificity of virtue. If, that is, one is a born[17] herd-type then 'public spirit, goodwill, consideration, industry, moderation, modesty, clemency, and pity' (BGE 199) really are the virtues of one's station. For it is through such 'old maid's innocence' (see p. 94 above) that, in this case, one best contributes to the flourishing of the community as a whole.

RELIGION IN THE NEW SOCIETY

Whatever the details, then, the healthy society of the future must be, unlike the 'levelled' society of today, hierarchical. What now, to come to the centre of our concerns, of the place of religion in it?

The first thing to be said is that there *will* be a place for religion. The religious life, says Nietzsche, requires 'idleness with a good conscience'. Modern industriousness, therefore – 'noisy, time-consuming, self-satisfied, stupidly proud industriousness' – kills the religious life. People of 'modern ideas' who approach religion with 'an air of superior, gracious amusement' have completely lost the 'reverential seriousness'

---

17 Brian Leiter has argued persuasively that for Nietzsche, as for Schopenhauer, the basic structure of character is innate and unalterable. See 'The Paradox of Fatalism and Self-Creation in Nietzsche' in Richardson (2001) pp. 281–321.

with which religion should be approached. They have stupidly lost all idea of why religion is important (BGE 58). So why is it important?

'Reverence (*Ehrfurcht*) of rank' is the best legacy of Christianity.

[The] involuntary hush, a hesitation of the eye and a quieting of every gesture, all of which indicates that the soul *feels* the presence of something deserving of the highest honours. The way in which respect for the *Bible* has on the whole been maintained in Europe might be the best piece of discipline and refinement in manners that Europe owes to Christianity. Books with this sort of profundity and ultimate meaning [*Zarathustra*, perhaps] need the protection of an externally imposed tyranny of authority: this way, they can *last* through millennia that are needed to use them up and figure them out. It is a great achievement when the masses . . . have finally the feeling bred into them that they cannot touch everything, that there are holy experiences that require them to take off their shoes and keep their dirty hands away.

Modernity, however, particularly that part of it afflicted by 'modern ideas', has completely lost this sense of reverence (BGE 263). Why should this matter?

A 'species' or 'type' of humanity establishes itself as such – i.e. as a Volk – only by competing successfully in what are 'essentially constant *unfavourable* conditions'. It must struggle long and hard both with its neighbours and with its own underclass. A precondition of success is

hardness, uniformity and simplicity of form . . . A tremendous range of experiences teaches it which qualities are primarily responsible for the fact that, despite all gods and men, it still exists, it keeps prevailing. It calls these qualities virtues, and these are the only virtues it fosters. (BGE 263)

Though this sounds exactly like Darwin one needs to remember that, for Nietzsche, 'life is will to power – self-preservation is only one of the indirect and most frequent *consequences* of this' (BGE 13). So what communal ethos ultimately facilitates is increase in the power of a Volk: its ability to 'rule and conquer and glitter, to the dread and envy of its neighbour' (Z 1 15).

So even a religion such as Christianity (and Buddhism) has a by no means negligible upside to it. With respect to the rulers it legitimises their rule and generates obedience (Nietzsche surely has in mind here the doctrine of the divine right of kings), with respect to potential rulers it provides a model of 'higher spirituality',[18] and with respect to the ruled it provides comfort for the hardship of their lot, meaning to their lives,

18 BGE 188 says that a 'long stupidity', a 'compulsion in one direction', is necessary to spiritual growth.

and legitimisation of the social order. By situating the lowly in 'an illusory higher order of things' it enabled them 'to stay satisfied with the actual order' (BGE 61).

Having acknowledged this upside to Christianity, Nietzsche is quick to remind us of the 'downside (*schlimme Gegenrechnung*)' which has made Christianity 'the most disastrous form of arrogance so far' (BGE 62). This consists in the fact that, historically, it became 'sovereign' – established ultimate values instead of being merely used as a means for 'breeding and education' (for preserving social order and leading potential leaders on the path to a 'higher spirituality') employed by enlightened rulers. What this must mean is that it came to be believed not only by the masses but by *everyone* – including the (on this account, *non*-enlightened) rulers.

The ill-effect of that, he reminds us, is that by validating the lives of society's 'failures' (i.e. instituting 'slave morality') it 'throws suspicion on the delight in beauty, skew[s] everything self-asserting (*selbstherrlich*), manly, conquering, domineering, every instinct that belongs to the highest and best-turned-out type of "human"' in favour of an '"unworldly", "unsensuous"' notion of the 'higher man' (BGE 62).

Nietzsche says that

> The philosopher as *we* understand him, we free spirits –, as the man with the most comprehensive responsibility, whose conscience bears the weight of the overall development of humanity,[19] this philosopher will make use of religion for his breeding and education work. (BGE 61)

Does this leave the 'philosopher' as an areligious, ironic outsider, as one who knows the 'noble lie' is a lie – although good enough for the contemptible masses? Not so, for then the 'philosopher' would be indistinguishable from the 'free thinker', the man of 'modern ideas' who, to repeat, looks down on religion 'with an air of superior, almost gracious amusement . . . mixed with slight contempt for what he assumes to be "uncleanliness" of spirit' (BGE 58: see, too, 263). He would be, that is to say, indistinguishable from the (post-modern) 'sceptic', whom, as we have seen (p. 130 fn. 12), Nietzsche regards as 'diseased'.

What, therefore, Nietzsche must mean is that the 'philosopher' of the future will make use of a religion for purposes of 'breeding and education' which possesses the upside *but not the downside* of Christianity and to

---

19 Notice again how far this figure is from the Goethe-figure whose poems alone supposedly provide humanity's 'meaning and justification'.

which, most importantly, the enlightened ruler can himself subscribe – a religion, in other words, which involves no 'noble lie'.

What, then, might this religion be? How do the enlightened stand to religion? What is Nietzsche's own religious position in *Beyond Good and Evil*?

He tells us in section 295, the positioning of which as the last section of the work (apart from a final coda) gives it especial significance.

'They tell me', Nietzsche begins by observing, 'that you do not like believing in God and gods, these days.' The point of the section is now emphatically to separate himself from such a-theists:

The genius of the heart as it is possessed by that great hidden one, the attempter god (*Versucher-Gott*) and born pied [Pan-] piper of consciences . . . that makes everything loud and complacent fall silent and learn to listen, that smoothes out rough souls and gives them the taste of a new desire – to lie still, like a mirror that the deep sky can mirror itself upon . . . the genius of the heart . . . that guesses . . . the drop of goodness and sweet spirituality under thick, dull ice, and is a divining rod for every speck of gold that has long been buried in a prison of mud and sand: the genius of the heart that enriches everyone who has come into contact with it . . . [and by whom] they are made richer in themselves, newer than before, broken open, blown on, and sounded out by a thawing wind . . .

And then Nietzsche interrupts himself to recall that – a hesitation appropriate to speaking of holy things – he has not yet brought himself to mention the name of his god. Finally he tells us:

the one I have just been talking about, who has crossed my path again and again [is] . . . nobody less than the god *Dionysus*, the great ambiguity and attempter god, to whom, as you know, I once offered my firstborn [*The Birth of Tragedy*] in all secrecy and reverence. I seem to be the last one to have offered him a *sacrifice* . . . In the meantime I have learnt much more . . . about the philosophy of this god . . . I, the last disciple and initiate of the god Dionysus.

The hushed reverence of this beautiful passage, as well as the reference to the sky, seems to me to link it to *Zarathustra*'s equally beautiful 'Before sunrise' (see pp. 107–11 above). What this suggests is that in *Beyond Good and Evil*, as in *Zarathustra*, the importance of the god Dionysus, the importance of Dionysianism, is that it enables one to perform the inseparable tasks of affirming both one's life and one's own death:

There are heights of the soul from whose vantage point even tragedy stops having tragic effects: and who would dare to decide whether the collective sight of the world's many woes would *necessarily* compel and seduce us into a feeling of [Schopenhauerian] pity [and world-denial]. (BGE 30)

This unmistakably repeats the notion in 'Before sunrise' that there are very high mountains from which one smiles down on all tragedies, 'real and imagined' (see p. 107 above). And so it returns us, I suggest, to the principal ideas contained in that passage.

The first of these ideas, to repeat, is that if one is fortunate enough to enter the 'high', 'intoxicated' state of the soul then one transcends the everyday, embodied self to become the all-embracing totality of things so that, in becoming 'eternal', one transcends mortality. Section 57 refers to this idea in saying that, 'as humanity's spiritual vision and insight grows stronger, the distance and, as it were, the space that surrounds us increases as well', as does section 56 in alluding to a perspective on things from which one *is* 'the whole play and performance'. And section 54 opens the way for such a perspective by endorsing the view of 'Vedantic philosophy' (Nietzsche, to repeat, always regards Dionysus as having emigrated to Greece from 'Asia' (BGE 238)) that the notion that there must be an individual 'subject' or ego corresponding to the 'I' attaches to grammar an ontological weight it by no means deserves.

The second main idea in 'Before sunrise' was that ecstatic identification with the totality of things takes one 'beyond good and evil' – beyond the *contrast* between good and evil – since that totality of things is experienced as absolutely good, 'perfect'. Ecstatic identification, that is, requires unconditional love, and 'everything', Nietzsche reminds us, 'done out of love takes place beyond good and evil' (BGE 153). This is why, in section 295, Dionysus is a 'philosopher', his philosophy being the 'Dionysian pessimism' which overcomes Schopenhauerian 'pity' and world-denial. It is, that is to say, the theodicy of *The Gay Science* that recognises the inevitability of pain but experiences itself as 'pregnant' with a future that will turn every 'desert' into 'lush farmland' (see pp. 103–4 above). Dionysus' philosophy is, in other words, the philosophy of the 'eternal recurrence', the philosophy which, in *Beyond Good and Evil*, cries out '*da capo* . . . to the whole play and performance' (BGE 56).

Nietzsche points out that the *da capo* is a circle, that Dionysian pantheism is 'God as a vicious circle' (BGE 56). In other words, since the world is divine every woe finds eventual 'redemption' in some joy, and since every woe finds redemption the world is divine. But this is just to say that Dionysianism, like every religion, is a *faith*; and, Nietzsche would add, is none the worse for that since, to repeat yet again, 'un- [or better non-] truth [is] . . . a condition of life' (BGE 4).

A final remark about the worship of Dionysus in *Beyond Good and Evil*. Since Christianity stems from pessimism and world-denial (BGE 59), what *ultimately* overcomes Christianity, for Nietzsche, is not positivism or 'modern ideas' or even Nietzsche's own exposé of its nefarious origins and terrible effects. What really overcomes Christianity – at least for Nietzsche himself – is a *satisfying* of the 'metaphysical need' for a solution to the problem of pain and death. Only now – as he understood already in *Zarathustra* (see p. 100 above) – he understands that it is not really a *metaphysical* need at all, that the problem of pain and death can be solved by entry into a (self-)transcendent *perspective* on the world rather than entry into a transcendent world.

THE FESTIVAL

What is the relation between Nietzsche's own religion, the religion of the enlightened ones, and the religion of the community at large? What has *Beyond Good and Evil* to say about the communal festival? Virtually nothing – there is, of course, no reason Nietzsche has to discuss everything in every work – until the very last stanza of the 'Aftersong' which concludes the whole work.

The poem finds its author on the 'lonely ledges' of a 'high mountain' waiting, somewhat mournfully, for '*new* friends' to arrive, the old friends having all disappointed or disappeared. And then the author, as it were, dreams that the awaited friends have arrived:

Now, communal (*vereinten*[20]) victory certain, we celebrate/the festival (*Fest*) of festivals:/ Friend Zarathustra came, the guest of guests!/Now the world laughs, the dread curtain rent,/the wedding day of light and dark was here. (BGE p. 180)

The reference to the festival links this back to *The Gay Science*'s new 'festivals and holy games we will have to invent' on account of the death of the old, Christian, festival (see p. 101 above), while the presence of Zarathustra links this festival back to the Ass Festival. One cannot, of course, celebrate a genuine festival without the gathering of an entire community to share in the celebration. But since modernity is incapable of the festival, the best that can be hoped for is, as I have called it, a mini-festival with a few 'friends' in whom 'spiritual vision and insight has grown stronger' (BGE 57). But this, one may surmise, is a model, a paradigm, out of which, one day, the festival proper will arise.

What kind of festival? Apollo being the shining god of light and Dionysus the god of dark incomprehensibility, the Hölderlin-echoing

---

20 Judith Norman fails to translate this crucial adjective.

mention of the 'wedding of light and dark' is, fairly clearly, a reference to the unification of the Apollonian and the Dionysian – as in Greek tragedy. So it seems, once again, that what Nietzsche is looking for is a new Greece, a new *polis* brought to unity and health by a re-created version of Greek religion.

Sounding a theme first sounded in *The Birth*, Nietzsche writes that 'What is amazing about the religiosity of ancient Greece is the excessive amount of gratitude that flows from it: – it takes a very noble type of person to face nature and life like *this*!' (BGE 49). And what he desires, above all, is the rebirth of a 'noble' society. So what he aspires to is the rebirth of a 'noble' religion.

In sum, then, it seems that what Nietzsche wants is something with the structure and function of the medieval Church but with 'Greek' – life-affirming – rather than Christian – life-denying – content. He wants something that will, in its Dionysian aspect, release us from anxiety about death, and in its Apollonian aspect, expound and empower community-creating ethos. What he wants is a synthesis of West and East – the Dionysian Greeks were, let us recall, 'Asia's best heirs and students' (BGE 238).

CHAPTER 8

On the Genealogy of Morals

The *Genealogy* is a rich and complex work. In the interests of focusing on the topic of religion, I shall ignore a great deal of what it has to say. The work's title, however, is something which cannot be ignored. What demand discussion are the questions of what 'genealogy' is, and what purpose – or purposes – it has.

GENEALOGY

The answer to the first question is straightforward: it is an investigation into the 'origins' of – in the *Genealogy* itself – 'our' morality. In *Human*, which is Nietzsche's first attempt at a genealogy of Christian morality, it is called 'historical philosophy' (see p. 62 above). The second question, however, has proved much more difficult to answer.

Most of the secondary literature (not to mention Nietzsche's deconstructionist disciples) assumes that there is just one purpose to Nietzsche's genealogy: critique. Thus Keith Ansell-Pearson, in his introduction to the Cambridge translation, claims that 'Nietzsche's aim in writing this book can be stated quite simply as one of presenting a novel critique of morality' (GM p. x). And Brian Leiter writes that 'in the genealogy of morals, his [Nietzsche's] aim is critical not positive'.[1] This monistic assumption seems to me to be mistaken. Certainly critique is *a* major purpose of Nietzsche's genealogy. But, so I shall suggest, genealogy has another purpose too, in particular a 'positive' one.

As far as critique is concerned – to touch briefly on a topic somewhat peripheral to our central concerns – the problem about genealogy is the following.

---

1 Leiter (2002) p. 167.

In the Preface to the work Nietzsche claims that his investigation of the origins of our current morality is motivated by the fact that it is one 'route' to answering the much more important question of the '*value*' of that morality (GM Preface 5).[2] Two things make this claim problematic: first, the fact that the idea that, in general, origins determine value is a fallacy – the so-called 'genetic fallacy'. And second, the fact that Nietzsche himself seems to recognise the genetic fallacy as a fallacy (at GS 345 and GM II 12).

Some readers, impressed by the – from the point of view of reason – fallaciousness of the 'genetic fallacy', have preferred to see genealogy as a non-rational, rhetorical critique. And that it surely is. The work's subtitle, 'A Polemic', gives this game away, disclosing Nietzsche's strategic knowledge that, as a *Nachlass* note puts it, while 'the inquiry into the *origins of our evaluations* . . . is in absolutely no way identical with a critique of them', none the less 'the insight into some *pudenda origo* [shameful origin] certainly brings with it a *feeling* of a diminution in value of the thing that originated thus and prepares the way to a critical mood and attitude towards it' (WP 254).

But genealogy is not just, or mainly, rhetoric. It is also, I think, in two ways, rational critique. In the Preface Nietzsche writes that he aims to answer the question

under what conditions did man invent the value judgments good and evil? *And what value do they themselves have?* Have they up to now obstructed or promoted human flourishing (*Gedeihen*)? Are they a sign (*Zeichen*) of distress, poverty and the degeneration of life? Or, on the contrary, do they reveal the fullness, vitality and will of life, its courage, its confidence, its future? (GM Preface 3)

This indicates the two directions of rational critique: one is concerned with what our morality 'promotes', with its effects; the other with what it is a 'sign' or symptom of – what promotes it. I shall discuss them in this order.

---

2 According to the 'motley' critique of modernity, as we have seen, modernity has *no* unifying morality. This is repeated at GM II 2 which quotes *Daybreak* I 9 to the effect that since the 'morality of custom' has evaporated, we live in a very 'immoral' age. At GM III 16 Nietzsche repeats (see pp. 121–2 above) the theme that the modern moral scene is one of confusion owing to the intermingling of Christian and pre-Christian values. What he must mean, I think, is that while Christian morality is the *dominant* morality of modernity it is no longer dominant *enough*: neither effective in eliminating rivals nor powerful enough in its grip on those for whom it is the only morality. Seen in this light, Nietzsche's critique is a matter of giving a helping push to that which is already falling. Of course, that it is on its way out anyway (compare GS 125) gives added weight to the idea that the *fundamental* aim of Nietzsche's genealogy is constructive rather than destructive.

Nietzsche writes that people adopt moralities because they 'instinctively strive for an optimum of favourable conditions in which to fully release [their] . . . power' (GM III 7). Thus people would not adopt a morality unless the effect, verified over generations, was to maximise their power. But, as we will shortly see, the origins of our current, essentially Christian, morality lay in the attempt by the sick and oppressed in society to increase their own power by crippling and disempowering the healthy nobility. So, Nietzsche suggests, the origin of Christian morality makes clear its 'sick'-making effect, the fact that it hobbles the healthy.[3]

As to what our morality is a 'sign' of, Nietzsche writes in the retrospective *Ecce Homo* that the *Genealogy* is a 'psychology of Christianity; the birth of Christianity out of the spirit of *ressentiment*' (EH XI). This, it might seem, is an unabashed plunging into the genetic fallacy – a quite unwarranted inference from the psychological *origins* of our system of moral judgments to the *current* motives on which people make such judgments. In fact, however, this seems to me not to be the case.

What I think Nietzsche is fundamentally doing is inviting the reader to examine his *own* motivation and that of his fellows. If we look into our own hearts, he is suggesting, we are likely to find the will to power at work, *ressentiment* against the target of our judgments. And if we do not find it in our own hearts we can surely recognise it in others of our acquaintance, particularly those who call themselves Christians.

The point of the reference to the origins of Christianity is to facilitate this acquisition of self-knowledge, to provide a pattern or dynamic that we can recognise in ourselves. In this respect, Nietzsche's speculative history functions in the way a great deal of literature functions. Dickens, for instance. Uriah Heep, for example, exhibits precisely the insatiable will to power disguised under the exterior of a 'very humble man' that Nietzsche is talking about. Dickens was a moral reformer. The point of his grotesque hypocrites, Mrs Jelleby, various headmasters and so on, is not merely to entertain but also to produce uncomfortable feelings of recognition in cases where the cap fits. And that is Nietzsche's point too.

In two ways, then, genealogy is intended as rational critique. It is intended to expose the deleterious effects on those subjected to Christian moral judgment and is intended to expose the unpleasant psychology that motivates them – thereby revealing the 'moralist' as someone we do not want to be. And, as already mentioned, it is also intended as rhetorical

---

3 I owe this insight into Nietzsche's methodology to Brian Leiter's book ((2002) pp. 176–8).

critique. In various ways, therefore, genealogy is intended, as Foucault and Derrida have emphasised, to liberate the reader from the (remaining) power of 'morality'.

As we know, the intended reader of Nietzsche's works is by no means just anyone, but rather the exceptional type, the potential free spirit, the 'random mutation' whom Nietzsche wants to rouse from innate human laziness by appealing to his pride and contempt. The *Genealogy* repeats this point: though Christian morality has long been the dominant moral-ity there still remain '*higher natures*' who disclose themselves as such by being a 'battle ground' for the struggle between Christian morality and the morality of antiquity that preceded it (GM III 16). It is, then, the potential free spirit who is the target of liberation through deconstruction.

What, however, has been missed by those who hold, with Ansell-Pearson, that the *Genealogy*'s aim is 'simply' a critique – Foucault bears the greatest responsibility for the widespread view that genealogy is a purely destruc-tive technique – is Nietzsche's fundamental axiom that 'only as creators can we destroy' (GS 58).[4] This is repeated in an emphatic way in the *Genealogy* itself. 'Is an ideal set up or destroyed here?', Nietzsche asks at the end of the second of the work's three essays. He answers that 'if a shrine is to be set up, a *shrine has to be destroyed*: that is the law', and goes on to discuss his hopes for a new ideal that will be the 'reverse' of the Christian ideal (GM II 24). Given this axiom (in the language of *Zarathustra*, the axiom that only as a 'child' can one be an effective 'lion') it follows that, together with the critical, there must be a *constructive* purpose to genealogy.[5] Moreover, as I mentioned earlier (footnote 2 above), there would be little point to a merely critical study since, in Nietzsche's view, Christian morality is collapsing quite successfully with-out his help. The question is, therefore: what constructive purpose could be fulfilled by identifying the – as we shall see, multiple and overlapping – origins of 'our' present morality?

---

4 Let me once again call attention to the 'can' – as opposed to 'may'. Nietzsche is not only pointing to the fact that destruction unmotivated by any constructive purpose is a waste of time but also pointing out that one *cannot* destroy without constructing. If one criticises an old thought structure without offering anything in its place then, however trenchant the criticism, the old structure will soon reassert itself in one form or another.

5 *Ecce Homo*, too, points to this ultimately constructive purpose by calling the *Genealogy*'s three essays 'preliminary studies of a psychologist for a revaluation [i.e. reversal] of values' (EH XI). An historian who wrote a book *merely* rubbishing Gibbon's account of the fall of the Roman Empire could not claim to have engaged in a 'preliminary study' for a new theory of its fall.

The *Genealogy* comprises two basic stories, each concerned with a different aspect of what Nietzsche calls 'the ascetic ideal'. The first, told in the first essay, tells the story of the origin of our judgments of good and evil; the second, told mainly in the second essay, tells of the origins of guilt and the bad conscience. I shall discuss them in this order.

NOBLES AND SLAVES

Originally, at the dawn of history, there were the noble warrior tribes. Their morality was a morality in which the fundamental contrast was between 'good' and 'bad'. Because their warrior existence was in harmony with their warrior instincts, their lives, though hard, were basically healthy and happy. So they called themselves and their warrior attributes – courage, self-confidence, intelligence, loyalty, ruthlessness towards enemies – 'good'. 'Bad' figured only as an afterthought in their valuations. The 'bad' were simply those unfortunates who were not like them – the weak tribes they had defeated and enslaved. Etymological evidence for this, claims Nietzsche, is provided by the derivation of '*schlecht* (bad)' from '*schlicht* (low, or plebeian)'. The 'pathos of distance' (sense of superiority) was what created the first value-distinctions and hence the first values.

'Noble' – good/bad – morality was the style of almost all moralities in the ancient world. An exception was the Jews, the nature of whose morality changed dramatically after the great misfortune of the Babylonian exile.[6] A priestly people, the Jews, too weak to gain physical revenge, gained the satisfaction of spiritual revenge on their oppressors through a radical reversal of values which they effected through redescription. The noble virtues of courage, self-confidence and intelligence now became the vices of cruelty, arrogance and pride, while the attributes they themselves, as slaves, *had* to display – impotence, timidity, fawningness and sheep-likeness, from the *noble* perspective – became the virtues of humility, patience, friendliness and solidarity with one's neighbour. Christianity completed this 'slave revolt' in morality by postulating a heaven which the meek would not only enter but from where they would be vouchsafed the sight of their earthly masters suffering the everlasting torments of hell (GM I 1–16).

---

6 This important distinction between pre- and post-'Exile' Jewish culture is added only in *The Antichrist* (see p. 178 below). In the *Genealogy* itself Nietzsche paints Jewish history with only the very broadest of brushes.

Whereas the fundamental contrast in noble morality is between good and bad, the fundamental contrast in slave/Christian morality is between good and evil (*Böse*). Nietzsche adopts this nomenclature to capture the difference between the attitude to the 'other' on the part of the nobles and slaves respectively. The nobles viewed the slaves with relative indifference: they no more *hated* 'bad' people than one hates 'bad' eggs.[7] The Greek word for the rabble, Nietzsche observes, expresses mildly sympathetic indulgence (GM I 10). Christian morality, on the other hand, grew out of an (of course understandable) 'cauldron of hatred' for their oppressors, making the hate-demanding 'evil' the appropriate word.[8]

The essential contrast between noble and slave morality, that is to say, is that whereas the nobles' morality is essentially *affirmative* – the 'bad' comes in only as a conceptually necessary 'afterthought', a 'complementary colour' – slave morality is fundamentally a *denial*: in slave morality 'evil' is (to use a phrase Nietzsche would have enjoyed) the 'trouser word' and 'good' comes in primarily only as a conceptually necessary contrast (GM I 10–11). In other words, whereas noble morality is the expression of 'a powerful physicality, a blossoming, rich, even effervescent good health' (GM I 7), slave morality is an expression of all-consuming hatred: 'the slave revolt starts when *ressentiment* becomes creative of values' (GM I 10).

So what is there of constructive value that we learn from this story? What hints as to the character of a 'counter ideal' (EH XI) to that of Christianity are to be found in it?

Health stops where resentment becomes creative. Nietzsche's paradigm of health is the eighteenth-century French politician the Comte de Mirabeau, who 'could not forgive' an insult 'simply because he – forgot' (GM I 10). What we learn, therefore, is that a healthy ideal must spring from esteem for oneself and one's kind rather than hatred for the 'other' and its kind. What we learn is that a healthy morality will be (a) self- rather than other-focused and (b) that it will be an expression of esteem rather than hate.

---

7 I believe I owe this felicitous way of putting Nietzsche's point to Arthur Danto, but regrettably, the reference is irretrievably lost.
8 Nietzsche's observation here tells us, I think, a considerable amount about the psychology of the target audience at which the phrases 'evil empire' and 'axis of evil', coined by the speech-writers of neo-conservative US presidents, are aimed.

Let us now turn to the second story. If we can identify the point at which cultural 'sickness' starts we will have simultaneously identified the point at which health stops, and will have gained thereby another at least hint of an 'opposing ideal' (GM III 25) to that of Christianity. This, to repeat, is the ultimate point of genealogy. As *Beyond Good and Evil* puts it, a serious thinker goes a long way 'backwards [as] . . . one who wants to take a great leap' forwards (BGE 280).

So now, in brief, the second story which is concerned with the origin of the 'bad conscience'.[9]

In the beginning, as we saw, were the noble societies. Reaffirming sections 9, 14 and 16 of Book 1 of *Daybreak*, Nietzsche says that what held them together was 'morality', that is to say, the 'morality of custom'; the morality of a community, says Nietzsche, just *is* its customary, traditional ethos. Obedience to such a morality is, he says, 'the first proposition of civilization' (D 1 16).[10] Without the 'breeding' of a reliable, 'predictable' animal, which can only come from the 'straitjacket' of morality, there can be no civilisation (let alone 'culture') (GM II 2).

The most fundamental aspect of the 'morality of custom', the most elementary form of 'predictability' required by any society, is the repayment of debts; that is, the keeping of promises. Originally, this needed to be 'burnt' into individual memories by the most horrendous of sanctions (GM II 3). The debtor–creditor relation was considered to hold, not just between individuals, but also between the individual and society as a whole: the individual received the benefits of social life – shelter, peace, trust and safety – in return for which he owed obedience to the customary law (GM II 9). And it was also considered to hold between the present generation and the ancestor who had founded the tribe. Since the tribe only existed through the ancestor's efforts, his spirit needed to be repaid in feasts and sacrifices (the sorts of thing he was likely to find entertaining). The more powerful and victorious the tribe the greater the debt and the greater the stature of the ancestor. Eventually, surrounded by an air of

---

9 In what follows I omit a great deal of the story in order to highlight that which is relevant to Nietzsche's positive philosophy of religion.

10 Nietzsche holds, of course, that the 'morality of custom' is not just any set of norms, but rather those which experience has shown to promote the survival and growth of the community: those which are, as *Zarathustra* puts it, both 'hard' and 'indispensable' (Z 1 15; see p. 112 above). It is this quasi-Darwinian theory that generates the central puzzle that the third of the *Genealogy*'s essays tries to solve: how it is that the life-denying 'ascetic ideal' could possibly be life-promoting. (Discussion of Nietzsche's answer would take us too far afield.)

'divine mystery and transcendence', he was 'transfigured into a god'. Here, suggests Nietzsche, is the probable first origin of gods (GM II 19).[11]

Having inherited the pagan idea of the creditor god, the Christian 'stroke of genius' was to invent the idea a 'maximal' God and hence a maximal debt, while at the same time making it a debt that, on account of our sinful, animal natures, in principle we *cannot* repay. (We are so despicable that *nothing* we do can be in any way pleasing to God.) Only God can repay the debt – and did through his own suffering and crucifixion. Christianity's 'master-stroke' was thus to turn the debt into an *undischargeable* debt, thus making us originally and inescapably guilty. Nietzsche refers to this as the 'moralization' of the concept of *Schuld* – the German word means both 'debt' and 'guilt'. It is the point at which a legalistic and pre-Christian notion becomes recognisable as the Christian notion of sin. And it is the point at which man becomes an intensely 'sick' creature, 'mad' even, since he has inflicted the whole crazy metaphysical–moral structure on himself (GM II 20–2).

What of a positive, constructive nature can we learn from this story? What can we learn of Nietzsche's hopes for the future, of his 'counter-ideal' to Christianity? How is the long look 'backwards' to facilitate the 'great leap' forwards?

Nietzsche's ambition, clearly, is to identify the historical point at which health gives way to sickness. But just where is that? It is clear that with the arrival of the Christian god sickness has set in. But what about the pagan creditor god? Is *it* entirely healthy? To answer this question we need, finally, to speak directly of the *Genealogy*'s positive philosophy of religion.

RELIGION IN THE 'GENEALOGY'

What is the place of religion (if any) in the *Genealogy*'s conception of a healthy future, in Nietzsche's 'opposing ideal' to that of Christianity?

Since Christianity has created, as we saw, an in principle unrepayable debt to God and consequently a sense of absolute guilt and worthlessness, 'atheism', suggests Nietzsche, must come as a kind of 'second innocence' (GM II 20). Is, then, the *Genealogy* an atheistic work?

---

11 Nietzsche seems here to have abandoned (or forgotten) the animist hypothesis as to the origin of gods propounded in section III of the first volume of *Human* (see p. 63 above). Though *fear* of gods is common to both hypotheses, the idea that the first god was the spirit of the storm does not seem really compatible with the idea that the first god was the ancestor. Since both hypotheses seem, in themselves, highly plausible, I think one should rectify the inconsistency by allowing that different gods arise in different ways in different places.

After the self-ravaging of Christianity, atheism provides, certainly, a therapeutic pause. But it does not constitute a resting place. In the contemporary world 'atheism' is, indeed, simply a popular name for the lack of *any* ideal (GM III 27) – whereas the whole point is to discover an 'opposing ideal' to that of Christianity. The 'unconditional honest atheism' of the 'man of science', on the other hand, is simply a disguised *manifestation* of the Christian ideal (GM III 27).

What Nietzsche is getting at here, I think, is the idea that since both truth and falsity are each, on occasion, useful to life, the '*unconditional*' pursuit of truth can only be a legacy of the Christian value of being truthful at all costs. It is, therefore, a disguised perpetuation of Christian morality. And since this makes no sense without the metaphysical structures on which that is based, scientific atheism is also unconsciously committed to the metaphysically transcendent, to precisely what it denies. This is, I think, psychologically acute. The *fervour* of the aggressive and passionate denier of God typically has the quality of *religious* fervour.[12]

The *Genealogy* is not, then, atheistic. But is it perhaps simply indifferent to religion? Is it simply uninterested in gods? Nietzsche's talk of destroying Christianity in order to set up a new 'shrine' (GM II 24) suggests otherwise. And, since religion played a central role in the life of the ancient world, so does Nietzsche's slogan 'Rome against Judea', as well as his identification of his own 'counter-ideal' with the 'noble', that is, 'classical' ideal (GM I 16).

Let us return to the creditor god of the tribes of 'pre-history'. Since the debt to such gods is capable of being discharged through festivals and sacrifice, there is, Nietzsche holds, no 'sickness' in the tribe's relation to its god. On the other hand, he says, there is something ignoble about the relationship since it is based on 'fear' – the first origin, he suggests, of the worship of gods. 'Piety', he adds, does not come into the picture (GM II 19). Later, however, among the 'noble' tribes (Nietzsche clearly has in mind, here, the creation of the Olympian gods), a different relationship to the gods developed. Here they 'repay, with interest, their founders, their ancestors (heroes and gods), with all the attributes which, in the meantime, had become manifest in themselves, the *noble* attributes'.

---

12 Such fervour is not, however, shared by those for whom the Christian God has simply become 'unbelievable'. This, I think, is why Nietzsche says that 'only the comedians of the [Christian] ideal are its true enemies' (GM III 27). Only those who find traditional Christianity absurd, and not, therefore, in need of passionate opposition, are genuinely free of it.

Here, in this glorification of themselves, fear is replaced by authentic 'piety' (*ibid.*).

A little further on Nietzsche returns to the topic of the Greek gods. The Christian God, as the 'antithesis' of the natural, animal instincts in human nature, is an 'instrument of torture' (GM II 22). But, he adds,

there are *nobler* ways of making use of the invention of gods than man's self-crucifixion and self-abuse . . . this can fortunately be deduced from any glance at the *Greek gods*, these reflections of noble and proud men in whom the *animal* in man felt deified, did *not* tear itself apart and did *not* rage against itself. (GM II 23)[13]

And then, in the next section, Nietzsche talks of the desirability of a 'reverse experiment' – his 'counter-ideal' to Christianity – in which a new 'shrine' is set up and the bad conscience is attached to 'all those other-worldly aspirations, alien to the senses, the instincts to nature, to animals, in short to all that which up to now has been hostile to life'. And he speaks of 'the Antichrist' as the one who will institute this new ideal, thereby conquering both God and the 'nihilism' of modernity that arises from the combination of the yearning for God with his 'unbelievability' (GM III 24). (Note, in preparation for our discussion of *The Antichrist*, that this figure is no mere destroyer but a positive creator. Alternatively put, he is a genuine destroyer *because* he is also a creator.)

The contrast, here, between the self-tormenting creation of the God of Christianity and the self-glorifying creation of the gods of Greece takes us back, very clearly, to *The Birth* (see pp. 17–18 above). And so does the role envisaged for the gods in the 'reverse experiment'.

The positive result of the first genealogical story, it will be remembered, was that a healthy, a good/bad, morality needs to be, unlike the other-focused and other-hating morality of *ressentiment, self*-focused and self-*esteeming*. The discussion of the Greek gods at the end of the second essay makes precisely these points: that in the creation of their gods the Greeks portrayed and esteemed themselves in a 'transfigured', idealised form. In other words, taken together, the two stories return us to the idea that we have seen to go back to the beginning of Nietzsche's thinking: the idea that the ethos of a community is embodied in exemplary figures,[14] its

13 In the same passage Nietzsche calls the Greeks 'these marvellous lion-hearted children', which suggests (a) that it is the Greeks who are paradigms of *Zarathustra*'s final 'metamorphosis' from 'lion' into 'child' and (b) that what the 'child' creates is above all gods.

14 At GM III 22 Nietzsche deplores the way Christians *chat* to their God in familiar, first-name ('*Du*' as opposed to '*Sie*') terms. It is, he says, a lack of 'tact'. Eastern religions show much more

gods, and that a healthy ethos, rather than setting up an anti-human ideal, idealises the human, including the all-too-human.

There is, therefore, a powerful continuity between the *Genealogy* and *The Birth*. In both works community requires gods – a polytheistic array of gods – who embody the stratified yet unified ethos which creates and preserves the community.

COMMUNITY IN THE 'GENEALOGY'

I have said nothing explicit about communitarianism in the *Genealogy*. But lest it be thought to be absent let me quote section 22 of the third essay. Nietzsche explains his preference for the world of the Old Testament over that of the New Testament as follows. Whereas the latter is 'nothing but petty sectarian groupings, nothing but rococo of the soul, nothing but arabesques, crannies and oddities', in the former he finds 'Great men, heroic landscape and something of that which is most rare on earth, the incomparable naivety of the *strong heart*; even more I find a Volk.' And in section 9 of the second essay, reminding us that the preservation of the creditor–debtor relation (in brief, the relation of trust) is essential to any community, he reminds us too of the 'benefits of community (*Gemeinwesen*)', peace, trust and safety, that are not available to the 'man *outside*'. 'Oh, what benefits!', he continues, benefits we all too readily 'underestimate . . . today'. Unlike the 'radical individualist', therefore, the Nietzsche of the *Genealogy* neither forgets nor despises the need for community.

In the *Genealogy*, in sum, Nietzsche remains a communitarian. And he remains committed to the idea that ethos-embodying gods are essential to the existence and preservation of community. In a word, therefore, he remains, as I have called him, a religious communitarian.

POSTSCRIPT ON THE FREE SPIRIT

To this conclusion I should hasten to add that the *Genealogy* of course continues to care deeply about fostering the appearance of the strong/ healthy/higher/free-spirited individual. Not, however, as an end in itself,

---

respect by refusing to pronounce even the name of god. There are, I think, two points here. First, a point about genuine reverence. But second, a rejection of the 'power of prayer'. To the kinds of gods Nietzsche approves of one does not talk, does not ask for their intervention in human affairs. Rather, one imitates them in action.

but rather because, as we have repeatedly seen, it is on the free spirit, the random mutation or, as the *Genealogy* now calls him, '*man's stroke of luck*' (GM III 14; Nietzsche's emphasis), that the preservation and flourishing of the community depend. Potential free spirits should, he says, be allowed to develop and breed away from the 'bad air' emitted by the mediocre mass of modernity. (A reappearance, I think, of *Beyond Good and Evil*'s complaint against the dumbing down of education.) Not, however, because the appearance of a Goethe pleases our 'aesthetic' taste, but rather because free spirits 'alone are *guarantors* of the future' and because 'they alone have a *bounden duty* [not themselves but ultimately] to man's future' (GM III 14).

According to the theory of cultural development that we have seen to be consistently maintained through many works, only the production of the 'lucky' mutation guarantees a culture's future existence and growth. This view is reaffirmed in the *Genealogy*:

All good things [i.e. things currently called 'good'] used to be bad things at one time. Marriage, for example, was for a long time viewed as a crime against the rights of the community . . . Each step on earth, even the smallest, was in the past a struggle that was won with spiritual and physical torment . . . required countless martyrs. (GM III 9)

Martyrs, one might add, on both sides. Cultural change claims both Thomas Mores and Thomas Cranmers.

CHAPTER 9

The Wagner Case

The Wagner Case[1] (the title is intended to suggest, presumably, the idea of a psychiatric report) was written in May 1888. It is a diatribe against Wagner, in intention a negative polemic. As usual, however, constructive notions lie in close connexion with criticism and, with a little digging, emerge by way of contrast. Out of Wagner's failings emerges the contrasting outline of a positive conception of the artwork and its role in a healthy society, a conception which bears on our concern with Nietzsche's view of the role of religion in such a society.

WAGNER'S FAILINGS

Though the work is 'contra Wagner', Nietzsche represents the source of Wagner's failings as lying, to a considerable degree, not in himself but in the audience he finds himself saddled with. So – a point Nietzsche has made many times before – Wagner has to deal with the exhausted, work-weary audience of machine-minded modernity, an audience capable of responding only to cheap thrills, 'convulsive' 'hysterics', *theatrical* effects in the worst sense of the word. Wagner, however, makes the audience even more 'decadent' by supplying these effects. The effects leave them even more exhausted and demanding of ever 'stronger spices'. Wagner makes the sick sicker (WC 5).

One of Nietzsche's most frequent accusations against Wagner is that he is an 'actor', a man of the theatre. Since that was not, in fact, Wagner's profession, 'actor' must here be used in the sense of 'fake'. And this is indeed what Nietzsche says: as an actor what Wagner offers is never 'true', never 'authentic (*echt*)' (WC 8).

---

1 Or, in Kaufmann's translation, *The Case of Wagner* (*Der Fall Wagner*). I prefer my translation as more economical and as having more of a forensic ring to it.

157

Zarathustra says that the people who reign in the market place are the actors. Idolised by the masses, the actor

possesses spirit but little conscience . . . tomorrow he will have a new faith. He has a quick perception as the people have, and a capricious temperament. . . he believes only in gods who make a great noise in the world. (Z 1 12)

So the actor's lack of authenticity is the lack of an anchor, the lack of any genuine convictions he seeks to express. Lacking an inner compass he has no alternative but to follow the degenerate tastes of the masses.

But then, how *could* the artist of modernity have any inner 'truth' to impart to his artwork? The artist of modernity lives in a 'decadent' society, a society that has lost all organic unity, a society that is nothing but

the anarchy of atoms, disintegration (*Disgregation*) of the [communal] will, 'freedom of the individual' . . . expanded into a political theory, '*equal* rights for all'. Life, *the same* vitality, the vibration and exuberance of life pushed back into the smallest forms; the rest, *poor* in life. Everywhere paralysis, arduousness, torpidity *or* hostility and chaos: both more obvious the higher one ascends in forms of organization. The whole no longer lives at all: it is composite, calculated, artificial, and artefact. (WC 7)

It is produced, in other words, by that Volk-usurping unity, the 'cold monster' (Z 1 11) of the modern state (see p. 113 above). So Wagner is 'no arbitrary play of nature, a whim or accident'. His own decadence – in reality he is a gifted miniaturist, the operas being miniature moments pasted together into artificial wholes – simply reflects the decadence of modernity as a whole (*ibid.*).

Another oft-repeated criticism is that Wagner replaces the 'lawfulness' of music – the 'logic' of sonata form, for instance – with formless rhetoric (WC 8).[2] (As Nietzsche recognises, this is deliberate policy on Wagner's part, explicitly defended in the defence of Walter's prize song against, as Wagner represents them, the pettifogging rules of the *Mastersingers*.)

So Wagner's music lacks clarity of form (the Apollonian surface which *The Birth* so admires in Greek tragedy). And it is the same with content. Wagner is Hegel's successor. He offers not clarity of thought but 'intimations'. Among Germans, 'clarity is an objection . . . a refutation'

---

2 This criticism may in part derive from Wagner's opponent, the formalist music critic Eduard Hanslick, whom, as Christoph Landerer and Marc-Oliver Schuster have shown, Nietzsche read and was impressed by even before writing *The Birth*. (Their theme is that Nietzsche had his doubts about Wagner, doubts he suppressed in *The Birth*, as early as the *Nachlass* note 7 12 [1] of 1871.) See Landerer and Schuster (2002).

(WC 10). Such mistiness enables Wagner to appeal to the nihilistic instincts of his audience by offering them – above all in *Parsifal* – a counterfeit transcendence (WC Postscript).

POSITIVE LESSONS

What positive results emerge from this critique? Above all, that what healthy art needs is a non-decadent society, that is, a society which (a) possesses a communal will rather than dissipating its energy in the frenzied but directionless activity of its smallest units (individuals), and (b) is held together by the unity of a culture or Volk rather than by the 'artificial' means of the modern state. And secondly, that what is needed is a society that brings a serious degree of attention to the artwork, that is not looking for a cheap narcoticising of its work-weariness but seeking instead to discover in the work some kind of essential 'truth'. As already mentioned, Nietzsche partly excuses Wagner on the grounds that he lacked such an audience. He lacked, specifically, Corneille's audience (WC 9).

Pierre Corneille belonged to the seventeenth-century French classical revival and is regarded as the founder of French tragedy. He believed in creating types rather than individuals through the sparing use of local and historical detail. He believed, in other words, in creating the universal types of Greek tragedy (see p. 26 above).

In *The Gay Science* Nietzsche remarks that 'in the age of Corneille . . . the French took possession of Roman antiquity' in the way in which 'Roman antiquity itself . . . took hold of everything good and lofty in Greek antiquity' (GS 83). *Daybreak* provides the contrast between the modern audience and Corneille's audience to which *The Wagner Case* refers. 'They tell me', says Nietzsche, 'that modern art provides momentary oblivion for harassed men'.

> How much more fortunate was Corneille . . . how much more exalted was his audience, whom he could improve with pictures of knightly virtue, stern duty, magnanimous self-sacrifice and heroic self-restraint. How differently did he and they love existence: not out of a [Schopenhauer's] blind, dissolute 'will' which is cursed because it cannot be killed, but as a place where greatness and humanity are *possible* together. (D 191)

What we meet here is a picture of a non-decadent society, a society consisting not of chaotic 'atoms' but bound together, rather, by communal ethos, an ethos which is embodied in role models: *this*-worldly models – there is, says Nietzsche, to be none of Wagner's quasi-Christian 'transcendence'. Such models of 'the great and beautiful soul' (HH II a 99) will be models of restraint and moderation – there will be no hysterical histrionics. The artist will make them 'shine' and so, 'through the excitation of envy and emulation' (*ibid.*; see pp. 74–5 above), encourage individuals to aspire to the ideals of communal ethos.

That this by now familiar picture is the positive background against which Wagner and his age are judged and found wanting is confirmed by a note Nietzsche added to section 9 of *The Wagner Case*. Commenting on Wagner's taste for big gestures and dramatic action he remarks that

> It has been a real misfortune for aesthetics that the word *drama* has always been translated as 'action'. It is not Wagner alone who errs at this point: the error is world-wide and extends even to the philologists who ought to know better. Ancient drama aimed at scenes of great *pathos* – it precluded action (moving it *before* the beginning or *behind* the scene). The word *drama* is of Doric origin, and according to Doric usage it means 'Event (*Ereignis*)' or 'Tale' – both words in the hieratic [sacred] sense. The most ancient drama represented the legend of the place, the 'holy story' on which the foundation of the cult rested.

So authentic drama – music-drama or otherwise – requires a 'place', a community, with a founding 'cult'. The holy legend of the place is told through exemplary, mythic figures, figures who, as *The Birth* puts it, by 'abbreviating appearances' (see p. 26 above), expound the ethos of the community.

The background to the critique of Wagner in *The Wagner Case*, in other words, is just *The Birth*'s picture of the healthy community as a community created and preserved by the religious artwork. Religious communitarianism which, in *The Birth*, is used to defend and promote Wagner is now used, essentially unchanged, to attack him. The Wagnerian ideal remains, but *qua* man and artist, Wagner now fails to match up to it.

CHAPTER 10

Twilight of the Idols

'Medical' in character, like nearly all of Nietzsche's thinking, the reflections in *Twilight* respond to, and arise out of, a diagnosis of the ills of modernity, out of 'cultural criticism'. Many earlier themes reappear: we live in an *Erlebnisgesellschaft* – German students drink too much beer (TI VIII 2) – we have become a 'machine-minded' (TI IX 37) society capable of finding stress-relief only at seaside resorts and Bayreuth (TI IX 29–30), and so on. Over and above these relatively random hits, however, is a central theme focused on the word 'democracy', which, for Nietzsche, is a synonym for '*décadence*'.

THE DECADENCE OF DEMOCRACY

For all that Plato is his great antagonist, Nietzsche never escapes his profound influence. (The four most frequently discussed figures in his published works are Wagner, Goethe, Schopenhauer and Plato. Aristotle comes twenty-first on the list, after, *inter alios*, Epicurus, Sophocles and Aeschylus, which speaks volumes about 'What I owe the Ancients' – the title of *Twilight*'s section x.[1])

In the *Republic*, Plato famously holds that state and soul are structurally the same, that they stand to each other as macrocosm to microcosm. And he also famously holds that democracy in the soul (a condition in which all the instincts are given equal weight) and democracy in the state (the world of, as Nietzsche puts it, 'equal rights') are conditions of decadence. The reason the democratic soul is decadent is that it is incapable of focused and concerted – 'long-willed', Nietzsche would say – action. Until one has instituted a disciplined hierarchy in the soul, until one has become 'one man', one will butterfly from one whim to the next, will

---

1 I owe this information to Brobjer (1998) p. 317, fn. 40.

be the starter of many projects and finisher of none. And the same with the democratic state. In an environment of war – as Nietzsche emphasises, the Greek city-states were constantly at war with each other (TI x 3) – it will lack the power to sustain itself and will constantly threaten, therefore, to collapse into demagogic tyranny.

Nietzsche's discussion of democracy (by which he means a characteristic of both state and society) is a repetition of this line of thinking. Socrates (i.e. Plato), he says, lived at the time of Athens' descent into decadence. The instincts in the individual were in a state of 'anarchy'. Socrates' elevation of 'reason' to a position of dominance in the soul was a symptom of this fear of anarchy (TI II 9). We are in the same situation today. The instincts 'contradict' each other; we lack 'self-mastery'; there is no organising principle in the modern soul (TI IX 41).

Plato sees unity of soul – selfhood – as demanding rigorous self-discipline, since each and every instinct ('appetite') desires to play the tyrant. Nietzsche is of the same view. Each and every 'drive' 'craves mastery' over all the others (BGE 6, WP 481). So 'freedom as I understand it', he says, is certainly not the 'anything goes' negative freedom of today (TI IX 41). It is, rather, positive freedom, 'mastery' over the tyranny of the instincts (TI IX 38) by a single dominant instinct, so that the entire soul is organised in a 'straight line' towards a single 'goal' (TI I 41).

Nietzsche has, to be sure, a serious disagreement with Plato. Whereas the latter made reason a 'tyrant' and sought, like Christianity, to *exclude*, exterminate, 'castrate' the 'evil' instincts, Nietzsche's view is that they should be 'spiritualised', *incorporated* into the economy of the soul, but in a sublimated form. Thus the spiritualisation of sex is love; the spiritualisation of 'enmity (*Feindschaft*)' 'consists in profoundly grasping the value of having enemies; in brief, in acting and thinking in the reverse of the way one formerly acted and thought' (TI v 3). The need for 'enemies' is based, of course, on the Heraclitean thought that spiritual 'war is the father of all things', that the self can only be defined through difference.

In spite of this disagreement, however, the idea that both self and society require the victory of order over anarchy is common to both Plato and Nietzsche. Moreover, both believe that 'order' means the order of the pyramid. Plato, of course, believes in aristocracy, in 'rule by the best', specifically by the philosopher-king. And similarly, Nietzsche holds that 'democracy' is a 'declining form of the power to organise' (TI IX 39), since true order in both self and society is always hierarchical, always involves 'separating . . . opening up chasms . . . ranking above and below' (TI IX 37).

COMPASSIONATE CONSERVATISM

Like the modern individual, then, modern society is in decay. What is the remedy? Though in these days of 'equal rights' all differences are being levelled out, '[t]he chasm between man and man, class and class, the multiplicity of types, the will to be oneself to stand out – that which I call *pathos of distance* – characterises every *strong* age'(TL IX 37).

One of the few virtues Nietzsche allows to nineteenth-century Germany is that, more than anywhere else in Europe, it remains still a place of the '*virile* (*männlich*)' virtues, 'inherited ability', a place where there is still

a good deal of cheerfulness and respect for oneself, a good deal of self-confidence in social dealings [e.g. clearly defined rules about the use of the familiar and formal 'you'[2]] and in the performance of reciprocal duties . . . I would add that here people can still obey without being humiliated by obeying . . . and no one despises his adversary. (TI VIII 1)

So the first thing required for a healthy ('virile') society, as for a healthy soul, is a strongly hierarchical order, aristocracy. But it also needs to be a society in which everyone accepts the class in which they find themselves. As de Tocqueville also saw, what is needed is a society without (in the language of the recent popularisation of de Tocqueville's insight) 'status anxiety'. It is also a society of mutual respect between classes,[3] and of self-respect even if one finds oneself in a position of subordination. It is a society of service without servility, a society where people are valued for their contribution to the social organism whatever form it takes.

Of significance here is Nietzsche's abandonment of the – always silly – thesis that a healthy, hierarchical society requires slavery, or at least 'slavery in some sense' (see p. 132 above). It is, he says, an absurd trait of modernity that 'whenever the word "authority" is heard one believes oneself in danger of some new form of slavery' (TI IX 39).

Nietzsche only ever had two arguments for the necessity-of-slavery thesis. First, that the flowering of things of the spirit is the product of leisure, which can only be generated through servitude – an argument overtaken by the washing-machine[4] – and second, that only where there is social 'pathos of distance' can internal pathos of distance, the striving for personal excellence, occur. To the earlier criticism of this argument

---

2 Rules that were, to some degree, deconstructed in the 1960s and 1970s.
3 One might recall, here, Zarathustra's constant demand that he free himself from 'contempt' towards those 'lower' than himself.
4 Wagner had already realised this in his *Art and Revolution* of 1849.

(see p. 125 fn. 6 above) can now be added Nietzsche's own implicit self-criticism – that subordination does not necessarily imply servitude. (The second violin in a string quartet takes the lead from the first but, unless things are going seriously wrong, does not thereby feel abused.)

What, above all, the healthy society requires are *leaders*, individuals who stand for 'ascending life', people with whom the future of society stands or falls. For the production of such leaders exceptional measures are justified, measures that will sequester them off from the universal levelling of contemporary society (TI IX 33). In the specifically German context what this requires is a *genuinely* 'higher' education; in other words, exactly the opposite of the dumbed down university – the adjustment of instruction and the curriculum to 'the most dubious mediocrity' – that is the inevitable consequence of its 'democrat[isation]' (TI VIII 5; compare p. 43 above).

These leaders, or at least forerunners of leaders, are of course, as I have emphasised before, Nietzsche's intended readers. It is to these potential leaders that he addresses, in the first section of the book, the '*first* question of conscience':

You run on *ahead*? Do you do so as a shepherd or as an exception? A third possibility would be as a deserter.

And lest one misses the point, the 'third question of conscience' asks whether one 'sets to work' or 'looks away' (TI I 37, 40).

The distinction between 'shepherds' and 'exceptions' is fairly clearly the distinction between the two kinds of 'philosophers of the future' drawn in *Beyond Good and Evil* (see pp. 128–30 above). The 'exceptions' are the 'random mutations', as I have called them; those who, though judged 'evil' by the reigning ethos of their community, represent its hopes of survival into the future, of being able to survive and thrive in a changing environment. 'All *healthy* morality', Nietzsche reiterates, responds to 'some commandment of life' (TI v 4). The 'exception' is one who enables a morality to continue to so respond, to remain healthy.[5] The 'shepherds',

---

5 Nietzsche continues by saying that 'anti-natural morality . . . turns on the contrary precisely *against* the instincts of life'. This seems to me to represent a radical modification of the thesis, maintained, as late as *On the Genealogy of Morals*, that *every* morality 'serves life' – the motivation for the third essay attempts to show that, paradoxically, even the 'ascetic priest' serves life. And given the identification of life with the will to power, it represents a dramatic modification of the thesis that the will to power is the human essence, the underlying motive for every action. (See further, sections 2 and 6 of *The Antichrist*.) It seems to introduce, that is, alongside the will to life/power something like the Freudian death instinct. The universality of the will to power also appears to be abandoned in the odd discussion of art at TI IX 10 which seems to introduce a

on the other hand, are the 'philosopher-kings' ('philosophers triumphant', as I call them), where 'philosopher' is understood broadly enough to include Napoleon. The shepherd is the 'philosopher' who has achieved a position of actual leadership, whether spiritual or overtly political, the 'legislator of values' who has graduated from being the 'exception' to being the new 'rule' (see p. 96 above). In *Twilight*, while the former are called 'beginnings' (TI IX 44), the latter, Napoleon (*ibid.*) and Goethe (TI IX 50) for instance, are regarded as 'termini'. (I shall have more to say about the status of the philosopher-king as a 'terminus' in discussing *The Antichrist*.)

What needs to be noticed about Nietzsche's 'leadership manual' – especially by anyone still inclined to the view that Nietzsche is interested only in the flourishing of the exceptional few and has an 'almost anarchistic' (Leiter (2002) p. 296) attitude to social life – is the extraordinary weight of social responsibility he places on the shoulders of the exceptional person. The demand that he has a 'conscience' is clearly the demand that he has a *social* conscience, that he accept the responsibility not just for his own flourishing but for the flourishing of the community as a whole. To do otherwise, to fail to return to Plato's cave, to fail to come down from Zarathustra's remote heights, to fail to overcome Spinoza's icy detachment (see p. 130 above), is to be a 'deserter'. It is to *abandon* one's status as a higher type.[6]

Underlying the above, 'compassionately conservative' account of the healthy society is the Volkish, communitarian conception of a society in which the good of the organic, social whole takes precedence over – or, better put, constitutes – the good of each and every individual, including, above all, that of its leaders. It is a society in which inequality of station, rights, duties and virtues is compensated for by equality of respect, and in which the loss of the freedom of liberalism to do and be whatever one wants is compensated for by a sense of meaning and authentic fellowship that comes from a shared conception of the good life.

---

threefold impetus to art: the visual and plastic arts which arise out of Apollonian 'intoxication', the musical and performing arts which arise out of Dionysian 'intoxication', and finally architecture, which arises out of 'the intoxication of a strong will'.

6 A similar demand is made in the second essay of *The Genealogy* where the 'sovereign individual', the creator of new values, is required also to be aware of his 'extraordinary privilege of *responsibility*' to the community as a whole. Since the essay portrays the 'bad conscience' of the Christian as a sickness Nietzsche goes out of his way to make the point that he is far from being opposed to *conscience as such* by calling the sovereign individual's sense of social responsibility his 'conscience' (GM II 2).

So Nietzsche's conservative communitarianism is alive and well in *Twilight*. The next question is: how do the gods show up in the work? Is it still a religious communitarianism to which Nietzsche subscribes?

Themes in Nietzsche come and go. They press into the foreground of one work and recede into the background of another. In *Twilight* the gods remain in the background. None the less, enough tips of the iceberg remain visible to show, I think, that the persistent idea that authentic community is impossible without 'gods of the hearth' to provide it with a 'mythical home' (BT 23) survives.

In contrast to modernity, a healthy society needs, we have seen, hierarchy and spiritual leadership. But it also needs rootedness in the past:

Criticism of modernity. – Our institutions are no longer fit for anything . . . For institutions to exist there must exist a kind of will, instinct, imperative, which is anti-liberal to the point of malice; the will to tradition, to authority, to centuries-long responsibility (*Verantwortlichkeit*), to *solidarity* (*Solidarität*) between succeeding generations backwards and forwards *ad infinitum*. If this will is present there is established something like the *Imperium Romanum*. (TI IX 39)

Authentic 'institutions' are, that is, *immutable* social structures. By this standard modern marriage has ceased to be an 'institution' since, built on the shifting sands of love, it has lost the 'indissolubility in principle' that used to be its rationale (*ibid.*).

The idea, here, that a society thrives only in the light of a 'will to tradition', to 'backwards and forwards' solidarity between generations, is a repetition of the thesis that community requires (self-modulating) communal ethos. And according to what we have understood to date, the preservation of ethos requires its embodiment in 'monumental' figures, in role models or 'gods'.

Gods are not mentioned explicitly in *Twilight*. But 'educators' are. These, as we saw, are role models: it is Schopenhauer *the man* rather than Schopenhauer the philosopher, remember, whom Nietzsche describes as his 'educator'. Specifically, they are 'educators' for the small elite of potential leaders, those who are worthy of a genuinely higher education. Far from being mere scholars, *Twilight* says, genuine educators such as Jacob Burckhardt are themselves educated,[7] are, that is, 'superior, noble

---

7 As such, Nietzsche says, they are representatives of a 'culture ['*Cultur*', interchangeable with '*Kultur*' in nineteenth-century German], grown ripe and sweet'. Nietzsche uses 'culture' in

spirits, who prove themselves every moment by what they say and by what they do not say' (TI VIII 5). So 'gods' in the sense of role models survive at least in the context of the education of potential leaders.

But they survive, I think, in a more general context as well.

Once again (see p. 134 above), Nietzsche attacks 'art for art's sake' as 'decadent'. The 'meaning' of art is not itself but rather *life*. Art that is of any value, that is to say, 'selects', 'highlights', 'idealises', 'perfects', 'praises' and 'glorifies' aspects of life. (Hence there can be no Christian art. Raphael? 'Let us not be childish . . . Raphael said Yes, Raphael *did* Yes, consequently Raphael was no Christian.') By doing all this it '*strengthens* or *weakens* certain valuations'.[8] This is not an accidental feature of art but belongs to the 'basic instinct' of the artist, is a prerequisite of the artist's being an artist at all (TI IX 24; see, too, 8–9).

This passage is clearly a fairly exact repetition of *Human, All-to-Human*'s view that the function of ('Apollonian') artists is to influence action by ' scent[ing] out those cases in which, in the *midst* of our modern world . . . the great and beautiful soul is still possible, still able to embody itself in the harmonious and well-proportioned and thus acquire visibility, duration and the status of a model', thereby exciting 'envy and emulation' (HH II a 99; see pp. 74–5 above). In other words the – or at least a major – function of art (of 'the media' we might say today) is to 'raise to the status of a [role] model' certain figures who embody communal ethos. It can be inferred, therefore, that the idea of communal gods, of a community-preserving humanistic religion, is alive and well in *Twilight*.[9]

---

different ways. Often it seems interchangeable with 'people'. Here (TI IV 5), however, it is described as the product of 'education (*Erziehung*)' in the sense of 'personal formation or cultivation (*Bildung*)'; a *Bildungsroman* is a novel (*Roman*) of 'education' in the sense of being a tale of the hero's growth from naivety to maturity through undergoing a series of 'learning experiences' – 'self-overcomings', as Nietzsche would put it. To possess 'culture' in this sense is to be a fine, a 'noble', human being (*ibid.*). Of course, culture in the sense of immersion in great art is, for Nietzsche, an essential part of *Bildung*. Not, however, as an end in itself, but because great art, by definition, is art which 'serves life' (see pp. 167, 207 below). (We read Homer and Sophocles, remember, only as a 'polished mirror' in which to learn about ourselves (see p. 15 above).) Those who think that all Nietzsche cares about is the product of a few great works of art misunderstand, among other things, his notion of culture.

8 This view of art, to repeat, makes a nonsense of the claim that Nietzsche's ultimate end is the production of a couple of great artists every few centuries. His view is in fact the exact *opposite* of the view that art is the end which justifies life. What he holds is *not* that the meaning of life is art but rather that the meaning of art is life.

9 Nietzsche observes, in the famous, already quoted, passage, that while 'the Englishman' strives for pleasure what 'man' needs is meaning (TI I 12). What we need is meaning, not happiness, a 'goal', that is to say, which will overcome nihilism (compare WP 4) by giving purpose and direction to

THE LAW OF MANU

Section VII of *Twilight* is entitled 'The "Improvers" of mankind'. 'In all ages', Nietzsche writes, 'one has wanted to "improve" men; this above all is what morality has been about' (TI VII 2). Two ways of doing this, he continues, have been attempted: 'breeding' and 'taming'.

A priori, one would think that no one is more of an 'improver' of mankind than the proponent of the idea that 'man is a rope tied between beast and superman'.[10] And since Nietzsche talks on many occasions of the need for 'breeding' – both in the biological sense of eugenics and in the cultural sense of education (*Bildung*)[11] – one would expect him to reject taming but approve of breeding. In *The Antichrist*, he goes as far as to say that '*the* problem' is 'what type of man shall be *bred*' (A 3; first emphasis mine). What is puzzling about the *Twilight* passage, however, is that it at least appears to criticise both taming *and* breeding.

To call taming, the method of the medieval Church, 'improvement', Nietzsche writes, is a bad joke. Animals are not 'improved' by being put in a zoo (TI VII 2). Thus far we are offered a predictable sentiment.

our lives. Particularly in *The Gay Science*, Nietzsche frequently talks about 'self-creation', about giving meaning to one's life by organising it so it has the coherence of a well-written work of literature. One of the objections often raised to this idea is what might be called 'the problem of the immoral script'. If a life-'script' determines my life's meaning why should I not choose *being a serial murderer* as my life-defining goal? What resources does Nietzsche have to condemn *this* kind of meaning? The answer is: communal ethos. The ideals around which we script, 'idealise' (see p. 45 above), our lives are the communal gods. And for obvious reasons none of those are going to be serial murderers. Of course, the free spirit worships at the shrine of an 'unknown god' (see p. 90 above) but mass murder is not an option for him either, since, as we have seen, he is bound by a tremendous sense of 'responsibility' to the communal good.

10 In *Ecce Homo* (Foreword 2) Nietzsche says that since he erects no 'new idols' he cannot be counted as one who seeks to 'improve' mankind. How then are we to understand his constant affirmation of 'classical values', his call for a return to 'Greek' values? Via, I think, the remark that classical ideals are to constitute the 'all-embracing golden ground upon which alone tender *distinctions* between the different embodied ideals would then constitute the actual *painting*' (HH II a 99) – i.e. morality. Classical ideals, his point is, provide the *form* of any healthy morality. But as to giving that form content, embodying it in concrete role models, he has nothing to say. Conceivably with his positivist predecessor, Auguste Comte, in mind (Comte canonised 559 positivist 'saints' in his 'religion of humanity') Nietzsche goes out of his way to emphasise that he erects no 'idols', canonises nobody (though, in fact, he comes very close in the case of Goethe and Burckhardt).

11 Like most of his contemporaries, Darwin included (see Richardson (2004) p. 84), Nietzsche was a Lamarckian. He believed in the inheritability of acquired traits (see, for instance, GS 143, BGE 213, WP 995). Given this presupposition, the two forms of 'breeding' merge into each other: characteristics acquired through education can be biologically transmitted to the next generation. That he thinks of this as a rather hit or miss process is, I think, the reason Nietzsche often emphasises that the breeding of 'higher types' is a process that takes many generations.

But then he goes on to discuss the *Lawbook of Manu* – the foundational text of Hindu society, supposedly given by a god to the first ancestor – which Nietzsche describes as 'the most grandiose example' so far of the attempted 'breeding of a definite race and species' (TI vii 3). What surprises is that, though observing the world of Manu to be 'a hundred times' more healthy than the world of 'the Christian sick house and dungeon atmosphere', he then proceeds to level two criticisms against Manu. The first is that it essentially involves genocide: genocide against 'the non-bred human being . . . the Chandala' (Untouchable) (TI vii 3). And the second is that, like 'every means hitherto employed' to 'improve' mankind, it involves the 'pious fraud', what Plato calls the 'noble lie' (TI vii 5).

Up to now, I have been emphasising that Nietzsche's vision of a healthy alternative to 'democratically' levelled modernity is a society marked, as in pre-modernity, by hierarchy, by strong class – or as he sometimes says 'caste' – differences. And I have emphasised Nietzsche's approval of the pyramidal society led by the philosopher-king of Plato's *Republic*. But Hindu society is also strongly hierarchical, is a caste system. And since Nietzsche criticises it for employing precisely what Plato sanctions, the 'noble lie', this has led Thomas Brobjer (1998) to argue that there are in fact *no* 'political ideals' in Nietzsche's philosophy, a position endorsed in Brian Leiter's already quoted claim that Nietzsche has an 'almost anarchistic' attitude to political life (Leiter (2002) p. 296). Since the Brobjer–Leiter position is (certainly with a broad and even, I think, with a narrow understanding of 'political') incompatible with the central, communitarian thesis of this book, I need to say why I reject their interpretation of the 'Law of Manu' discussion.

Though Hindu society is infinitely healthier than Christianity, the Law of Manu, Nietzsche observes, allows the Chandala to drink only at swamps, forbids them to wash, forbids them to help one another in childbirth. This, he says, 'outrages our feelings' (TI vii 3).

Coming from the firebrand 'immoralist', this last remark is perhaps more of a comment than a criticism. Nietzsche's real criticism takes the form of a surprising shift from India to the Roman Empire. The conception of Aryan 'pure blood' that underlies Manu's exclusion of the Chandala from communal life is, he says, 'the opposite of a harmless concept'. For it was in and through the (metaphorical) Chandala of the Roman Empire that Christianity grew to power. Christianity, 'sprung from Jewish roots and comprehensible only as a growth on this soil', was the Empire-destroying reaction of the outcasts and of the Roman Empire, was – as we know from *The Genealogy of Morals* – the 'Chandala revenge' (TI VII 4).

In discussing *Twilight*'s 'compassionate' communitarianism (pp. 163–6 above), I emphasised its rejection of slavery. *Everyone* in the healthy society, as Nietzsche conceives it, occupies a position that is accorded respect both by its occupier and by others. Services are performed without servility. We now understand the reason why a healthy society must be, though hierarchical, all-inclusive. For a society that excludes, a society that creates an underclass of *Untermenschen*, creates thereby the seeds of its own collapse. (The origins of this thought go back to *The Birth* where Nietzsche predicts the collapse of capitalism through the revolt of the industrial slaves (BT 23; see, too, HH II b 285–7 discussed on pp. 70–1 above).)

Notice that Nietzsche's demand for all-inclusiveness in the macrocosm, in society at large, parallels his views on the microcosm, the soul. For with regard to the latter, as we have seen (pp. 25, 162 above), he absolutely rejects the tyrannisation of the 'lower' appetites, the exterminationist, as it were genocidal, war waged against them by both Socrates and Christianity, requiring instead their incorporation, assimilation, into the soul by way of 'spiritualisation'. In both cases, I suggest, the identical motive is at work: ultimately, the excluded always react with tremendously destructive effect. In the end, tyranny and exclusion never pay.

Notice, too, that Nietzsche's anti-anti-Semitism is not some relatively superficial reaction to the stupid vulgarity of people like his brother-in-law but is rooted in the heart of his communitarian thinking. As the Romans destroyed themselves by treating Jews and slaves as *Untermenschen*, so we, if we indulge in the notion of 'Aryan . . . "pure blood"' – 'the opposite', to repeat, 'of a harmless concept' will do the same.

Nietzsche's critique of Manu's treatment of the Chandala is, then, a criticism made not from the point of view of someone who has no views on the proper order of society. It is, on the contrary, a criticism made from the point of view of a 'compassionate' communitarian.

So far as the 'pious fraud' is concerned, what Nietzsche says is that, hitherto, none of the 'improvers' of mankind – Manu, Plato, Confucius, Jewish and Christian priests – have doubted their right to tell lies, so that the means 'of making man moral have always been thoroughly *immoral*' (TI VII 5). This amounts to the charge of hypocrisy against Christianity, since it, Nietzsche believes (somewhat dubiously), is committed to truthfulness as an unconditional virtue. But Nietzsche himself is not so committed, emphasising many times, as we have seen, that 'untruths' are a 'condition of life' (BGE 4), that myths and 'errors' often serve life better than truth. And neither is there any reason to suppose that he takes Manu to be committed to the unconditional value of truthfulness. So the noble lie discussion is not, on the face of things, a direct criticism of Manu.

None the less Nietzsche actually does, I think, object to the noble lie and intend its discussion as a criticism of Manu. The source of his objection, it seems to me, is the following. What a noble lie does, in one way or another, is to provide divine sanction for a particular morality (Moses and the burning bush, God appearing himself in the world in human form, and so on). By doing so it places that morality beyond criticism. In *On the Genealogy of Morals* Nietzsche says that a major purpose of his genealogical tracing of current morality to its human, all-too-human, origins is to debunk the notion that it has other-worldly origins and sanctions (GM Preface 3). This is important to Nietzsche, I think, because, as we have seen, it is essential to a strong society that its morality should, with the aid of the free spirit, be capable of flexibility, of modulating itself in the light of new circumstances. From this point of view, the last thing we need is religious fundamentalism.

There remains considerably more to be said about Nietzsche's objections to the 'noble lie'. I shall however reserve further discussion until the next chapter, since both Manu and its 'lie' come to the fore, once again, in *The Antichrist*.

DEATH AND THE DIONYSIAN

Topics, as I have observed, recede and advance as one moves from one text to the next. Two topics that come to the centre of Nietzsche's attention in the closing pages of *Twilight* are death and the Dionysian, pages in which Nietzsche affirms the essential identity of his final thoughts on the subjects with those first expressed in *The Birth*.

Philosophers, says Nietzsche, have always been obsessed with being. Becoming they hate. Their 'Egyptianism' makes them think they honour something when they eternalise it. 'Death, change, age as well as procreation are for them objections – refutations even' (TI III 1). So what philosophers do is to relegate all forms of becoming to the realm of (mere) 'appearance'. Behind or beyond this realm they postulate a 'true world' (TI IV) which is simply the 'contradiction' of the apparent world

(TI III 6). To it, that is to say, all forms of becoming are foreign. It is the world of being, a world of absolute permanence and unity, a world, in a word, of absolute 'substance'. The conceptual foundation of this world is the projection of the ego. Starting with the idea of there being an ego behind every deed, philosophers project this 'ego-substance' onto everything. In particular, they project the God of Christian 'monototheism' and the absolute ego, the immortal soul. Turning from metaphysics to physics, Nietzsche remarks that the material atom is similarly a permanentising projection of the ego (TI III 5).

The interesting question is why philosophers have 'always' done this, have always been metaphysical Platonists. Grammar, Nietzsche observes, is the seduction. It encourages us to think that behind every predicate lurks a subject (though it is not actually so clear why it should seduce us into thinking that one and the same subject lies behind every predicate), which leads Nietzsche to say that 'we are not yet rid of God because we still believe in grammar' (TI III 5).

The question, though, is *why* philosophers still 'believe in grammar'. It is, after all, not compulsory. Heraclitus, for one, did not. Whereas other philosophers rejected the senses because they showed no absolute 'duration' (TI III 5) Heraclitus rejected them for precisely the opposite reason – that they showed at least relative duration, permanence, substance. Though this was unjust, a 'high reverence' is none the less due to Heraclitus for his denial of absolute being, his insistence that *ultimate* reality is becoming (TI III 2). The question arises, therefore, as to what distinguishing characteristic Heraclitus possessed that Plato and the Christians did not.

Great philosophy, Nietzsche observes, is always autobiography (BGE 6). One should ask not what is said but who is speaking. The Platonists he calls 'brainsick . . . morbid cobweb-spinners' (TI III 4). (In the *Phaedo* Socrates says that philosophy is a long 'preparation for death'.) This places death in the centre of the picture. The reason philosophers (and others) insist on the true world of absolute permanence is to overcome fear of death. (Recall Schopenhauer's claim that fear of death is the most powerful impetus to religion; that people would readily give up gods if they turned out to be incompatible with personal immortality.) So Nietzsche's interesting extension of this thesis is that even scientific atomism is ultimately the product of a neurotic compulsion to project permanence onto becoming, a compulsion which is ultimately the product of fear of death. So what makes Heraclitus deserving of special 'reverence' – as philosopher but much more as man and 'educator' – is that he has overcome fear of death.

The important question, however, is the question of *how* he did this. Nietzsche says that a 'true world' is 'absolutely indemonstrable' (TI III 6). 'Perspectivism' – the view that our knowledge is always mediated by a conceptual 'horizon', a 'corner' we can never get around – of course commits him to there being 'other' worlds, a point we saw him acknowledging in 'Our new infinite' (GS 374; see pp. 105–6 above). But since, as we saw, these are totally unknown, there is no reason to attribute to any of them fear-of-death-calming properties. So what was it Heraclitus did – what are we to do – about fear of death? This question is, of course, a particularly pressing one for Nietzsche. For since, to repeat, ecstatic, unconditional love of life is his highest desiderata, and since death is inseparable from life, his highest desiderata cannot be achieved until we have overcome fear of death.

Nietzsche remarks that life-denigrating Christian morality is a 'blasphemy of life' (TI V 5). This indicates that Nietzsche's attitude to 'life' is a religious one. As many others have observed, Nietzsche subscribes to a 'religion of life', a religion which, as we shall see, regards the object of its reverence as good, as, indeed, perfect.

He is, however, clear that the proposition that life *merits* such reverence can never be established. The value of life, he says, cannot be estimated. It cannot be estimated by the living because they are 'a party to the dispute'. (There is no horizon-free knowledge, no 'immaculate perception' as *Zarathustra* called it, and all our horizons, Nietzsche believes, are determined by our needs, desires and emotions.) And not by the dead 'for another reason' (TI II 2). One would have to be situated outside life – and not be dead – to be justified in making such a judgment (TI V 5).

Yet judgments concerning life's value are extremely valuable, valuable as 'symptoms', as 'semiotics' (TI VII 1). That a philosopher values life negatively is an 'objection' to *him* (TI II 2), a sign of spiritual sickness. We 'immoralists', however, continues Nietzsche (we who have freed our natural *joie de vivre* from the depressive effects of Christianity), 'open our hearts to every kind of understanding, comprehension, *approval*'. 'We have come more and more', he continues, 'to appreciate the economy which needs and knows how to use . . . [how to] derive advantage' from even the most 'repellent'. We even approve of the priests since they have given rise to – us (TI V 6). In other words, Nietzsche claims, those who reach his own level of spiritual development, of spiritual health, love life without qualification, *unconditionally*.

Nietzsche says – thinking of Christianity in the first instance, but the point is generalisable – that though one is wont to attribute one's 'feeling of plenitude and strength' (being on top of things) to one's faith in God, it is actually the other way round. One's sense of the divine is a projection of one's feeling of plenitude and strength (TI v 6). So a pantheistic sense of the 'economy' of things as perfect, as an object of unconditional love, is an expression of spiritual health.

The reason, however, that a sense of the world as divine can never constitute knowledge – that it is, in Nietzsche's terminology, a 'faith' – is that, as finite beings, *we* can never know that Auschwitz, for instance, will find a necessary place in the economy of the whole. This means that we can never *know* that it will be justified in the way in which the priests are justified by their having given rise to 'immoralists'. This is the point Nietzsche is making in saying that only from a position outside life could one know its value; only from such a God's-eye point of view could one grasp the whole. (Note that this is not only because, as finite beings, we can never grasp the *temporal* totality of things. On account of perspectivism it is also the case that we can never grasp what we might call the 'disclosive' totality of things – the 'new infinity' of all those aspects of reality which lie beyond our 'horizon'.)

So supreme health expresses itself in a supreme faith: the faith that *The Gay Science* calls *amor fati* (GS 276) – love of what is 'necessary', that is to say, of everything that has happened up to now. In other words, Goethe's

Joyful and trusting fatalism . . . [his] *faith* [Nietzsche's emphasis] that only what is separate and individual may be rejected, that in the totality everything is redeemed and affirmed . . . Such a faith is the highest of all possible faiths; I have baptised it with the name *Dionysus*. (TI ix 49)

But what has such a pantheistic theodicy got to do with overcoming fear of death? What, indeed, has it got to do with the Dionysian which, in *The Birth*, as we saw (pp. 20–4 above), had that as its essential function?

Nietzsche says – expanding, as it were, on 'Goethe's faith' – that 'the fatality of man's nature', the fact that 'he cannot be disentangled from all that has and will be', means that one belongs to, that one *is*, the whole, a whole that is of course eternal. There exists '*nothing*', we need to realise, '*apart from the whole*' (TI vi 8). Once one overcomes the illusion that one's everyday self, one's ego, is more than an incident in the interwoven totality of things (an illusion fostered by the illusion of 'free will'), once one overcomes the painful hubris of thinking that, ontologically, the ego counts for something, then one sees that one just *is* the totality and hence that death is of no concern. If one accepts the Christian package of the ego/soul as ontologically ultimate, as possessing a free will in the sense of being itself a 'first cause', and as subject to judgment, then fear of death can only be overcome by postulating the eternality (and virtue) of that ego. But since there is no reason at all to believe in the package, the ego had better not be ontologically ultimate.

Notice that in *Twilight* Dionysus has become, as he was not in *The Birth*, a *philosopher* – 'Ariadne's philosophical lover' (TI IX 19; see too BGE 295). The philosopher is of course Nietzsche himself: after his breakdown he began to style himself as Dionysus and his secret love, Cosima Wagner, as Ariadne. But the philosopher is also, I believe, Heraclitus. The special 'reverence' for Heraclitus the man is due to the fact that he saw that there is nothing permanent, save the totality of things itself, and faced death – and was therefore able to love life – because he realised his own identity with *that* permanence.

But how are *we*, at least some of us, to enter this Dionysian state? Nietzsche claims that he was the first to understand the 'wonderful phenomenon' of the Dionysian as fundamental to the Hellenic instinct. Only in the Dionysian mysteries, he says, did the Greeks express their fundamental 'will to life'. For in such mysteries

The Hellene guarantee[d] himself . . . *eternal* life, the eternal recurrence of life; the future promised and consecrated in the past; the triumphant Yes to life beyond death and change; *true* life as collective continuation of life through procreation . . . This is why the sexual symbol was so important to the Greeks [and, one might add, to the world of Manu]. It was the symbol of a world that was experienced religiously. (TI X 5)

This, however, just repeats the foregoing description of the death-conquering character of the Dionysian state. How, to repeat our question, did the Greeks *enter* this state?

The key, says Nietzsche, is the 'psychology of the orgy' (TI X 5), in other words 'intoxication (*Rausch*)' (TI IX 10). This, he continues, was his 'bridge' to the understanding of the tragic effect, an effect which Aristotle, in particular, had misunderstood. *Not* catharsis, but rather 'the will to life rejoicing in its own inexhaustibility through the *sacrifice* of its highest types . . . the eternal joy in becoming'. And here Nietzsche says – the concluding words of the whole book – ;

I again return to the place from which I set out – *The Birth of Tragedy* was my first revaluation of all values: with that I again plant myself in the soil out of which I draw all that I will and *can* – I the last disciple of the philosopher Dionysus – [i.e.] I the teacher of the eternal recurrence. (TI x 5)

The eternal recurrence, the ability, that is to say, to will the eternal return of one's life and the world *down to the very last detail* (GS 341), is the ultimate test of one's Dionysianism, of one's Dionysian *faith* in the perfection of the whole.[12] It is the ultimate test of one's faith in there being an 'economy' to the whole according to which everything 'terrible and questionable' in the past and present will find its 'redemption' in the future, an economy which will turn every 'desert' into 'bountiful farmland' (GS 370).

I have identified two discussions in *Twilight* relevant to our central concerns. First, the discussion of the nature of a healthy alternative to our present, sick society, the role of 'the gods' in such a healthy society and of (in the language of *The Birth*) the 'Apollonian' art that uncovers such gods and allows them to shine. Second, the discussion of death and the role of the Dionysian (and implicitly of Dionysian art) in enabling one to love life without that love being spoilt by fear of death. While the first discussion concerns the communal, the second might seem to be addressed only to individuals. As far as *Twilight* goes, that is, these two themes might seem to be independent of each other. When we turn to *The Antichrist*, however, written almost concurrently, we shall see that this appearance is misleading.

---

12 Notice how completely irrelevant to the central role of the eternal recurrence in Nietzsche's thinking is the question of whether or not it is intended as a 'cosmological' truth.

CHAPTER II

The Antichrist

The Antichrist was completed in September 1888, just three months before Nietzsche's mental collapse on 3 January 1890. It is full of vitriolic attacks on Christianity, most of which I shall ignore. But it is also highly informative as to his positive alternative, his views on the healthy society and the place of religion in it. That *The Antichrist's* ultimate purpose is constructive rather than destructive ought to come as no surprise since in the *Genealogy* Nietzsche has informed us that the 'Antichrist' is not just the 'conqueror of God' but represents also 'the great health', that is to say, the 'redemption of . . . reality' (GM II 24).

HEALTHY VERSUS UNHEALTHY GODS

'A people', says Nietzsche

which still believes in itself [i.e. possesses a unifying ethos in which to believe] still also has its own god. In him it venerates the conditions through which it has prospered, [i.e. as we know from *Zarathustra's* 'Thousand-and-one goals'] its virtues – it projects its joy in itself, its feeling of power, onto a being whom one can thank for them. He who is rich wants to bestow; a proud people needs a god in order to *sacrifice* . . . Within the bounds of such presuppositions religion is a form of gratitude. One is grateful for oneself: for that one needs a god. – Such a god must be able to be both useful and harmful, both friend and foe. (A 16)

Clearly Nietzsche is talking, here, about what the *Genealogy* called a 'noble' religion, the religion of a healthy people, paradigmatically the Greeks (see pp. 152–5 above). He is speaking of the religion of a people who 'repay with interest their founders, their ancestors (heroes and gods) with all the attributes which, in the meantime, had become manifest in themselves, the *noble* attributes' (GM II 19).[1]

---

1 As we are about to see, Nietzsche has in mind, in this passage, the God of the Old Testament. An indistinctness in his assimilation of ancient Judaism to Greek religion, however, is caused by the

There is a slight puzzle, here, as to why the god has to be capable of being both friend and foe. The answer is that 'one would not understand' a god 'who knew nothing of anger, revengefulness, envy, mockery, cunning, acts of violence'. One needs a natural god as opposed to the '*anti-natural*' god of Christianity (A 16). This is just the point, first expressed in *The Birth*, that a *non*-human role model is an *anti*-human role model since the effect of such a figure is depressing rather than inspiring: the point that a genuinely inspiring model with whom we can identify must be human, indeed all-too-human (see pp. 65–6 above).

Section 25 reveals that it is primarily the Jews Nietzsche is thinking about in the above passage, that he is placing ancient Judaism in the same 'noble' category as the Olympian religion:

Originally, above all in the period of the Kingdom, Israel stood in a *correct*, that is to say, natural relationship to all things. Their Yaweh was the expression of their consciousness of power, of their delight in themselves, their hopes of themselves: in him they anticipated victory and salvation, with him they trusted that nature would provide what the people needed – above all rain . . . These two aspects of a people's[2] self-affirmation find expression in festival worship: it is grateful for the great destiny which has raised it on high, it is grateful towards the year's seasons and all its good fortune with livestock and husbandry. (A 25)

With 'the Exile', however, this original, healthy, 'correct' relationship to 'all things' – to earth, sky, gods and mortals[3] – disappeared. The world became a place of misery which the priests interpreted as 'punishment' for 'sin'.[4]

---

difference between polytheism and monotheism. According to Nietzsche's 'stratification of the virtues' thesis, as we have seen, a healthy community has *many*, station-relative virtues by no means all of which can be instantiated by the same person (see p. 117 above). So really, a healthy community has to have *many* role models and cannot venerate all its virtues in a single God. If Nietzsche had worked out this passage more carefully, I think he might have said that a monotheistic people give thanks to their (capital 'G') God *for the existence of their (lower case 'g') gods and heroes*, for 'the famous men and the fathers that begat us'.

2 '*Volk*', not '*Nation*'. Hollingdale's 'nation' is less than ideal.

3 The phrase is of course Heidegger's. I use it here, however, because Nietzsche at this point seems to me to come close to the Heidegger/Hölderlin conception of 'the festival' as the 'wedding feast' of earth, sky, gods and mortals. See Young (2002) chapter 3.

4 In Jewish history, 'the Exile' refers to the deportation of a large segment of the Jewish upper class to Babylon, the capital of the Chaldean empire, following the capture of Jerusalem by Nebuchadnezzar in 597 BC. Nietzsche's view of the traumatic significance of the event is supported by historians. Richard Hooker comments that 'the Jews in Babylon creatively remade themselves and their world view. In particular they blamed the disaster of the Exile on their own impurity. They had betrayed Yahweh and allowed the Mosaic laws and cultic practices to become corrupt; the Babylonian Exile was proof of Yahweh's displeasure' (http://www.jewishvirtuallibrary.org.jsource/Judaism/Exilic.html).

In a cynical attempt to increase their power,[5] they invented 'the *lie* of a "moral world order"' and preached that God forgives those who repent, that is, submit to priestly authority. This provided the fertile soil out of which, with St Paul as the chief gardener, Christianity grew (A 26–7). (This is a repetition of the firemen-lighting-their-own-fires critique of the priesthood – see p. 67 above.)

Nietzsche ends the discussion of healthy religions by complaining that the 'stronger races of Northern Europe have not used their "god-creating" powers' to create an alternative to the Christian God. 'Almost two millennia and not a single new god!' he laments (A 19). His conclusion is that Europe is still sick. But what is also clear from the discussion is that a god, not of self-vilification but of self-celebration, a 'noble' religion, is viewed as essential to a healthy society. One might even be tempted to sum up his discussion of sick and healthy gods with Heidegger's famous slogan that 'only a god can save us'.

THE LAW OF MANU AGAIN

The argument I have been advancing throughout this book is that the heart of Nietzsche's philosophy is his response to the 'nihilism' of modernity, his view of what it is that would reconstitute us as a healthy society. And that view, I have suggested, is part of the conservative anti-modernism that was widespread among German thinkers in the late nineteenth and early twentieth centuries. Nietzsche's vision of a healthy society, that is, is a vision of a hierarchically organised community in which everyone knows and takes pride in their station within it, a society created, preserved and unified by an ethos-embodying communal religion. What I have been suggesting, therefore, is that the heart of Nietzsche's philosophy is, in a broad sense, a *political* vision, a vision, albeit relatively abstract, of the shape and structure of the healthy *polis*.

As mentioned in the previous chapter, however, this reading has recently been challenged by Thomas Brobjer (1998), who has received support from Brian Leiter ((2002) pp. 292–7). As the title of his article puts it, Brobjer wishes to argue for the (apparently total) 'Absence of Political Ideals in Nietzsche's Writings'.

---

5 Here, I think, we come to the heart of Nietzsche's consistently virulent (and given that his own father was a priest, personally problematic) anti-clericalism: priests (of all denominations) he sees as exploiters, and therefore increasers, of human misery.

The issue, as we saw, turns on Nietzsche's discussions of the Law of Manu in *Twilight*, but even more centrally in the closing pages of *The Antichrist*. I shall first give my reading of the passage and then turn to considering the Brobjer–Leiter objections.

The context of the discussion of Manu is again provided by a more general discussion of the warrantability or otherwise of the 'holy lie'. Ultimately, says, Nietzsche, what matters

is to what *end* a lie is told. That 'holy' ends are lacking in Christianity is *my* objection to its means. Only *bad* ends: the poisoning, slandering, denying of life, contempt for the body. . . It is with the opposite feeling that I read the Law-book of *Manu*, an incomparably spiritual and superior work such that to *name* it in the same breath as the Bible would be a sin against the spirit. (A 56)

Nietzsche offers Manu as, in at least two ways, an 'antithesis' to Christianity. First, whereas in Christianity it is the priests who rule, in Manu (or so Nietzsche represents the matter) it is 'the *noble* orders, the philosophers and the warriors who keep the *mob* under control'. And secondly, whereas Christianity despises the body and, in particular, sex, Nietzsche says he 'knows of no book [certainly not his own!] in which so many tender and kind remarks are addressed to women' (*ibid.*).

Nietzsche goes on to praise the empirical foundations of Manu. It does what every good lawbook does: it 'summarizes the experience, policy, and experimental morality of long centuries, it settles accounts, it creates nothing new', constitutes, that is, 'a *truth* slowly and expensively acquired'. 'At a certain point in the evolution of a people', he continues,

the most enlightened, that is to say the most reflective and far-sighted class declares the experience in accordance with which the people is to live – that it *can* live – to be fixed and settled. Their objective is to bring home the richest and completest harvest from the ages of experimentation and *bad* experience. What, consequently, is to be prevented above all is the continuation of experimenting, the perpetuation *ad infinitum* of the fluid condition of values, tests, choices, criticizing of values. (A 57)

For three reasons, this is an important passage. First, it seems to confirm Nietzsche's commitment to the 'philosopher-king', the idea introduced in *Beyond Good and Evil* that we must hope for (in Nietzsche's broad, Napoleon-including, sense of the term) the 'philosophers of the future' who will be, in one way or another, the leaders of society (see pp. 129–32 above).

Second, it serves to confirm the theory of cultural development I have been attributing to Nietzsche and to bring out its almost Popperian coloration. The 'random mutations', as I have been calling them, the 'philosophers of the future' in the sense of the philosophers who *look towards* the future (see pp. 129–32 above), are the 'experiments', many of whom come to a bad end as their experiment is 'falsified' at the tribunal of experience; fails, that is, to promote the health and success of the community. The growth of a culture, as we saw, entails many 'martyrs' (see p. 156 above). And it is the 'philosophers of the future', in the sense of the philosophers who *inhabit* the future, who bring the age of experimentation to an end.

The third reason the passage is important is that it serves to deepen our understanding of Nietzsche's Heracliteanism. In a famous *Nachlass* note Nietzsche says that 'To impose upon becoming the character of being – that is the supreme will to power' (WP 617). According to Nietzsche's Heracliteanism, being is, strictly speaking, an 'illusion' (WP 708) since change, eternal flux, is the metaphysical condition of reality. (This, to repeat, is the reason the 'superman' is only a *façon de parler*. As with all life there is no terminus to human life, no 'end of history'.) None the less, becoming can be given the '*character*' of being. And this moment when a people 'become[s] perfect' (A 57) is the highest moment human beings can achieve.

Perfection is a very important notion for Nietzsche. In the *Genealogy* he prays for a 'glimpse . . . just one glimpse of something perfect, completely finished, happy powerful, triumphant' (GM I 12). In *Beyond Good and Evil* he complains that modernity's craving for novelty 'biases' it against

that perfected and newly ripened aspect of every art and culture, the genuinely noble element in works and people, their moment of smooth seas and halcyon self-sufficiency, the gold and the coldness seen in all things that have perfected themselves. (BGE 224)

Historically, Nietzsche believes, there have been several 'glimpses' of such high and perfect moments, several glimpses of 'transfigurations of human life as they light up every now and then, those moments and marvels when a great force stands voluntarily still in front of the boundless and limitless' (*ibid.*): fourth-century Athens, the Italian Renaissance, and – the briefest of glimpses – Napoleon. And the meaning-giving goal of our efforts, he believes, must be to aim at another such effort.

The metaphysical image underlying Nietzsche's Heracliteanism is, it seems to me, that of a wave. The wave gathers and, at its peak, seems to

attain a moment of stasis. The appearance is deceptive, of course –
droplets of water are already falling away from the crest – but (as any
surfer knows) the supreme moment is the moment of seeming stasis. This
is what Nietzsche venerates in *The Gay Science*: 'the desire for fixing, for
immortalising, for *being*' that springs from 'gratitude and love' and which
one also finds in 'the [Apollonian] art of apotheosis', the art of Rubens,
Hafis or Goethe (GS 370).

It is at this point in the discussion of Manu that we arrive at the 'holy
lie'. The enlightened leaders realise that to preserve the moment of stasis,
to endow becoming with the character of being, the law must be given
absolute authority. And so it is asserted that, far from being the product of
years of experimentation, the law was given by God, whole and complete,
to the ancestor who lived it (A 57).

That which is authorised by the holy lie is 'the order of castes'. But at this
point Nietzsche makes what could be a criticism of Manu. The order of
castes, he says,

Is only the sanctioning of a *natural order*, a natural law of the first rank over
which no arbitrary caprice, no 'modern idea' [such as feminism or socialism] has
any power. In every healthy society, there can be distinguished three types of
man of divergent physiological tendency which mutually condition one another
and each of which possesses its own hygiene, its own realm of work, its own sort
of mastery and feeling of perfection. Nature, not Manu, separates from one
another the predominantly spiritual type, the predominantly muscular and
temperamental type, and the third type distinguished neither in the one nor the
other, the mediocre type – the last the great majority, the first the select few
(*Auswahl*). (A 57; compare KSA 14 [221] and BGE 61–2)

What is odd about this passage is that while Nietzsche speaks of three
castes Manu actually has four: in descending order of purity, the Brah-
mins (priests), Kshatriyas (warriors) and Vaishyas (merchants), and finally
the most numerous caste, the Shundras (peasants and artisans). Below
them are the Untouchables or Chandala who are considered too polluted
to be accorded any place at all within the caste system.

The reason Nietzsche ignores the fourfold structure of the Indian caste
system is that what is at the front of his mind is no longer Manu but
rather Plato's *Republic* in which there are just three classes, cemented
in place by the 'noble lie' of the gold, silver and bronze people (section
414b–415d). Nietzsche even matches up his 'natural' hierarchy of classes
quite specifically with Plato's. Every high culture, he says, is a broad-based
pyramid. At the bottom are the great majority, Plato's 'craftsmen' or as

Nietzsche puts it 'the entire compass of *professional* activity'. Above them are the – Nietzsche uses exactly Plato's word – 'guardians', the keepers of order and security and the executive. And at the top, in a position of leadership, are 'the most spiritual human beings'.

So what we now have, in fact, is a discussion of Plato's *Republic* whose social order Nietzsche appears to endorse in its general form. And the reason appears to be that Plato's scheme is a formalisation of his own validation of the pre-modern, hierarchical society which, he believes, maximised *everyone's* well-being, even those belonging to the lowest class: 'to be a cog . . . is a natural vocation; it is not society, it is the *happiness* of which the great majority are alone capable, which makes intelligent machines of them'. And Nietzsche adds (following his 'educator', Schopenhauer[6]) that what he hates most is 'the socialist rabble, the Chandala apostles who undermine the worker's instinct, his pleasure, his feeling of contentment with his little state of being, who make him envious' (A 57).

One interesting divergence from Plato, however, appears in Nietzsche's account of the ruling caste. While both he and Plato agree that 'only the most spiritual human beings' are permitted to rule, Plato defines this in terms of knowledge of the 'Forms'. Nietzsche on the other hand defines spiritual elevation in terms of being able to affirm that '*The world is perfect*'. In such an affirmation, he says,

speaks the instinct of the most spiritual, the affirmative instinct . . . 'imperfection, everything beneath us, distance between man and man, the pathos of this distance, the Chandala themselves, pertain to this perfection'. The most spiritual human beings, as the *strongest*, find their happiness where others would find their destruction. (A 57)

In Plato, knowledge of the Forms is necessary to the ruler because, the highest Form being the good, it is knowledge of the good. Nietzsche too, I think, has the good in view because he says that 'only the most spiritual human beings are permitted beauty, beautiful things; only in their case is benevolence not a weakness. *Pulcrum est paucorum hominum*: the good is a privilege' (*ibid.*).

If one does not believe in democracy, if one believes, to call a spade a spade, in dictatorship, the question arises as to how to ensure it is a *benevolent* dictatorship. Plato's answer is essentially mystical: knowing the Forms will somehow make you good. Nietzsche, on the other hand,

---

6 Schopenhauer's will left money to the widows of soldiers who died putting down the workers' uprising of 1848.

believes that what is needed is supreme health.[7] And such health is defined as being able to affirm that 'The world is perfect.'

In many earlier works Nietzsche has argued that Christian displays of benevolence or compassion are fake: not, in fact, benevolence at all but exercises in 'egoism'. Upon examination they turn out to be, for example, techniques of humiliation, of increasing dependence or of increasing the sense of one's own superiority. In the hands of the supremely healthy, on the other hand, benevolence and compassion are *genuine* displays of these virtues. 'He who is rich [in health] wants to bestow' (A 16), writes Nietzsche. He is full of what Zarathustra calls the 'gift-giving virtue'. Whereas 'cats and wolves . . . the all-too-poor, have a hungry selfishness that always wants to steal, . . . [a] sick selfishness', the healthy possess 'the highest virtue', the virtue of 'bestowing love' (Z 1 22).[8] It is, that is to say, in the nature of good fortune that one wants others to share in it.

So, for example, the healthy leader 'handles the mediocre more gently than he does himself or his equals' (A 57). That they should be oppressed or unhappy would, considered in isolation, be a blot on his horizon. But that their unhappiness creates an occasion for his love to 'overflow' is part of the world's perfection. Notice that when *The Gay Science* talks of the supremely healthy type desiring and being confident of his ability to turn any 'desert' into 'bountiful farmland' (GS 370) this is capable of a quite *literal* reading, an affirmation of the value of social welfare. (Recall that in *Human, All-too-Human* Nietzsche appeared to favour something resembling a modern Scandinavian state (see pp. 70–1 above).)

So the rulers of a healthy society are to be able to affirm that 'The world is perfect.' But this wanting *nothing* to be different from the way it is is just what willing the eternal recurrence – i.e. '*amor fati*', 'my formula for greatness . . . that one wants nothing to be other than it is (EH 11 10) – comes to.

This, I think, shows something important about the way in which Nietzsche's thinking about eternal recurrence fits into his thinking about

---

7 Or in other language, 'happiness': 'a well-constituted human being, a "happy one", *must* perform certain actions and instinctively shrinks from other actions . . . In a formula: his virtue is the *consequence* of happiness' and not the other way round as moralists try to persuade us (TI VI 1).

8 *Zarathustra* represents the difference between takers and givers as a difference between sick and healthy 'selfishness'. This seems to me a confusion which, as already remarked, runs through nearly all of Nietzsche's works. He seems to assume that anyone who does what he *wants* to is *a fortiori* being 'selfish'. In fact, of course, what makes an action selfish or not is not the fact that one wants to do it, but rather whether or not what one wants involves harming the interests of others in pursuit of one's own.

community. It is not *everyone* who has to be able to will the eternal recurrence; not everyone is criticisable for failing to be able to do so. Rather, it is required only of the highest spiritual types charged with governance. The 'mediocre' have different 'laws of spiritual hygiene' of their own. The reason is that since it is *sick* 'selfishness' that is the human cause of human misery, only the super-healthy can be trusted with power. So ultimately, the test of willing the eternal recurrence is a test of fitness to lead. (Of course, to repeat the point that Nietzsche's target audience is confined to potential leaders, for all his proper readers, willing the eternal recurrence *is* an ideal, or an ideal, at least, for those of whom they are the forerunners.)

Manu, says Nietzsche, is a 'religious legislation the purpose of which is to "eternalise" a grand organisation of society, the supreme condition for the *prosperity* of life'. The 'grandest (*grossartigste*) form' of such an organisation so far achieved, he adds, was the Roman Empire. This 'most admirable of all artworks in the grand style' was fit to last for millennia. But (Nietzsche agrees with Gibbon) it was destroyed by its 'vampire', Christianity, by the Chandala revenge, by Paul's 'Chandala hatred against Rome' (A 58). Thus 'the whole labour of the ancient world was in vain'. The Greeks and Romans had existed for nothing. Christianity robbed us of 'the harvest of the culture of the ancient world [as] it later robbed us of the culture of *Islam*' (A 60), and as Luther later robbed us of the golden age of modernity, the reborn classicism of the Renaissance (A 61).

This passage confirms several theses I have been advancing: the centrality of community to Nietzsche's thinking, his conviction that life can only 'prosper' within a healthy, hierarchically organised society (and of course state); the 'cosmopolitanism' theme – the desire for *global* community, a 'grand' politics aimed at an 'artwork' that is, like Rome, in the 'grand style'; Nietzsche's classicism, his desire for a future that will, as it were, simply *cancel* the Christian era and return us to an *authentic* European culture, a re-created classicism. And it also reveals the deepest ground of his hatred of Christianity – that it destroyed the world of antiquity.

THE NACHLASS

As observed, Thomas Brobjer argues that the Law of Manu discussion in *The Antichrist* does not express any 'political ideal'. Rather, he claims, the function of the discussion is simply to use it as a stick to beat

Christianity with,[9] 'to make the reader realise that even the laws of Manu . . . is [sic] higher and more humane than Christianity. Whereas Christianity destroys, the intention at least of the laws of Manu was to save and protect' (Brobjer (1998) pp. 312–13).

Brobjer points out that Manu cannot represent Nietzsche's ideal society since it is subject to a great deal of criticism in the *Nachlass*. These criticisms boil down to four central and interconnected points. First, that Manu is a priest-ridden society: it is more priestly than any other (KSA 13 14 [204]), even farmers and soldiers have to study theology for nine years (KSA 13 14 [203]), and Manu is *not* motivated by human well-being, does not genuinely seek to 'improve' mankind but is rather a cynical system of oppression used to enforce priestly power (KSA 13 15 [45]). Second, that Manu excludes the Chandala class (and so, as we saw in discussing *Twilight*, prepares the seeds of its own destruction) (KSA 13 14 [199], KSA 13 15 [44]). Third, that Manu is ascetic, anti-sensualist, the priest's exclusion of the Chandala representing his fear of sensuality (KSA 13 14 [199]). And fourth, that

the whole book rests on the holy lie . . . The most cold-blooded self-control has here been effective, the same sort of self-control which Plato had when he thought out his 'Republic' . . . The classical pattern of thought here is specifically *Aryan* . . . the *Aryan influence* has ruined the whole world. (KSA 13 15 [45])

By means of this lie (the tale of the transcendent god who gave the laws to the ancestor), 'the whole of life is cast in the perspective of the beyond so that it is understood as *rich in consequences* in the most horrible manner' (KSA 13 14 [216]). And in a related passage Nietzsche comments that Islam learnt from Christianity to use the 'beyond' as an 'organ of punishment' (KSA 13 14 [404]).

These remarks give a picture of Manu strikingly different from that presented in the published remarks in *The Antichrist*. What they confirm is that Nietzsche hates (a) priests, (b) exclusionary and oppressive (as *opposed to* hierarchical) social systems, (c) anti-sensuality and (d) 'holy lies'.[10] And the *Nachlass* remarks confirm that in his unpublished thoughts he finds all these objectionable features manifested in Manu.

---

9 Given that Nietzsche has so many sticks already one is inclined to wonder why he should need yet another – rather indirect – stick.

10 There are, I think, two points here. First, Nietzsche objects to *holy* lies, lies – this, I think is the force of '*holy* lie' and opposed to the less objectionable '*noble* lie' – that use the transcendent as an instrument of fear and punishment. But second, in his later writings, I think Nietzsche objects to

But does it follow from this that what appears in the published text is not an account of Nietzsche's conception of the outline of a healthy society? Here it seems to me that Brobjer makes far too big a leap.

The question to ask is why Nietzsche chose to suppress his private critique of Manu. And the answer, I think, is a very Nietzschean one. In the published text he has chosen to 'idealise' Manu (and Plato's Republic at the same time), to use his 'art' to 'transform into the perfect' (TI ix 8–9) by highlighting certain features and drawing a veil over others. In doing so he hopes to 'strengthen [and] . . . weaken certain valuations' (TI ix 24); that is, to point his audience of potential 'creators of the future' towards a certain kind of hierarchical society and away from the levelled society of 'democratic' modernity.

The most conspicuous aspect of this idealisation is the total disappearance of the priests from idealised Manu. Those who rule, in Nietzsche's representation, are not priests but, as we saw, 'the *noble* orders, the philosophers and the warriors', otherwise described as 'the most enlightened and far-sighted'. Furthermore, there is no mention in the published text of the exclusion of the Chandala – the blurring of the boundary between Manu and Plato's Republic serves to represent it as an all-inclusive social system. And finally, there is no mention of Manu's alleged anti-sensuality. On the contrary, the published text emphasises Manu's 'tender' dwelling on 'a woman's mouth' and a 'girl's breast' (A 56).

The only point at which a criticism in the *Nachlass* is allowed to appear in the published text concerns the content of the 'holy lie'. Nietzsche comments in the *Nachlass* that

The order of the castes rests on the observation that there are only three or four kinds of human being each determined and best developed for different kinds of activity . . . the order of the castes is merely a sanctioning of a natural division between different psychological types. (KSA 14 [221])

And as we have seen (p. 182 above), this comment appears almost unchanged in the published text.

As I read it, the comment amounts to a criticism because what it says is that the 'holy lie' is *unnecessary*. It is unnecessary because a society allowed to develop without ideology will *naturally* fall into a hierarchy of classes. Or rather it will fall into a 'rank ordering'.

'lies' as such. Lies, that is, are different from life-enhancing 'faiths', 'errors' and 'myths', all of which he is thoroughly in favour of. With respect to these, no one is trying to fool anyone. I shall return to this point in a moment.

Brobjer quotes from a draft of a letter to the first person to lecture on his philosophy, Georg Brandes: Nietzsche writes in December 1888 that '*If we win*, then we will have the world government in our hands – including world peace . . . We have overcome the absurd boundaries between race, nation, and class (*Stände*): there exists from now on only order of rank (*Rang*) between human beings, and in fact, a tremendously long ladder of rank' (Brobjer (1998) p. 313). This is interesting as one of the clearest expressions of Nietzsche's cosmopolitanism. But it is relevant to the current discussion on account of the distinction between 'class' and 'rank'. In this context, I take it, a 'class' is something established by birth and so does not necessarily correspond to the natural order of needs and abilities, whereas a 'rank' is a class that does – is, that is to say, the product of an authentic meritocracy.

So Nietzsche's overall conception of the healthy society is a hierarchy of classes where one's position in the hierarchy is determined by *natural* need and ability. The actuality of Manu does not satisfy this requirement – this, I suggest, is Nietzsche's criticism – because it ossifies the natural with a rigid legalism that become unnatural and oppressive by making class boundaries impermeable. But democratic modernity, the levelling induced by 'modern ideas' (A 57) such as socialism and feminism, is equally unnatural. If society were only allowed free experiment it would soon return to a *naturally* pyramidal society – and, Nietzsche would wish to add, to a *natural* division between the roles of men and those of women.[11]

I should like to conclude this chapter by returning to *Twilight's* observation that the 'holy lie' is a 'pious *fraud*' (TI VII 5; my emphasis). What motivates the use of this word, I think, is the fact that, whether he be Plato's philosopher-king, the codifier of Manu, or Dostoevsky's Grand Inquisitor, the lie does not fool the lie-*teller* for otherwise it would not be a 'lie'. Though it may have some benefits for the lied-to, the supposedly enlightened ones are left over in a position of cynical detachment. This means (a) that their own lives are meaningless, consigned to the 'disease' of post-modern 'scepticism' (BGE 208) and (b) that they have no genuine commitment to the social order that is based on the lie, in other words,

---

11 At the time of writing (January 2005), the president of Harvard University is reported as being in trouble for suggesting, as a hypothesis worth researching, the possibility that some major gender differences may not be, as twentieth-century feminists maintained, the product of culture, but might actually have some basis in biology. As a good 'liberal' parent, he is said to have added, he gave his baby daughter two toy trucks to play with, only to find that she immediately christened one 'mummy truck' and the other 'baby truck'.

that like, in Nietzsche's view, the 'priests' of all denominations, their rule is based on the lust for dominion for its own sake. But this makes them despotic rather than enlightened rulers, entirely devoid of the 'gift-giving virtue' essential to the proper leader.

A society based on what is perceived to be a *naturally* hierarchical order, on the other hand, has none of these implications. To a natural hierarchy the benevolent ruler can have a genuine commitment.

In sum, therefore, the fundamental mistake in the Brobjer–Leiter position is this. Correctly perceiving that Nietzsche objects to the hierarchical society based on the holy/noble lie, they wrongly conclude that Nietzsche has no axe to grind in favour of hierarchical societies as such. They are mistaken. He does.

CHAPTER 12

Ecce Homo

Since we have now reached the end of Nietzsche's path of thinking – *Ecce Homo*[1] is the final major work – let me attempt to sum up the issues that have been at stake throughout.

WHY NIETZSCHE IS NOT AN 'INDIVIDUALIST'

On the negative side, what I have been attacking is the 'individualist' reading of Nietzsche. What exactly is this reading?

There is, of course, what one might call society-friendly individualism. This is the position one might attribute to Freud, to the non-fraudulent Indian Guru, or, on a humbler level, to Joseph Pilates. Each in their own way offers a recipe for achieving at least an aspect of individual flourishing. What makes this kind of individualism unchallenging is that there is no hint of a conflict between the flourishing of one individual and that of others. Indeed nothing would please an 'improver of mankind' of this ilk more than that *everyone* should take up their form of meditation, yoga, diet or whatever.

The 'individualism' that has been so often attributed to Nietzsche – let us call it 'anti-social individualism' – however, is not of this innocuous variety. It differs from it in that individual flourishing is not taken to be compatible with the flourishing of society as a whole, but to be, on the contrary, incompatible with it. Specifically, Nietzsche is taken to hold that:

1. Only a very few, exceptional types are capable of any kind of significant flourishing, of living worthwhile lives.

---

1 'Behold the man'. As the title indicates, Nietzsche is concerned in the work to present himself – in 'idealised' form, of course – not just as a thinker, but as a *man*. Remembering that 'educators', role models, have to be rounded human beings and not just thinkers (p. 47 above), it is arguable that the George Circle were not too far from Nietzsche's aspirations when they mythologised him into a heroic role model himself (see further, p. 211 fn. 9 below).

2. The promotion of their flourishing is all that has intrinsic value and is the final end of human existence.

3. Their flourishing can only be accomplished at the cost of the well-being of the majority. It requires 'slavery in some sense'.

The view I have been defending, on the other hand, arrives at the following conclusions:

1. is false. Nietzsche believes in different levels of flourishing, believes in a 'stratification' not only of the virtues but also of well-being. Of course Nietzsche believes, too, that there are exceptional individuals and that, on account of their scarcity and indispensability to the development of society as a whole, they are of vastly greater value to the social whole than average human beings. And he also believes in a 'naturally' hierarchical, pyramidal, order to society. But to think that only those at the apex of the pyramid are capable of flourishing is precisely the kind of universalism about the good (in the sense of both virtue and well-being) against which Nietzsche protests on many occasions.

2. is false. Exceptional measures do indeed need to be taken to produce and promote the higher types, but that is not because their flourishing is, in itself, the intrinsic good. Rather, it is because either they are the 'random exceptions', the 'experiments', who promote the adaptability, hence the survival, and hence the flourishing of the community as a whole, or – in rare cases – they are the political (in at least a broad and sometimes a narrow sense) leaders and conservers of a community that has reached a state of perfection. Not the flourishing of the higher individual but the flourishing of a 'people' or 'culture' as a whole is Nietzsche's highest goal; the higher types (who may well, in the case of unsuccessful 'experiments', find themselves 'martyrs') are merely an essential means to this end.

3. is false. While higher types need exceptional privileges and while a healthy society retains privilege and relations of subordination, to occupy a subordinate position is by no means contrary to, indeed it is likely to be just what is required for, one's own kind of flourishing. Some people are destined by nature to be prima donnas, but most are destined to be, and to find their happiness in being, second violins.

So, it seems, a healthy society preserves an 'order of rank' that is in *everybody's* best interest. But what else do we know about it? According to the reading I have been presenting, it requires a shared community-creating ethos that is embodied in role-modelling gods who form the focal point of communal festivals of worship. The Middle Ages, of course, had such festivals but, according to Nietzsche, their gods were the unhealthy embodiments of an unhealthy ethos. What a healthy society requires is a *healthy* ethos embodied in *healthy* gods; gods who represent, not a non- and so anti-human ideal, but rather an idealisation of humanity itself, so that what the healthy society worships are its own potentialities for ('polytheistic') excellence. What we need, in short – this 'Wagnerian' conclusion, first arrived at in *The Birth* is, I have argued, maintained *throughout* Nietzsche's career – is a rebirth of something resembling the religion of the Greek temple and amphitheatre, something with the life- and humanity-affirming characteristics of Greek religion.

It seems to me reasonably clear that this is the view that receives its final affirmation in *Ecce Homo*. But before showing this to be the case let me attend to certain themes that might seem to go against the reading I have been presenting.

COUNTER-INDICATIONS

My business, says Nietzsche, is overthrowing, not erecting 'idols' (EH Preface 2). And in a similar vein he says that he/Zarathustra is no 'prophet', offers no 'faith'. Zarathustra, he reminds us, tells his pupils not to 'believe' him, that a teacher is badly rewarded by eternal pupils (EH Preface 4). Again in the same vein: 'there is nothing in me of the founder of a religion – religions are affairs of the rabble[2] . . . I do not want "believers"' (EH xiv 1).

These remarks might be taken to show that religion plays no role in Nietzsche's aspirations for the future. But of course, that Nietzsche does not see *himself* as the founder of a religion by no means shows that he does not want, one day, a new one to be founded. (To repeat his reproach: 'Almost two millennia and not a single new god!' (A 19).)

In terms of his categories of higher types Nietzsche generally casts himself in the role of a 'free spirit'. He is, he says, not a man but 'dynamite' (EH xiv 1). So he is a destructive force, a 'lion'. But is he a free spirit merely of the 'second rank' (see p. 96 above)? Is he *merely* destructive, or is he also creative?

Nietzsche's/Zarathustra's problem in answering this question is, as earlier observed, the problem of the 'creative writing' class: how do you teach *creation*? What Nietzsche wants to promote, that is, is 'free spirits of

---

2 This affirms, once again, the select nature of Nietzsche's target readership.

the first rank', in other words *creators* of new values[3] that will lead us out of the morass of modernity. But if you *teach* creation then, surely, *you* are the creator and the pupil merely your creature. The answer to this conundrum was first given in Kant's *Critique of Judgment* (section 46), in his account of the way in which great art is a model for future generations: it inspires imitation, he says, but since 'genius' cannot be 'reduced to a rule' it simultaneously baffles it. Nietzsche's way of combining inspiration with bafflement is to offer a very abstract sketch rather than a blueprint for the future, a few 'signposts' as he puts it (EH v 1).

Nietzsche is, *of course*, a free spirit of the first rank, but he deliberately leaves the creative side of his thinking vague and sketchy. That is why anything as concrete as 'founding a new religion' or enunciating a set of articles of faith to be subscribed to by his 'believers' would be completely counter-productive. (And futile, since Nietzsche, one would think, hardly had the kind of personal charisma necessary to becoming a guru.)

Nietzsche admits this deliberate formalism in his work. One day, he says, chairs will be set up for the interpretation of *Zarathustra* – a prospect he seems to view as not only satisfying but also necessary. He records that a contemporary critic, Karl Spitteler, called *Zarathustra* an 'advanced exercise in style' but requested that its author 'might later try to provide it with some content'. Nietzsche's reply is that 'no one can extract from . . . books more than he already knows' (EH iii 1), which I take to be the Kant-echoing point that while Nietzsche may 'signpost', it is up to the reader to create – in terms of his own historical situation, cultural context and horizon of experience – the precise destination.

A second theme in *Ecce Homo* that might be taken to tell against the reading I have been offering is Nietzsche's insistence on his 'anti-political' nature, his insistence that he is 'the last anti-political German' (EH 1 3). But all he means by this is that he is against 'petty' politics, the politics of European nationalism that had plagued the continent for at least a millennium. What Nietzsche is especially against is the politics of *Deutschland, Deutschland über alles* (TI viii 1): the aggressive, jingoistic, *Reichsdeutsch* politics of Bismarck's Germany – and, in particular, of Richard Wagner.[4] In opposition to such nationalism he calls himself, once again, 'a good European' (EH 1 3).

---

3 *Relatively* new values, that is. Whatever values are created they must, remember, be 'European' values. The creation Nietzsche seeks is creation *within* what he regards as the authentically European tradition (see p. 120 above).

4 When Nietzsche calls *The Birth* a 'politically indifferent work' (EH v 1) he means, I believe, to distinguish it from the petty, *Reichdeutsch* politics of the later Wagner.

Far, however, from representing apoliticality as his preferred alternative (being a 'good European' is itself, of course, a political stance), he says that what concerns him is 'grand (*grosse*) politics' (EH xɪv ɪ; see BGE 208 discussed on pp. 123–4 above). Grand politics is the 'war of spirits' ((EH xɪv ɪ) – something like Samuel Huntingdon's 'clash of civilizations', only, I think, not specifically with Islam (towards which Nietzsche is unexpectedly well disposed) but with other world-cultures in general.

Heidegger claims that 'poetry in politics is the highest and most authentic sense' (Heidegger (1977–) vol. 39 p. 214). Though he would prefer to use the word 'philosophy', Nietzsche, I believe, usually thinks along similar – essentially Platonic – lines. The quest for 'spiritual' dominion is the *essence* of politics. Get the 'spiritual' side of things right, develop a healthy culture, and the nuts and bolts of practical politics (which are not the concern of the philosopher[5]) will follow.

Of course Nietzsche's own war to the spiritual death with Christianity – his struggle for the redemption of the European 'spirit' – is an instance of 'grand', world-historical, politics (see, further, pp. 214–15 below). This observation makes it clear that Nietzsche's grand politics operates from the bottom up rather than from the top down. It is, as we have seen before, a matter of setting 'fish hooks' for those 'related to me', for potential free spirits (EH x ɪ), for 'bold venturers and adventurers . . . with cunning sails'[6] (EH ɪɪɪ 3).

Nietzsche never, he says, speaks to the masses (EH xɪv ɪ). In spite of its name, there is nothing of the Nuremberg Rally about grand politics. Zarathustra, let us recall, tried the Rally approach in the Prologue and found that it did not work. Rather, he speaks to exceptional individuals and hopes that, like a virus, the new word will gradually spread among those with spiritual influence, until, in time, it comes to infect the whole of society.[7]

---

5 In the 1930s, Heidegger thinks of a chain of command descending from 'poet' to philosophical 'thinker' (who interprets the great poet) to 'state-founder' (Heidegger (1977–) vol. 39 p. 144). The nuts and bolts of the construction of the state come in only at the third level. Nietzsche, I think, usually operates with a similarly fastidious conception of nuts and bolts political theory as existing beneath the concerns of philosophy.
6 Those who can set 'cunning sails' are skilled 'sailors' rather than enthusiastic amateurs. Not everyone – this seems to me Nietzsche's point – who would like to be a free spirit has the education and talent to become one.
7 The George Circle thought of themselves as an underground network of individuals devoted to the revival, through art, of a renewed spirituality, individuals with talent and influence vastly out of proportion to their numbers. Though some members disgraced themselves when the Nazis came to power, in this respect at least, they were true Nietzscheans. (See further, p. 211 below.)

THE RETURN OF DIONYSUS

I want now to look at the positive indications in *Ecce Homo* that the religious communitarianism I have argued to be at the heart of earlier works is preserved to the end of Nietzsche's career.

Various remarks in *Ecce Homo* have a strongly apocalyptic, world-historical tone. Section 8 of 'Why I am so wise', for example, speaks of Nietzsche/Zarathustra's need for solitude, necessary to prevent his being overcome by his 'greatest danger', disgust for the dirty, evil-smelling rabble of today. But he also speaks of a 'redemption' from disgust in the certainty that 'like the wind will I one day blow among them and with my spirit take away the breath of their spirit', which looks to anticipate not just a few 'clean' individuals but a 'clean' *society* in the future. The first two sections of the retrospective reflections on 'Daybreak' are even more apocalyptic. In *Daybreak*, Nietzsche says, he seeks 'a new dawn a whole world of new days, a great coming to himself on the part of man, a great noontide'. And in section 4 of the reflections on *The Birth* he speaks of the need for a 'higher breeding of humanity in order to bring about the 'Zarathustra event (*Ereignis*)'. All of these remarks possess a Hegelian grandeur which, I think, is difficult to reconcile with the idea that all Nietzsche seeks is the appearance once in a while of a few great individuals. In section 8 of 'Why I am destiny' he explicitly calls himself a 'world-historical event'. And of course, the whole conception of 'great politics', as we have just seen, is world-historical in scale.

But what will the 'great noontide' look like? I have referred already to Nietzsche's need to remain relatively abstract, but a 'signposting' cannot be a signposting without *some* informational content. What does *Ecce Homo* offer us?

Let us listen to section 4 of the reflections on *The Birth*. I hope, says Nietzsche,

For a Dionysian future of music . . . Let us suppose that my assasination (*Attentat*) of two millennia of anti-nature and the violation of man succeeds. Then that party of life which takes in hand as its sole aim the higher breeding of humanity together with the remorseless destruction of all degenerate and parasitic elements[8] will again make possible on earth that *superfluity of life* out of which the Dionysian condition

---

8 This is a worrying turn of phrase, but I think that by 'element' Nietzsche means, not individuals, but rather traits. As we have already seen, he sometimes displays an inclination to believe that there should be a strict 'promoter and preventer of marriages' which will result in the 'amputation' of 'negative' traits (HH 1 243; see p. 69 above). This is bad (though most of Nietzsche's contemporaries, and not just in Germany, thought along similar eugenic lines), but the passage should not, I believe, lead one to think of death camps.

must again proceed. I promise a *tragic age*: The supreme art in the affirmation of life, tragedy, will be reborn . . . A psychologist might add that what I in my youthful years heard in Wagnerian music had nothing at all to do with Wagner; that when I described Dionysian music I described *that* which *I* had heard – that I had instinctively to translate and transfigure into the latest idiom all I bore within me. The proof of this . . . is my essay 'Wagner at Bayreuth': in all the psychologically decisive passages I am the only person referred to – one may ruthlessly insert my name or the word 'Zarathustra' wherever the text gives the word Wagner . . . the 'Bayreuth ideal' had likewise transformed itself into something that those who know my Zarathustra will find no riddle: into the *great noontide* when the most select dedicate themselves to the greatest of all tasks – who knows? The vision of a festival I shall yet live to see . . . Everything in this essay is prophetic: the proximity of the return of the Greek spirit, the necessity for *counter Alexanders* to *retie* the Gordian knot of Greek culture after it had been untied . . . Listen to the world-historic accent with which the concept 'tragic disposition' is introduced: there are in this essay nothing but world-historic accents.

Here, unmistakably, at the end of Nietzsche's journey, are all the themes I have been emphasising throughout this book. That Nietzsche's ultimate concern is for community, for the flourishing of a 'people' in general rather than the flourishing, merely, of a few individuals, that what he wants is a revival of the great age of Greek culture, a culture whose greatness has at its heart the religious festival, and that consequently Nietzsche remains, all his life, committed to the Wagnerian *ideal* of the revival of society through the rebirth of Greek tragedy and so remained, in *that* sense, all his life a Wagnerian.

The end of Nietzsche's path of thinking is, in other words, in essential respects, the same as the beginning. Here, as there, the ideal is the existence of a healthy – 'Dionysian' – people and culture: a healthy *herd*, in Nietzsche's own language – note, once again, that herds, both literal and figurative, can be healthy as well as sick.

In the second section of the observations on *Human, All-too-Human* Nietzsche reflects on the first Bayreuth Festival. 'I recognised nothing', he says. Nothing remained of the cloudless days at Triebschen or of the original 'little band of *initiates* . . . who did not lack fingers for delicate things'. All that was there was a degenerate audience who wanted to forget themselves 'for five or six hours' (EH VI 3) on Wagner's 'hashish' (EH III 6). His complaint against Wagner, Nietzsche sums up, is that 'music has been deprived of its world-transfiguring, affirmative character, that it . . . no longer plays the flute of Dionysus' (EH XIII 1).

In *Human, All-too-Human*, the first book after his flight from Bayreuth, Nietzsche says, he laid an axe to the root of the 'metaphysical need'. He adds, as earlier noted, that he sent two copies of this anti-Schopenhauerian, anti-Wagnerian work to Wagner (EH vi 6). But to no avail, since Wagner – by now the composer of the text of the world-renouncing, quasi-Christian *Parsifal* – had become 'pious' (EH vi 5). Why, one wonders, did Nietzsche bother? The answer, as I observed, is surely that – naively – he hoped to show Wagner that with his 'pious', 'narcotic', transcendentalist, life-denying music he had precisely betrayed his own ideal, the life-affirmation of the Greek festival.

So, above all, Nietzsche's future society is going to be one in which values are revalued (EH ii 9), more exactly re-re-valued, given that Christianity was the 'first revaluation of values'. It is going to be one where Christian life-denial is replaced by the 'counter-ideal' (EH xi) of Dionysian life-affirmation. But what is the Dionysian? What are we to understand by *Ecce Homo*'s final sentence: '*Dionysus against the Crucified*' (EH xiv 9)?

One thing we are to call to mind is the *whole* of Greek art. In the reflections on *The Birth* Nietzsche claims that in the book he was the first to understand the 'Dionysian phenomenon' as 'the sole root of the whole of Hellenic art' (EH iv 1). This, to put it charitably, is a failure of memory. For in *The Birth* there are quite clearly *two* kinds of art with two different origins, the Apollonian art of 'dreams' and the Dionysian art of 'intoxication', which achieve a synthesis for the first time in Greek tragedy. This is why it comes as a shock when, in *Twilight*, Nietzsche proposed to conceive 'the antithetical concepts *Apollonian* and *Dionysian* which I introduced into aesthetics' *both* as 'forms of intoxication', one which animates 'above all the eye so that it acquires the power of vision', the other 'the entire emotional system' (TI ix 9). This brings the two forces closer than they had been in *The Birth* but still keeps them separate. So it is actually a new idea, introduced for the first time in *Ecce Homo*, to represent the Dionysian as having given birth to the whole of Greek art. Be that as it may, the result is that both Dionysian and Apollonian art will be of importance in the future society. (This means that the theme of the raising of ethos-embodying figures to the status of role models through the glamorising effect of Apollonian art, though not explicitly discussed in *Ecce Homo*, can be assumed to be implicitly present in Nietzsche's final views on the relation between 'art and Volk, myth and morality' (BT 23).)

Absent from much of Nietzsche's work before the final year, Dionysus occupies centre-stage in *Ecce Homo* as he had done at the end of *Twilight*. In the foreword Nietzsche again introduces himself as 'the disciple of the philosopher Dionysus'. Later on he says that the Dionysian is his 'innermost experience' – the, as Schopenhauer would put it, 'hidden illuminism' (PP II pp. 9–11) of which Nietzsche's entire philosophy is an articulation.

Nietzsche recalls that in *The Birth* he, for the first time, solved the problem of the tragic effect, discovered – here he quotes *Twilight* (see p. 175 above) – 'the bridge to the psychology of the *tragic* poet'.

Since, as we first saw in chapter 2's discussion of *The Birth*, one of the two essential features of the Dionysian state is that it provides a solution to the 'riddle' of death, Nietzsche, after some hesitation along the way concerning his first account of the tragic effect (see p. 103 above), here once again affirms *The Birth*'s solution as his final position. One over-comes fear of death through *transcendence*; not *à la* Schopenhauer, transcendence to an extra-mundane, noumenal thing in itself, but rather transcendence of the everyday ego to identification with the totality of life. Nietzsche refers to this transcendence in the discussion of *Zarathustra*, where he says that in the Dionysian state out of which *Zarathustra* is written (this is why he regards it as his most 'inspired' work) one becomes 'immortal'. And in the same discussion he refers to the state as 'an ecstasy [*ex-stasis*] . . . a complete being outside of oneself . . . a *wide-spanning* rhythm . . . a feeling of . . . divinity' (EH IX 3).

In section 6 of the same discussion he experiences himself as perform-ing 'the supreme creative deed', in other words as giving birth to – the world. His own creation of *Zarathustra* is, that is, a recapitulation, in microcosm, of *The Birth*'s artist-child who gives birth to the world. And in the same section he experiences himself as the world-soul, 'the soul that loves itself most and in which all things have their ebb and flow'. It comes as no surprise, therefore, that while Nietzsche claims to be the first 'tragic philosopher' - as opposed, perhaps, to tragic poet - he feels 'warmer and more well' in the vicinity of Heraclitus than anywhere else (EH IV 3). It was, remember, 'the dark Heraclitus' who compared 'the forces that shape the world to a playing child who . . . builds up piles of sand only to knock them over again' (BT 24).

In a word, one becomes, in the Dionysian state, God. The author of *Zarathustra* was, Nietzsche says – 'speaking as a theologian – pay heed, for I only rarely speak as a theologian' – 'God himself' (EH X 2). Notice, once again, that many of the supposedly crazy and megalomaniac remarks made after his breakdown – his claim that he would rather be a Basle professor than God but in fact has 'not dared to push . . . [his] private egoism so far as to desist for its sake from the creation of the world', his apology to the inmates of the sanatorium for the bad weather and promise to 'prepare the loveliest weather for tomorrow' – exhibit a strong continuity with this experience, which leads one to Isadora Duncan's hope (see p. 110 fn. 2 above) that it was, perhaps, not such a dark night Nietzsche entered on 3 January 1899.

Like many of the German idealists, whom he purports to despise, like Schelling and Hegel and in a certain strange way Schopenhauer, Nietzsche's 'faith' is, as I have claimed before, pantheism, a pantheism which receives its fullest expression in *Ecce Homo*. Abuse of sex, he says, for example, is the cardinal sin against 'the holy spirit of life' (EH III 5). *Zarathustra* is 'music', the kind of music he wrote during the same period in his – note the religious title – 'Hymn to Life' (EH IX 1). Again, a Dionysian spirit has, he says, to speak in the language of the dithyramb (*religious* language, note), the kind of language Zarathustra spoke in 'Before sunrise' (EH IX 7; see pp. 107–11 above).

So Nietzsche is a pantheist. But if the world is a holy place what about the 'problem of evil', the massive amount of pain it contains? (Remember that according to Schopenhauer's definition, the central problem any adequate religion has to solve is the problem of death *and pain*.)

Nietzsche claims that, already in *The Birth*, he had discovered, in 'the wonderful phenomenon of the Dionysian . . . a formula of *supreme affirmation* born out of fullness, of superfluity, and affirmation without reservation, even of suffering, even of guilt, even of all that is strange and questionable in existence', and that 'this ultimate, joyfullest boundlessly exuberant Yes to life is . . . the highest insight' (EH IV 2). In other words he claims that already in *The Birth* he had discovered the idea of willing the eternal recurrence. But this can only mean *implicitly* discovered as part and parcel of the Dionysian state, since a little later he says that the articulation of '*the idea of eternal recurrence*, the highest formula of affirmation that can possibly be attained – belongs to the August of the year 1881' (EH IX 1).

In the Dionysian state, says Nietzsche, one has the experience that 'nothing that is can be subtracted, nothing is dispensable' (EH IV 2), that everything – even the most terrible – has its 'necessary' (EH IX 3) place in, as *Twilight* called it, the 'economy' of the whole. With Zarathustra, that is, one 'redeems' all 'It was' as 'Thus I willed it' (EH IX 8). As I pointed out earlier, since most of the 'it was' happened before its birth, the 'I' that 'will*ed* it' cannot be the individual ego but must be the ecstatic, individual-transcending, divine 'I'. And as I also pointed out, given that many of the questionable things in life – Auschwitz, Hiroshima, Abu Ghraib – must find their redemption, if anywhere, in the *future*, the affirmation of the 'formula' (test) of the Dionysian state, the eternal recurrence, must be based on 'faith' rather than knowledge, since the future is unknown. The affirmation issues from an extraordinary release of ecstatic energy – 'fullness, superfluity' (EH IV 2) – which generates 'positive thinking' about the future, an intuitive certainty that things *will* all find their 'redemption'.

So, to sum up, Nietzsche's response to the 'problem of evil' which confronts the pantheist as much as the Christian theist (in Nietzsche's case even more starkly, since he cannot appeal to the 'free will defence') remains that of performing a theodicy. The world is – as the most healthy, *The Antichrist*'s spiritual rulers, for example, experience it – *perfect*. The eternal recurrence is 'the formula for supreme affirmation' because to 'crave nothing more fervently' than the eternal recurrence (GS 341) of all that is and has been is to affirm that there is no possible way in which the world could be better than it is.

Epilogue: Nietzsche in history

The argument of this book has been that, though Nietzsche rejects the God of Christianity, he is not anti-religious. On the contrary, I have argued, he is *above all* a religious thinker. Accepting (as he should) Schopenhauer's twofold analysis of religion as an affective-intellectual-institutional construction which (a) responds to the existential problems of death and pain and (b) expounds and gives authority to community-creating ethos, Nietzsche (a) offers 'Dionysian' pantheism as the solution to the problems of death and pain, and (b) argues that we must hope and work for the new 'festival': that flourishing and authentic community, absent from modernity, can only be restored through the rebirth of a life- and humanity-affirming religion modelled on that of the Greeks. This, I have argued, is the view presented in his first book and – a more controversial claim – is a view that is maintained, essentially without alteration or interruption, up to and in his last book.

Since this account of the kind of philosopher Nietzsche is is radically unlike anything that has appeared to date in the Anglophone reading, I want to conclude this book by positioning Nietzsche within German intellectual history. I want, that is, to add plausibility to my reading of Nietzsche by showing that the views I attribute to him have a great deal in common with those of many of his German contemporaries who were similarly alive to, in Hölderlin's word, the 'destitution' of modernity. I want to show, in other words, that the views I attribute to Nietzsche are very much the views one would expect from someone with his perceptions and anxieties, writing at his time and in his place.

It has to be said, however, that I do this only with a certain reluctance. The reason for this – as I have indicated at various points in the above discussion – is that the tradition in which I believe Nietzsche has at least one foot firmly planted is that of the 'Volkish' thinking of the conservative anti-modernists of late nineteenth-century Germany. And the fact is that it is this tradition, more than any other, which prepared the intellectual climate – and much of the language – out of which Nazism grew. This raises the spectre – the spectre Walter Kaufmann devoted a lifetime to banishing – that when Nazi philosophers like Ernst Bertram, Richard Oehler, Heinrich Härtle and Alfred Bäumler (along with Elizabeth Förster-Nietzsche) claimed Nietzsche as one of their own they were right.

Fortunately, however, I think I can show that the genuinely wicked aspects of Volkish thinking[1] were ones that Nietzsche not only did not share but vehemently opposed. Nietzsche can, I believe, be located in the German tradition of anti-modernist, religious communitarianism without being turned into the godfather of Nazism. If this is right then a partial rehabilitation of the Volkish tradition seems called for: a recognition that, along with the vicious, it also contained noble impulses.

We need to begin with the eighteenth-century Enlightenment, three aspects of which are especially relevant to our concerns. First, its glorification of reason as a faculty in principle capable of solving every human problem ('Socratism', in Nietzsche's language). Second, its assumption that human nature – with reason as its essence – is universal in character. And finally, its deployment of reason to challenge and eventually demolish the authority of religion. After Kant had shown, it was felt, that the existence of God could not be proved, it became possible for a figure such as Goethe (1749–1832) explicitly to declare himself a non-Christian. (In its place, as Nietzsche points out (p. 174 above), he affirmed a pantheistic sense of the immanent holiness of the totality of things.) In the 1840s Kant's critique of religion was supplemented by Ludwig Feuerbach's persuasive account of gods as entirely human constructions, projections of human ideals.

The roots of Volkish thinking lie in the mainly – but not entirely – critical reaction to the Enlightenment that constituted German romanticism. (The following account of the Volkish tradition, of its roots in romanticism and its emphasis on the need for a new communal faith, is heavily dependent on the work of the German intellectual historian Thomas Rohkrämer.[2])

---

1 More properly, the genuinely wicked aspects of the thought of *some Volkish thinkers*. This incautious phrase indicates the dangerously homogenising potential of the history of ideas: an innocent thinker comes to share a label with a vicious one and so becomes guilty by association. As Heidegger says: whenever there is an 'ism' a powerful danger exists that 'inauthentic' (bad) thinking is underway.

2 In part on his groundbreaking *Eine Andere Moderne?* (Rohkrämer (1999)) but much more on the manuscript of his forthcoming study of the seeds of Nazism in the Volkish tradition, part of which he generously allowed me to read prior to publication.

The romantics objected, in the first place, to the Enlightenment's deification of reason. Acutely sensitive to the dark underside of modernity, they attributed this darkness to the glorification of reason, in particular to the invasion of all aspects of human life by instrumental reason. Novalis (1772–1801), for example, described the modern bureaucratic state with its capitalist economy as a 'mill as such, without a builder and without a miller, a real *perpetuum mobile*, a mill which grinds itself'. And Schelling (1775–1854) described modern society as 'a machine which . . . though built and arranged by human beings . . . act[s] . . . according to its own laws as if it existed by itself'. The objection to this, in Nietzsche's phrase, 'machine culture' is that it dehumanises, reduces human beings to atomic cogs in the giant mechanism, and so condemns them to isolated, miserable and meaningless lives.

The romantics rejected social contract theory – the idea that social life is and ought only to be the product of atomic individuals' game-theoretic calculations of what best promotes private advantage. Social life, they felt, cannot be the *product* of individual calculation since it is social life that first produces the authentically human individual. And neither does contract theory represent how society *ought* to be, since it is actually nothing but a *post facto* rationalisation of the machine society.

In place of the machine state the romantics wanted an 'organic' society. They wanted, in Jürgen Habermas' recent formulation of the demand, a society in which capitalism and state power are embedded in the 'life world' of a communal culture. In the language I employed earlier (p. 5 above), that is, they affirmed the primacy of Volk over state. Only in such an 'organic' society could individuals find community, identity and meaning.

For many of the romantics, the rediscovery of authentic community, of Ferdinand Tönnies' *Gemeinschaft* as opposed to modernity's *Gesellschaft*,[3] depended essentially on religion. Problematically, however, while rejecting the Enlightenment's excessive glorification of reason as well as its cosmopolitanism, most of the romantics accepted its critique of traditional Christianity, accepted that Christian dogma is unbelievable in the modern age.

But they saw this, as Thomas Rohkrämer puts it, not as the end of religion but rather as a temporary crisis. Hölderlin (1770–1843), for instance, spoke not of the 'death' of God but of the 'absence', the

---

3 Tönnies first drew this distinction in his 1887 *Community and Civil Society*, a work inspired by *The Birth of Tragedy* – see Aschheim (1992) pp. 39–41.

'default', of 'God and the gods'. Though we live in a time of 'night', it is a 'holy' night, a place to which, one day and in one shape or another, the gods will return.

The return of the godly, the rediscovery of community-creating religion, required, the romantics saw, the creation of 'a new mythology',[4] a post- but also in some respects pre-Christian mythology. As in many other areas, Herder was a forerunner of the romantics' interest in mythology. As early as 1767 he called for the revival of mythology, of in particular a 'political mythology', as an intuitive, allegorical and accessible way of discussing metaphysics and ethics. (Recall early Nietzsche's account of Wagner as thinking 'mythologically', the way, he says, the Volk has always thought (p. 53 above).) Dissecting Enlightenment reason should be balanced by the 'fictional spirit' and 'synthesising faculty' of the poet. Similarly, one of the founding documents of romanticism, 'The Oldest Programme of German Idealism' (probably written by Schelling), calls for 'a new mythology' which is to provide a 'new eternal gospel' that will found a 'new religion'. And in the same vein, Friedrich Schlegel (1771–1829) wrote that

Our poetry, I claim, lacks a centre, as mythology was for the Ancients, and all essential points in which our modern poetry is inferior to that of classical Greece can be summarised with the words: we have no mythology. But I add we are close to getting one; or rather it is time we all seriously participate in creating one. (Schlegel (1958–) vol. 2 p. 312)

As Rohrkrämer points out, 'new mythology' is a phrase pregnant with connotations. First of all, 'mythology' refers to a past which the Enlightenment had dismissed as superstition. Above all it refers to ancient Greece which, for romantic Graecophiles such as Winkelmann and Hölderlin, is a prime example of a community created and preserved by a communal artwork.[5] On the other hand, 'new' implied a certain acceptance of the Enlightenment critique of the religion of the past. A 'new mythology' did not claim the authority of divine revelation and neither would it take the form of any precise doctrine or dogma. Rather, it would allow us allegorical glimpses of metaphysical and ethical truths. (Recall that this 'mythological interpretation' of religion is the one Schopenhauer offers.) Finally, 'mythological' suggests something whose origins are lost in the

---

4 See in particular Frank (1989).
5 Frank (1989) pp. 88ff.

dawn of time, so that their authorship may be regarded as the work of the Volk as a whole rather than the invention of any individual.

Politically speaking, romanticism had the capacity to move either to the left or to the right. Hölderlin, for example, was a passionate admirer of the French Revolution. Unsurprisingly, however, many romantics became – to employ the phrase I applied to Nietzsche – 'compassionate conservatives'. Adam Müller, Friedrich Schlegel, Achim von Arnim and Franz von Bader, for instance, all idolised the Middle Ages. Inspired by Burke, they emphasised that rapid social change, loss of the past, produced deracinated, alienated individuals. Pointing out that the modern state with its emphasis on legal equality in a free market only served to disguise and cement the structural advantages of wealth, they idolised what Müller called the 'heartfelt association' of medieval feudalism, a harmoniously hierarchical community that guaranteed economic security to all.

Alongside the religious communitarianism of conservative romanticism, Volkish thinking found a second root in nationalism. At the beginning of the nineteenth century Germany found itself divided into thirty-eight independent states. French was the language of society and the differences between the various dialects of German were so strong that communication between people from different regions was difficult or impossible. The success of the French and American revolutions gave a new impetus to the idea of nation in general. But what really created for the first time a pan-German nationalism were the crushing defeats at Jena and Auerstedt in 1806 and the injustices of French rule that followed. As a result, German nationalism grew up as the other side of the coin of hatred of Napoleon and the 'French vermin', as the historian/poet Ernst Moritz Arndt called them.

This was the climate in which Fichte made his famous 'Speeches to the German Nation' in 1807–8, calling for 'not the spirit of calm, bourgeois love of a constitution but the consuming flame of a higher life of the fatherland . . . for which the noble-minded sacrifices himself joyfully'. Postulating Germany's cultural and moral superiority to all other nations – Schleiermacher called the Germans 'a chosen tool and God's people' – Fichte identifies world-hegemony as the German mission.

Notice here the Volkish thesis I earlier called the thesis of the priority of Volk to individual. By the time Volkish thinking had crystallised into the 'Ideas of 1914' – the efforts of Volkish thinkers to show that a German victory in the First World War was both desirable (to redeem Europe from decadence) and inevitable – this thesis, together with the perception of the English as a nation of shopkeepers with only the social contract to support their apology for social life, led to the representation of the war as a conflict between, in Werner Sombart's words, *Helden* (heroes) and *Händler* (traders).

The ideals of conservative romanticism and German nationalism coalesced into Volkish thinking proper in the mid-nineteenth century. Key figures in bringing about this coalescence were Heinrich Riehl (1823–97), Paul de Lagarde (1827–91) and Richard Wagner (1813–83).

Riehl, like Herder, opposed the Enlightenment's postulation of a cosmo-politan human nature. Human beings are products of local cultures and these in turn are as richly varied as are the landscapes they inhabit. Writing in the wake of the worker insurrections of 1848–9, Riehl saw farmers and the nobility as forces productive of stable environments in which human beings could flourish. Cities he viewed as places of alienation and instability.

Paul de Lagarde's main concern was the need for a new national religion. Like many in the Volkish tradition he broke with Christianity but remained in search of a substitute. Scholarly study of the origins of the Bible enabled him to continue the deconstructive work of David Strauss (see pp. 34–6 above). Pointing to contradictions between the gospels, between the Bible and church dogma, as well as to the fact that the Bible contains no eyewitness accounts of the life of Jesus, he sought to undermine its authority.

Most fundamentally, however, Lagarde's objection to the Christianity of his day was motivated not by doubts about the Bible but by its tepid and fractured character. He was not content to allow religion to remain a private affair but neither did he want an international religion. What he wanted was a *single*, powerful, communal faith that would unite the German nation and determine its historical destiny. Concerning the content of this new faith, however, Lagarde was vague, suggesting merely that we could discover God in exemplary others.

Like virtually everyone in the Volkish tradition, Lagarde called for strong, non-democratic leadership. 'Only the great, firm and pure will of one man can help us, the will of a king not parliaments, not laws, not the aspirations of a powerless individual.'

As with many in the Volkish tradition, Lagarde was viciously anti-Semitic (the term 'anti-Semitism' was first coined by Wilhelm Marr in 1879). As with many anti-Semites, his attitude to Jews was a mixture of admiration and hatred. On the one hand, as an ethnic group united by a single faith, they precisely matched his ideal of a Volk. But on the other he saw them as, for that same reason, an obstacle to his ideal of a communal Germanic faith. They had, therefore, either to assimilate or to be expelled from Germany. Lack of success in realising his ideals led him, in later life, to unbounded loathing of Jews, even to exterminationist fantasising. Lagarde was none the less admired by Thomas Mann who used many of his ideas in *Observations of an Unpolitical Man*, by the respected Protestant theologian Ernst Troeltsch, who approved of his ideas on the regeneration of religion, and by Franz Overbeck, Nietzsche's lifelong friend.

In opposition to the prevailing belief in relentless progress, Richard Wagner, influenced by the conservative romantics, experienced the modern age as a time of decadence, a falling away from the cultural glory of the past, in particular of the Greek past. It was an age desperately in need of 'regeneration', of 'redemption'.

Like the romantics, Wagner saw religion as the key to such redemption. Strongly influenced by Feuerbach's critique, however, he rejected traditional Christianity. Religions, he saw, were always a human creation, a projection of human dreams and ideals onto an imaginary realm. For human beings, he wrote in a letter of 1849, God has always been 'what they communally recognise as the supreme, the strongest communal emotion, the most powerful communal belief' (Wagner (1975) p. 182).

Rather than taking Feuerbach's analysis as a refutation of religion as such, Wagner took it instead as a guide to the construction of a new religion. Religion, as he understood it, is essentially mythology – and need be none the worse for that.

Wagner was a nationalist. He sought to create a national religious mythology. Though he believed in Germany's special mission to redeem humanity as a whole, it could only become worthy of the task by first of all redeeming itself. And, like Lagarde, he held that that could only come about with the appearance of a religious mythology that would unite all Germans into a communal whole.

Influenced again by the romantics, Wagner held that art should have a decisive role in creating this new mythology. Art, that is to say, should *not* be '*pour l'art*'. Rather it should be, as it had been in Greece, the place of the community's reflection on the proper shape of its life. Hence, as we saw in chapter 2, his own music dramas were conceived as the rebirth of Greek tragedy, the focus of a new national religion. Only art, that is to say, can save religion in the modern age. One could say, Wagner wrote, that at a time when religion has become artificial, art reserves itself the right to save the core of religion by interpreting the mythical symbols which the former want to be believed as true, in an allegorical way. Through an ideal presentation of these symbols, art can reveal the deep truth hidden in them.[6]

It was this religious conception of art that guided the Bayreuth project. Wagner, as we have seen, conceived the Festival as the focus of an annual pilgrimage, described the Ring Cycle as 'a stage festival drama for three days and a fore-evening', and called *Parsifal* a 'holy festival for the stage (*Bühnenweihfestspiel*)'.

Like Lagarde, Wagner was anti-Semitic, perceiving the strong identity of Jewish culture as an impediment to the national unity he sought. In his essay 'The Jews in Music' he called for the complete '*Untergang*' of Jewish culture, which could simply mean assimilation but could also mean extermination. After Wagner's death, the 'Bayreuth Circle', the group of his disciples now led by his widow Cosima and Houston Stewart Chamberlain – a group which until his death in 1887 included Nietzsche's friend Heinrich von Stein – emphasised the extreme nationalism and anti-Semitism of Wagner's later years.

Two further aspects of the Volkish outlook need to be mentioned. First the increasing prestige of the German army, particularly after victory over the French in 1870–1, which it did everything to promote with pompous, carefully choreographed marches and parades designed to display its discipline and efficiency. Increasingly, Volkish thinkers came to see fighting for one's country as the highest form of service to the nation.

Second, the close connexion between Volkism and the 'life-reform (*Lebensreform*)' movement. Appalled by the materialism and mechanism of God-less modernity, many of Nietzsche's contemporaries began to explore a variety of 'alternative', potentially more satisfying, ways of life. The focus was on the body. Through such things as the wearing of loose clothing, spending time close to nature, nudism, vegetarianism, teetotalism, giving up smoking and the abandonment of stressful work practices, the life-reformers wanted to improve individual lives. In the long run, however, such new ways of living were supposed to bring about communal regeneration, a revival of the Volk coming together in a non-materialistic, religiously inspired way of life.

The publishing house of Eugen Diederichs was set up to provide a focus for the new spirituality: Diederichs wanted, he wrote, to create 'a

6 Quoted in Friedländer (1986) p. 6.

space for the gathering of modern spirits . . . against materialism and for romanticism and a new renaissance'.

As well as providing a chapel-like structure in which the visitor could find the works of Paul de Lagarde prominently displayed, Diederichs organised festivals of seasonal celebration, folk dances, medieval songs and the delivery of pantheistic sermons.

Diederichs conceived of his publishing house as a 'laboratory for religious modernity'. Like his leading author, Paul de Lagarde, he wanted a new communal religion, above all one that affirmed life. 'Religion', he said, 'is a kind of perspective which allows one to say Yes to life.'

How, to return now to our central preoccupation, does Nietzsche stand to this romantic-Volkish tradition of thought and feeling? Clearly there are a number of strong affinities.

First, Nietzsche shares with the tradition a sense of modernity as a sick culture, a culture that has declined from a healthier past. And many of the specifics of his diagnosis – the description of modernity as a machine culture, for instance – reach back to writers such as Novalis in the late eighteenth century. Like the Volkists, he views ancient Greece, and to some extent the Middle Ages (see p. 137 above), as the golden age from which we have declined. And like them, his thinking is shaped by the fundamental trope of fall and the hope of 'redemption'.

Second, Nietzsche rejects democracy, viewing it as militating against the production of eminent human beings who might possibly lead us out of contemporary nihilism, and as offering ordinary people not genuine well-being but only economic insecurity (p. 137 above) and status anxiety (p. 163 above).

Third, Nietzsche deplores 'stateism', the state that has ceased to recognise the priority of the Volk, the state that claims to *be* the principle of social unity rather than to be an 'organic' outgrowth of the Volk, as its vehicle and expression.

Fourth, Nietzsche deplores the 'shopkeeper' mentality, the pursuit of private, 'worm'-like advantage (p. 35 above) that has come to replace the community as a whole as the object of primary commitment (p. 112 above).

Turning to the redemptive side of Nietzsche's thinking, we find further strong similarities.

First, like many of the Volkists, Nietzsche thinks that attending to small things to do with (in his broad sense) bodily 'hygiene', things such as diet, dress and bodily movement (particularly dance), will make an important contribution to fostering a new spirituality. Nietzsche's discussions of diet, clothing and climate, his hatred of industry, the effects of modern technology and the city, as well as his attraction to mountains and nostalgia for rural life, place him in close relation to the 'life-reform' movement. Indeed after his death, along with Tolstoy, he became one of the heroes of the artists' colony in the Swiss village of Ascona, a centre for such devotees of 'life-reform' as D. H. Lawrence, Hermann Hesse, Carl Gustav Jung and Isadora Duncan.[7]

Second, Nietzsche's pantheism links him to romantics such as Hölderlin and Schelling, and to many, such as Eugen Diederichs, who belonged to the life-reform movement.

Third, as for nearly all of the Volkists, the obverse of Nietzsche's rejection of democracy is the desire for a return to an hierarchical society under the rule of a wise, benevolent and strong leader.

The heart, however – so I have been arguing – of Nietzsche's remedy for the destitution of modernity lies in the return of a communal religion. Yet if Thomas Rohkrämer is right, religious communitarianism, the yearning to reintegrate the Volk through the establishment of 'one communal faith', is the single most decisive and unifying feature of the Volkish tradition in general. It seems, then, that the most important affinity between Nietzsche and the Volkists is the shared conviction that, while God is 'dead', the fundamental solution to the sickness of modernity lies in a 'return of the gods'.

As has often been observed, the building of great amphitheatres and the staging of events like the Nuremberg Rallies, as well as the films of Leni Riefenstahl, suggest that the attempt to recreate, through art, a new, vaguely Greek, communal quasi-religion belongs somewhere near the heart of the Nazi phenomenon.[8] In a famous book entitled *Nietzsche:*

---

7 See Aschheim (1992) pp. 58–62.
8 As Steven Aschheim points out, however, it is a confusion of the post-Nazi imagination to suppose that all political architecture is fascist. After his death, Aschheim points out, the most grandiose Nietzsche project was organised by Count Harry Kessler. He commissioned the famous Belgian architect Henry van de Velde to design a gigantic festival area as a memorial to Nietzsche, consisting of a temple, a large stadium and a huge statue of Apollo. Thousands were intended to pour into this stadium where art, dance, theatre and sports competitions would be combined into a Nietzschean totality. As Kessler conceived it, with remarkable accuracy in my view (save for the literalism of the statue), this was Nietzscheanism translated into mass action. The point about Kessler, however, is that he was a passionate cosmopolitan and anti-nationalist. He loathed the Nazis and was drawn to Nietzsche as a 'good European'. The plan attracted the support of other 'good Europeans' such as André Gide, Anatole France, Walter Rathenau, Gilbert Murray and H. G. Wells. In the end it came to nothing, partly through the opposition of the jingoistic Elizabeth Förster-Nietzsche who remarked that 'the aping of Greekdom through this rich, idle mob from the whole of Europe is horror to me' (Aschheim (1992) pp. 48–9).

Attempt at a Mythology (1918), the philosopher Ernst Bertram, who later played a decisive role in the appropriation of Nietzsche by the Nazis, representing the view of the George Circle in general, emphasised, as I have done, the quest for a new religious mythology as belonging to the heart of Nietzsche's thought.[9] Should we, then, begin once again to think of Nietzsche as the father of Nazism, or perhaps even as an actual Nazi?

Walter Kaufmann devoted his life to demolishing what he calls 'the legend' of Nietzsche as a proto-Nazi. In his view, the legend, a figment constructed by Bäumler, Bertram, George and Elizabeth Förster-Nietzsche, is in every aspect a complete misreading, a total misappropriation of Nietzsche to the Nazi cause. In reality, he suggests in his classic *Nietzsche: Philosopher, Psychologist, Antichrist* (1950), Nietzsche was utterly apolitical: 'the leitmotiv of Nietzsche's life and thought [was] the theme of the antipolitical individual who seeks self-perfection far from the modern world' (p. 418). (Revealingly, 'politics', like 'eugenics', receives not a single entry in Kaufmann's index.) It is hard to overestimate the dominance of Kaufmann's view of Nietzsche as an apolitical thinker over approaches to Nietzsche by Anglophone academic philosophers. (Brobjer and Leiter, for instance, clearly operate within this parameter (see pp. 179–80 above).)

Though Kaufmann's heart was in the right place, the trouble with his Nietzsche – a Nietzsche sanitised, as Michael Tanner[10] and Walter Sokel[11] point out, so as to be incapable of causing offence to anyone of a 'liberal humanist outlook' – is that it becomes impossible to understand how anyone could have made a connexion between Nietzsche and Nazism in the first place.

My locating of Nietzsche in proximity to the Volkish tradition has the virtue of making this connexion intelligible. Yet while I regard Kaufmann's attempt to construct an apolitical Nietzsche as being as bad a misreading and misappropriation as that of which he accuses the Nazi Nietzscheans, his fundamental point that Nietzsche is neither a Nazi nor a

---

9 George and Bertram, noting as I have Nietzsche's formalism, his reluctance to prescribe a specific content to the new mythology, to 'canonise' particular role models, made the interesting move of turning Nietzsche *himself* into the central role model in their 'new mythology'. Nietzsche was to become the 'educator' for the higher types of the future. (Walter Hammer, an important figure in the life-reform movement, actually wrote a work entitled *Nietzsche as Educator* in 1914.) It should be said, here, that by no means all members of the George Circle became Nazis. George himself did not and many members were Jews. Claus von Stauffenberg, who was hanged after attempting to assassinate Hitler in July 1944, was, together with his two brothers, also a member. It is said that his last words were 'for the secret Germany', the motto of the George Circle.

10 Tanner (1986).   11 Sokel (1983).

proto-Nazi seems to me indisputably correct. The discussion of this book reveals three decisive reasons why this is so.

The first is Nietzsche's anti-anti-Semitism. Though he says some hard things about the Jews – mainly that after the Babylonian Exile they became a priest-ridden people who, by inventing Christianity, destroyed the classical world – it is clear, as I have argued, that the need for a non-discriminatory, non-exclusionary social system, the need to offer full membership of society to all who come within its orbit thereby avoiding the creation of a 'Chandala' class of *Untermenschen*, belongs to both the beginning and the heart of his social thinking (see pp. 169–70 and p. 185 above). The concept of 'pure blood' is, remember, 'the opposite of a harmless concept' (TI vii 4). Nietzsche's anti-anti-Semitism[12] is therefore, to repeat, no superficial reaction to the vulgar stupidity of the likes of his brother-in-law but something rooted in the deepest levels of his thought. But Nazism without anti-Semitism is not Nazism.[13]

Second, in spite of his moustache and the bellicose language of 'war' and 'will to power', Nietzsche is deeply anti-militaristic. He lost school friends barely out of their teens in the Franco-Prussian war and, as a medical orderly, had regular dealings with men with their brains blown out. Hence the *Nachlass* remarks on the 'criminal . . . madness' of squabbling dynasties which place the flower of a nation's youth in front of the cannons (KSA 13 25 [15], 13 25 [19]). Peace, indeed, as the letter to Brandes written during his last sane moments puts it, 'world peace' (p. 188 above), is something for which he has the deepest of yearnings. As we saw, the yearning to be able to say 'peace all around me and goodwill to all things' is a leading motive for his cosmopolitanism, since, as he sees it, only global community offers the possibility of demilitarisation (HH ii b 284, 350; see p. 82 above).

Abhorrence of physical violence belongs to the beginning of Nietzsche's thought – the Greeks, remember, distinguished themselves from the 'barbarians' by giving *artistic* expression to Dionysian violence (see p. 25 above) – and it belongs to the end in the form of the repeated

---

12 Anti-anti-Semitism is one of the many surprising affinities between Nietzsche and George Eliot. Though abused by him as a 'bluestocking' who could not bring herself to accept the consequences of the death of God (TI xi 5), Eliot shared not only his anti-anti-Semitism but also his distress that the hierarchical society of the past was being destroyed by 'modern ideas' and modern technology. (Though a hero to the feminists of her time, Eliot in fact *opposed* female suffrage.) See Karl (1995).

13 As to whether Nietzsche might be committed to demanding an unwarranted degree of cultural assimilation, see the remarks on 'cultural totalitarianism' on p. ooo below.

insistence on the essential role of sublimation, 'spiritualization', in creating civilised individuals and a civilised society. Literal war, physical violence, Nietzsche regards as literally 'barbaric'. Let us recall here his remark that a church is a 'nobler' institution than the state since it 'secures the highest rank for the *more spiritual* human beings' and 'believes in the power of spirituality to the extent of forbidding itself the use of all cruder instruments of force' (GS 358; see p. 99 above). Nietzsche always favours 'soft' over 'hard' power. War, like politics, should always be 'of the spirit' (see p. 194 above). But Nazism without violence is not Nazism.

Third, after recovering from his infatuation with Wagner,[14] Nietzsche repeatedly and emphatically deplored the rise of nationalism, in particular the 'petty politics' of German nationalism and German imperialism. He loathed the *Deutschland, Deutschland über alles* spirit, the '*Vaterland* thinking' of Bismarck's Germany, loathed not only Wagner's anti-Semitism but also his *Reichdeutsch* politics and deplored the loss of the 'cosmopolitan taste' of his socialist youth (EH VI 2). And, far from thinking there might be a German 'mission' to rule the world, he believed Schopenhauer to be the last great German and modern German culture to be inferior to that of the French (TI VIII 4).

One might be tempted to follow Nietzsche's Nazi appropriators in interpreting his 'anti-German' remarks as 'angry love' of the German Fatherland, as a *deeply* nationalistic Nietzsche summoning the Germans, *à la* Fichte or the Heidegger of the 1930s, to rise from current decadence to their 'inner truth and greatness'. But at least three reasons tell against the postulation of such a hidden nationalism. First, there is no textual evidence whatsoever to support it. Second, since as we observed, German nationalism grew out of a loathing of the French in general and of Napoleon in particular, the depth of Nietzsche's opposition to German nationalism can be measured by his consistent admiration for Napoleon. (He admires Napoleon, it should be noted, not as a soldier – this he regards as belonging to the 'monstrous (*unmenschlich*)' side of his divided nature (GM I 16) – but as a cosmopolitan and a reviver of classical values.) And third, Nietzsche's love of France – of the Southern spirit, close to the Greek, of Bizet, of the 'gay science' of the Provençal minstrels – is no mere stick to beat the Germans with, but a deep and abiding theme in many of the major texts.

---

14 With Wagner, remember, *The Birth* spoke of the need for a '*rebirth of the German myth*' (BT 23; Nietzsche's emphasis). This helps explain why many of Nietzsche's Volkish and Nazi interpreters placed particular emphasis on *The Birth.*

Nietzsche is, then, neither an overt nor a concealed nationalist. But National Socialism without nationalism is not National Socialism.

Nietzsche loathed nationalism because he was (like Schopenhauer) an internationalist, a cosmopolitan. He wanted, as we have seen, a revived European culture to become the world culture. Though I have so far emphasised his strong affinities with the romantic reaction against the Enlightenment, his cosmopolitanism – as well as his rejection of 'metaphysics', his naturalism, his respect for science, and his deconstruction of the traditional authority – shows that he by no means abandoned Enlightenment ideals completely. Nietzsche's thinking is, in fact, a unique mixture of Enlightenment and anti-Enlightenment ideals, which makes it a mistake to imprison him in either one of these categories.

This raises the question of consistency. Is not, one might ask, his romantic yearning for religiously based community inconsistent with his Enlightenment cosmopolitanism? Is not community – something that can provide rootedness in tradition, fellowship, identity and a meaning to one's life – necessarily a *local* phenomenon that depends essentially on *difference* between one localised community and another? Is not the idea of 'world community' (like that expression which seems to have found favour with the modern police, 'the criminal community') a self-contradiction?

The answer, I believe, is that it is not. Recall, first, the remark in *Human, All-to-Human* that 'the greatest fact in the cultivation of Greece [was] . . . that Homer became pan-Hellenic so early' (HH I 262). And second, the remark that artists who 'signpost the future' are to make classical ideals the 'general all-embracing golden ground upon which alone the tender *distinctions* between different embodied ideals would then constitute the actual *painting*' (HH II a 99). What Nietzsche wants, both in the microcosm of the soul and in the macrocosm of human society at large, is, as he repeats often enough, neither undifferentiated unity nor atomic 'chaos', but rather 'unity in multiplicity (*Ganzheit im Vielen*)', the definition, he says, of human 'greatness' (BGE 212).

But is this not – to repeat the suspicion concerning the combination of communitarianism with cosmopolitanism – precisely what is impossible?

In the foregoing chapters we have repeatedly observed Nietzsche's admiration for the medieval Church. He admires it, of course, not for its doctrine but as a cosmopolitan institution (see pp. 44, 98–9 above). This, it seems to me, is what he wants: the rebirth of the medieval – or as he prefers to say, 'Roman' – Church with, of course, Christian gods supplanted by 'Greek' ones.

But, one might ask, is this not a kind of 'cultural totalitarianism' which (a) entails unacceptable intolerance towards minority (e.g. Jewish) cultures and (b) precludes precisely the kind of difference necessary to authentic community?

I believe not. The medieval Church had, as Nietzsche observes (see p. 152 above), a remarkable capacity to assimilate to itself local gods and pagan traditions, to reinterpret them within the generous outlines of Christian theology. Its power of assimilation, its flexibility, its 'plastic power' (UM II 10) to take on different colorations at different times and in different places, constitute the essence of the institutional strength that Nietzsche admires. On account of this remarkable flexibility, the Church, though global, was also local. Partly this was because particular saints became the patrons of particular places (the same is true of the Greek gods) and partly because – to translate Nietzsche's distinction between 'golden ground' and 'actual painting' into philosophers' jargon – saints, rituals and churches were 'types' which could tolerate a great number of markedly different 'tokens'. In this connexion, Nietzsche's 'Gadamerian' remarks about translation and interpretation as a 'fusion of horizons' which give birth to 'some third thing' (pp. 73–4 above) are an important indication of how he thinks of the possibility of combining 'unity' with 'multiplicity'.

As Nietzsche says, it is of course the case that 'all great spiritual forces exercise . . . a repressive effect' (HH I 262). Tautologically, unity must involve a deradicalisation of difference. But a religion which says, as Jesus said of his 'father's house', that in it 'many mansions' can dwell (John 14:2), a religion which disavows black-letter, doctrinal fundamentalism, can and has allowed comfortably enough difference for the existence of cultural plurality and genuine community. There is, in short, it seems to me, no inconsistency between Nietzsche's romantic communitarianism and his Enlightenment cosmopolitanism. On the contrary, one of the vital insights of this 'good European' is the compatibility of the two.

Bibliography

WORKS BY NIETZSCHE

The Anti-Christ in *Twilight of the Idols and The Anti-Christ*, trans. R. Hollingdale (Harmondsworth: Penguin, 1968).

Beyond Good and Evil, ed. R.-P. Horstmann and J. Norman, trans. J. Norman (Cambridge: Cambridge University Press, 2002).

The Birth of Tragedy in *The Birth of Tragedy and Other Writings*, ed. R. Geuss and R. Speirs, trans. R. Spears (Cambridge: Cambridge University Press, 1999).

The Case of Wagner in *The Birth of Tragedy* (with *The Case of Wagner*), trans. W. Kaufmann (New York: Vintage, 1966).

Daybreak, ed. M. Clark and B. Leiter, trans. R. Hollingdale (Cambridge: Cambridge University Press, 1997).

Ecce Homo, trans. R. Hollingdale (Harmondsworth: Penguin 1979).

The Gay Science, ed. B. Williams, trans. J. Naukhoff (Cambridge: Cambridge University Press, 2001).

Human, all-too-Human, trans. R. Hollingdale (Cambridge: Cambridge University Press, 1986).

Kritische Studienausgabe (15 vols.), ed. G. Colli and M. Montinari (Berlin: de Gruyter, 1999).

Nietzsche contra Wagner in *The Portable Nietzsche*, ed. and trans. W. Kaufmann (New York: Penguin, 1982).

On the Genealogy of Morality, ed. K. Ansell-Pearson, trans. C. Diethe (Cambridge: Cambridge University Press, 1994).

Thus Spoke Zarathustra, trans. R. Hollingdale (Harmondsworth: Penguin, 1961).

Twilight of the Idols in *Twilight of the Idols and The Anti-Christ*, trans. R. Hollingdale (Harmondsworth: Penguin, 1968).

Untimely Meditations, ed. D. Breazeale, trans. R. Hollingdale (Cambridge: Cambridge University Press, 1997).

The Will to Power, ed. W. Kaufmann, trans. W. Kaufmann and R. Hollingdale (New York: Vintage, 1968).

WORKS BY SCHOPENHAUER

The Fourfold Root of the Principle of Sufficient Reason, trans. E. Payne (La Salle: Open Court, 1974).

Parerga and Paralipomena, trans. E. Payne (Oxford: Clarendon Press, 1974).

The World as Will and Representation, trans. E. Payne (New York: Dover, 1969).

OTHER WORKS

Appel, F. (1999), *Nietzsche contra Democracy* (Ithaca: Cornell University Press).

Aschheim, S. E. (1992), *The Nietzsche Legacy in Germany 1890–1990* (Berkeley and Los Angeles: University of California Press).

Backman, E. L. (1952), *Religious Dances* (London: Allen and Unwin).

Bertram, E. (1918), *Versuch einer Mythologie* (Berlin: Bondi).

Brobjer, T. (1998), 'The Absence of Political Ideals in Nietzsche's Writings: The Case of the Laws of Manu and the Associated Caste-Society', *Nietzsche-Studien* 27, pp. 300–18.

Chambers, E. K. (1903), *The Medieval Stage,* vol. 1 (Oxford: Oxford University Press).

Coetzee, J. M. (1999), *Elizabeth Costello* (Sydney: Random House).

Dahlhaus, C. (1980), 'The Two-fold Truth in Wagner's Aesthetics' in *Between Romanticism and Modernism,* trans. M. Whittall (Berkeley: University of California Press), pp. 19–40.

Detweiler, B. (1990), *Nietzsche and the Politics of Aristocratic Radicalism* (Chicago: University of Chicago Press).

Durkheim, E. (1995), *Elementary Forms of the Religious Life,* trans. K. Fields (New York: Free Press).

Frank, M. (1989), *Kaltes Herz. Unendliche Fahrt. Neue Mythologie* (Frankfurt a.M.: Surkamp).

Friedländer, S. (1986), *Kitsch und Tod: Widerschein des Nazismus* (Munich: DTV).

Gilhus, I. S. (1990), 'Carnival in Religion. The Feast of Fools in France', *Numen* 37, pp. 24–52.

Heidegger, M. (1962), *Being and Time* (Oxford: Blackwell).

(1977–), *Gesamtausgabe,* ed. F. W. von Hermann (Frankfurt a.M.: Klostermann).

(1979), *Nietzsche* vol. 1, trans. D. Krell (San Francisco: Harper and Row).

(2002), *Off the Beaten Track,* ed. and trans. J. Young and K. Haynes (Cambridge: Cambridge University Press).

Karl, F. (1995), *George Eliot: A Biography* (London: HarperCollins).

Kaufmann, W. (1950), *Nietzsche: Philosopher, Psychologist, Antichrist* (New York: Vintage).

Landerer, C. and Schuster, M.-C. (2002), 'Nietzsche's Vorstudien zur *Geburt der Tragödie* in ihrer Beziehung sur Musikästhetik Eduard Hanslicks', *Nietzsche-Studien* 31, pp. 114–33.

Leiter, B. (2002), *Nietzsche on Morality* (London: Routledge).

Mosse, G. L. (1964), *The Crisis of German Ideology* (London: Weidenfeld and Nicholson).

Nehamas, A. (1985), *Nietzsche: Life as Literature* (Cambridge, Mass.: Harvard University Press).

Rawls, J. (1971), *A Theory of Justice* (Cambridge, Mass.: Harvard University Press).

Richardson, J. (2004), *Nietzsche's New Darwinism* (New York: Oxford University Press).

Richardson, J. and Leiter, B. (2001), *Nietzsche* (Oxford: Oxford University Press).

Rohrkrämer, T. (1999), *Eine andere Moderne* (Paderborn: Ferdinand Schöningh).

Russell, B. (1957), *A History of Western Philosophy* (London: Allen and Unwin).

Salaquarda, J. (1973), 'Zarathustra und der Esel: Eine Untersuchung der Rolle des Esel im Vierten Teil von Nietzsches "Also sprach Zarathustra"', *Viatorum* 11, pp. 203–38.

Schlegel, F. (1958–), *Kritische Friedrich Schlegel Ausgabe*, ed. E. Behler *et al.* (Paderborn: Ferdinand Schöningh).

Sokel, W. (1983), 'Political Uses and Abuses of Nietzsche in Walter Kaufmann's Image of Nietzsche', *Nietzsche-Studien* 12, pp. 436–42.

Swanton, C. (2005), 'Virtue Ethics, Role Ethics, and Business Ethics' in *Working Virtue: Virtue Ethics and Contemporary Moral Problems*, ed. R. Walker and P. Ivanhoe (Oxford: Oxford University Press).

Tanner, M. (1986), 'Organising the Self and World', *Times Literary Supplement*, 16 May, p. 519.

Wagner, R. (1975), *Sämtliche Briefe*, vol. III (Leipzig: VEB Deutscher Verlag).

Wicks, R. (2002), *Nietzsche* (Oxford: Oneworld).

Young, J. (1997), *Heidegger, Philosophy, Nazism* (Cambridge: Cambridge University Press).

(2002), *Heidegger's Later Philosophy* (Cambridge: Cambridge University Press).

(2005), *Schopenhauer* (London: Routledge).

Index